The Expressive Body

The Expressive Body

Physical Characterization for the Actor

David Alberts

St. Louis Community College
at Meramec
LIBRARY

HEINEMANN
Portsmouth, NH

Heinemann
A division of Reed Elsevier Inc.
361 Hanover Street
Portsmouth, NH 03801–3912

Offices and agents throughout the world

On the cover, a detail of Auguste Rodin's *The Burghers of Calais* at the Hirshhorn Museum and Sculpture Garden, Smithsonian Institution, Washington, DC.

Library of Congress Cataloging-in-Publication Data

Alberts, David.
    The expressive body : physical characterization for the actor /
David Alberts.
        p.   cm.
    Includes bibliographical references.
    ISBN 0–435–07030–4
    1. Movement (Acting).   I. Title.
    PN2071.M6A42   1997
    792'.028–dc21   97–16177
                                                                  CIP

Editor: Lisa A. Barnett
Production: Vicki Kasabian
Cover design: Jenny Jensen Greenleaf
Cover photo: Cheryl Kimball
Manufacturing: Louise Richardson

Printed in the United States of America on acid-free paper

Docutech T & C 2005

Contents

Introduction

Actions speak louder than words.
Anonymous

Acting is about human behavior. Acting is also about what people think and feel. Ultimately, however, acting is about what people do. As every experienced actor and director knows, the essential elements of a play—the plot, the character, and the theme—are revealed through the physical action of the play, not through the words. Words are often of secondary importance to the manner in which those words are expressed physically.

This is not to minimize the importance of the spoken word as a medium of communication and expression but to emphasize the expressive and communicative aspects of physical behavior in character development, character interaction, and the play as a whole. The total performance process is based on the interdependence of words and action. The words may be highly expressive, even poetic, but their true eloquence can only be realized in the way an actor physically presents them to the audience. Actors need to understand physical behavior because of the role that the body plays in the total communication process, the range and depth of information physical behavior can convey, and the tremendous potential for expression it affords. A raised eyebrow, a smile, or a touch may reveal individual characterization and character relationships more directly and in significantly less time than might be accomplished by several lines of dialogue.

In a theatrical context, the audience comes to know and understand the character through the interaction of verbal and nonverbal behavior. The lines that a character speaks either confirm or deny what is being expressed by the character's body. The interrelationship of words and action are what define the character, whatever that interrelationship may be.

Every human being's ways of moving are unique to that individual. No two people—not even identical twins—move in exactly the same way. These differences in human behavior are what make the characters in a play so interesting to watch. A person is not simply a collection of random movements and gestures but a "system" of interdependent behaviors, and these are, in turn, a clear and unmistakable reflection of the individual's essential character. Every movement a person makes reflects the character of that person as a whole. It demonstrates his relationship with his environment and to the people around him, and it reveals his emotional and psychological states—his relationship to himself. In fact, every action a person takes reveals something about his character. Even an untrained eye can discover a great deal about an individual simply by watching that person move. What a person does and how he does it speak volumes about who that person is. The best actors are those who understand human behavior and best represent that behavior to an audience.

The challenge for the actor, then, is to find ways to differentiate the movement of one character from another thereby defining who the character is. The first step, of course, is to become aware of the many different ways in which people move. The second step is to determine which of those differences are most applicable to a particular character. The third step is to develop a characterization that draws on those differences. The final step is to convey all this information to the audience in an interesting, compelling, and believable way.

This book is about discovering and exploring these differences in human behavior to help awaken the actor to the extraordinary range of communication and expression available through physical characterization and then applying these discoveries to the physical portrayal of the character. This book first differentiates between nonverbal and verbal behavior—to separate movement and gestures from words and the use of words—and then to demonstrate how expressive movement can greatly enhance the overall communicative and expressive process. It aims to enable the actor to communicate motivation, intent, expression, and the dramatic context of a play more effectively through physical characterization—to provide the actor with ways to find and develop whatever is needed in portraying a character in any production in any period and in any style.

The expressive potential of the body in performance and in relation to the spoken word is discussed in Chapter 1. Chapter 2 looks at the wide range of physical behavior, totally unrelated to speech, that can be analyzed in terms of character development and physical characterization. Chapter 3 is devoted to defining character relationships and character interaction through physical behavior. Chapter 4 examines the essential elements of physical characterization in relation to actual performance and to performance in period plays.

This book offers a practical approach to physical characterization that can be used by the actor, teacher, or director to free the actor's own creativity, spontaneity, and imagination so that she can truly "become" the character she wishes to portray—the embodiment of a living, breathing human being. The underlying motivation for this book is to encourage actors to investigate the body's expressive potential and to more fully realize that potential in performance.

Movement and Gestures 1

O ur verbal behavior accounts for only a small percentage of the overall communication process. In theatrical performance it is only in the context of physical activity that the expressive meaning and content of words can be fully understood.

Physical activity, the *how* words are said, provides a context for verbal behavior, but it can also be communicative in its own right. Some physical behaviors serve solely to convey information: we point, for example, when we give directions or to indicate an object or another person. Physical behavior is also a vital element of human expression. A clenched fist or a clenched jaw creates an emotional frame of reference for other actions.

Language and Behavior

Expressive movement is often referred to as language—"the language of the body," or "the universal language." In general, however, language is based on words, their pronunciation, and how they are combined to form cohesive, intelligible patterns. English, French, and Japanese, for example, contain particular words pronounced in a particular way that is understandable to those who speak these languages. Languages may contain the same words, but they are usually pronounced in different ways (unless they are "appropriated" directly from another language, such as *le week-end*) and often have completely different meanings.

Behavior refers to physical rather than language-based or word-based activity, and it is generally categorized as either movement or gesture. A *movement* is any physical action that involves large areas of the body, such as the legs or the torso, or uses the body as a whole in a series of organized activities intended to achieve a particular objective. Walking, running, opening a door, climbing stairs, and picking up a book are examples of movement. The term "movement" also applies to the eyes, although they are contained within the head and face and cannot move freely in space, as can other parts of the body.

A *gesture* is a physical action that involves using a limited area of the body—usually the fingers, hands, or head—to express or emphasize an idea, an emotion, or an attitude, or to convey information. A gesture may also involve other parts of the body used in the same way, for example, pointing with a foot.

By way of further definition, the term "nonverbal behavior" is used throughout this book to mean physical activity involving the body only. "Nonverbal communication" refers to movements or gestures of the body that are deliberately employed in an expressive or communicative endeavor.

Language and behavior have some similarities. Both involve identifiable patterns that can be analyzed and studied. In language, the patterns are formed by individual words; in physical behavior they are based on individual movements. Just as language can be understood without any accompanying movement or gestures, some patterns of movement can be understood without words. One distinction between language and behavior, however, clearly differentiates the two terms: individual words can be understood out of context, while individual movements and gestures cannot. Context gives meaning to physical behavior. To those who speak English, the word *hello* means "hello." A wave of the hand, however, has meaning only in the context in which it occurs. It might mean "hello," but it might also mean "good-bye." Physical behavior falls into discernible patterns, and it is those patterns, rather than individual movements, that hold significance for the observer. Each pattern is directly related to each individual's physical attributes, personality, and emotional and psychological states—his *character*.

Words and Movement

Communication through movement and gestures is an essential element of human interaction. Why do we place such emphasis on non-verbal behavior in our daily lives? Why do we rely so heavily on what we can apprehend from movement and gestures in our interactions with one another? Why? Because nonverbal behavior works. It's a quick, efficient, and effective way to communicate. Physical behavior represents our thoughts and feelings directly and instantaneously. It takes time to speak and to project speech to another person. In fact, by the time we say what we want to say, our feelings may have changed completely. We may not be saying what we think or feel at all. We may be lying. We sometimes say things we don't really mean, and our words can be ambiguous or misleading.

Seldom, however, does our physical behavior "say" things we don't mean. Our actions might say things that we don't mean to say, but they rarely express things we don't feel. Actions are seldom ambiguous except when they are taken out of context or when the context is unknown. We may point the wrong way in giving directions, but the act of pointing is clear.

In terms of their effect on an audience, verbal and nonverbal behavior are total and inseparable elements of the same communication process. In terms of the actual process, however, the verbal and nonverbal elements can be analyzed and studied separately. Like verbal behaviors, nonverbal behaviors can serve multiple purposes. Some nonverbal behaviors are intended to convey information. Others are intended to express emotions or to provide the emotional context for words or other actions. Physical behavior may be intentional or unintentional, functional or expressive, but it is in no way random, haphazard, or accidental. All physical activities occur in discernible patterns. Communication, too, is an ordered and continuous activity. Everything a person does reveals something about that person, even if it is not supposed to reveal anything at all.

Motivation and Intent

Physical behavior is categorized as either intentional or unintentional—goal-directed or not goal-directed. In day-to-day behavior, movements such as opening a door or eating a meal are goal-directed, whereas movements such as blinking are not. On stage, however, every movement is, or should be, intentional. Every movement an actor makes on stage is enacted consciously and directed toward illuminating the play through the character the actor portrays.

Actors and directors often speak in terms of a character's "motivation," particularly in reference to the blocking of a scene, the handling of props, or other onstage activities. Actors and directors also speak of "objectives" and "superobjectives"—the moment-to-moment, scene-to-scene, and overall goals of the character within the structure of the play. Because an actor wants to represent these motivations and objectives clearly to the audience through the physical activity of the character he is playing, he needs to know what the character wants and *why*.

That certain "something" is motivation, usually a compelling emotional need or desire. Motivation is the reason an activity is undertaken. "I want a new hat" or "I want to rule the world" are equally viable motivations. What is important is that the motivation is *compelling* enough to cause the person to pursue the need or desire. Why is the character doing this? What emotional force drives her forward and *causes* her to pursue a particular course of action? Love, hate, fear, revenge, and ambition are all strong emotions, and all are compelling motivations for action.

Every character wants something and firmly believes he deserves to have it. In his own mind, every character is a protagonist. The resulting battle of wills is what makes the interaction of characters so interesting to watch. Because of their personal desires, characters come into conflict with one another and serve as counterpoints to one another. They contradict each other, but they also complement each other. Characters in conflict need each other. Without conflict, there is no play.

Intent is purpose. It is the state of mind in which an activity is carried out, and it is also the design, objective, goal, meaning, and significance of each activity. What exactly does the character hope to accomplish through a particular course of action? What goal or objective does she wish to achieve? *What* does she want (not *why*, which is motivation)? What she wants defines her *intent*.

Motivation and intent, although often used interchangeably by directors and actors, are not the same thing. Motivation is the compelling reason for an action. Intent is the purpose of the action. Motivation is an *emotion*. Intent is an *objective*. The often-heard question, "What is my motivation?" addresses only half the problem. The rarely heard "What is my intent?" addresses the other half.

Expression

For the actor, expression is the manner in which an activity is made to be representative of an emotion or a physical state. The simple act of walking or sitting, or any movement or gesture (or spoken word, for that matter), is not inherently or fundamentally expressive. Many of our daily activities are purely functional, and we perform them without expressive intent. On stage, however, every movement means something within the context of the play. It expresses a character's motivation and intent. Therefore, every movement performed on stage is inherently expressive.

Every activity performed on stage holds expressive potential that an actor can tap. Any physical activity, in other words, can be consciously made to hold expressive significance. The simple act of breathing can become a sigh of relief, a yawn of boredom, or an expression of profound sadness. It is the manner in which the activity is performed that imparts meaning to it within a particular context, and it is the manner in which an activity is performed that can be controlled by the actor.

An actor is given specific activities to perform by the director—blocking and other movements and gestures relative to the set, the props, and the other actors. The actor has little control over the particular activity he is given, but he can exert considerable control over how he performs each activity. He can't control the movement itself, but he can control the expression of the movement.

The intent of an action is the means by which the motivation for the action is pursued. Physical activity is the means by which motivation and intent are expressed to the audience. These subtle distinctions between motivation, intent, and expression are best illustrated by a classic example: Shakespeare's *Macbeth*.

Macbeth's motivation for wanting to kill Duncan—the compelling reason and his driving emotional force—is ambition. Macbeth's intent in killing Duncan—the objective he hopes to achieve—is to be king. By actively pursuing his intent (to be king) Macbeth can fulfill his underlying motivation, his ambition. Macbeth can't simply wish Duncan dead or plan to kill him or wait around for Duncan to die of old age. He is compelled to act. To realize his ambition and achieve his goal, Macbeth actually has to do something, and he has to do it now. Macbeth has to kill Duncan, and, after some heavy-handed prompting by Lady Macbeth, he manages to do so. His action, killing Duncan, and the manner in which he does it are the expression of his motivation and his intent. Killing Duncan is the means by which Macbeth's motivation, intent, and essential character are revealed to the audience.

From Macbeth's actions and his interactions with other characters, the audience observes that he is essentially a moral man, basically good and honest, with one definitive and ultimately fatal emotional flaw—his ambition. His ambition (his motivation) and his *active* pursuit of the means to fulfill that ambition drive him to unspeakable acts—the murders of Duncan, Banquo, and Macduff's wife and children. In time, Macbeth's ambition proves his downfall. Achieving his heart's desire—"to be king"—was deceptively simple, particularly for someone with his apparent intelligence and resources. (True, Macbeth gets off to a fairly slow start—he has a few qualms about killing Duncan and is reluctant to do so—but he manages well enough after that.) Maintaining his position as king once it is achieved proves to be a far greater challenge. It is a challenge Macbeth is ill-prepared to meet, and for his failure, he pays with his life.

Like her husband, Lady Macbeth is ambitious, but ambition is a manifestation of an even more profound and unsettling character flaw—her psychological dysfunction. Lady Macbeth is distraught over the recent loss of a child (which occurs before the action of the play begins), and her husband has been away at battle for over four months. Perhaps her motivation is the need to fill this double void in her life—the loss of her child and the periodic loss of her husband. She is desperate, it seems, for some security and constancy in her life. She loves Macbeth passionately, but this does not fully explain her actions.

Lady Macbeth is a finely drawn, if somewhat enigmatic character. She is an interesting character to play, certainly, but she is not the tragic hero of the play. She goads Macbeth into acting in what she believes are his best interests, when, in fact, what she hopes to see fulfilled is her own desire to share the throne with him. She gets Macbeth's blood boiling with ambition and the promise of greater things to come, then turns him loose on the world. Macbeth *could* have said "No, thanks," and tucked Duncan into bed nice and cozy—but he doesn't. For better or worse, Macbeth makes his own choices. His motivations and actions, not Lady Macbeth's, drive the play forward.

One might argue that Macbeth's tragic flaw is one of moral corruption or emotional weakness, an inability to resist the urgings of his wife, for instance, or his easy surrender to the not altogether subliminal suggestions of the witches. Macbeth is superstitious, of course, in an age of superstition, so the witches' influence needs to be put in its proper perspective. Some have suggested cowardice—Macbeth is simply afraid of his wife—but emotional weakness, superstition, and cowardice hardly qualify as noble tragic flaws. It's what Macbeth does that counts, not what he's afraid of or what he doesn't do.

Another classic example is *Hamlet*. Why is Hamlet such a difficult role to enact? Often it's because an actor or a director chooses to characterize Hamlet's major shortcoming as "indecision." This characterization ultimately fails because it's virtually impossible to represent inaction, such as indecision, through action. The audience has absolutely no idea of what is going on in Hamlet's head because nothing happens! Hamlet doesn't do anything. He just mopes around the castle playing word games with Rosencrantz and Guildenstern, making fun of Polonius, and talking to himself.

If we think of Hamlet's motivation as ambition rather than indecision, however, then the thwarting of that ambition by those around him, coupled with his inability to fulfill his ambitions because of his own inner conflicts, illuminates his character and gives him something to do. His ambition motivates him to action. Likewise, if his motivation is revenge rather than ambition—revenge for the death of his father and the denial of his rightful throne—then Hamlet has something to do. He has plenty of reasons, plenty of motivations for his actions. An actor need only *pick* one and see where it takes him.

As the play opens, Hamlet has hurriedly returned from his studies in musical theatre at Wittenburg University to assume his rightful place on the throne of Denmark, except that his uncle, Claudius, is already *sitting* in it and married to his mom besides, thereby cleverly solidifying his own position as king and Hamlet's as nobody-in-particular. Hamlet wants to be king. By his birthright, he should be king. Both Hamlet (as we now know) and his father (as we are led to believe) have been wrongfully denied the throne. To make matters worse, Claudius won't let Hamlet go back to Wittenburg, follows him around the castle eavesdropping on his conversations with Ophelia, and later ships him off on holiday to England to have him killed—a plot that Hamlet discovers and sends Rosencrantz and Guildenstern to the Lord High Executioner in his place. (So much for old friends.)

To summarize: his father has been murdered by his uncle, his mother is married to this very same uncle, and Hamlet is denied the throne and his musical theatre career, and is nearly murdered besides. In the face of all this, Hamlet's problem is that he can't decide what to do?! 'Swounds! Hamlet knows well enough what to do: dump Claudius. He just can't figure out how best to do it. True, Hamlet spends the better part of four hours trying to figure it out, but his thwarted ambition (or his revenge) gives him a reason to live, and a reason, a motivation, to do something about it.

Motivation must be approached in a positive sense—what it is that the character wants or needs, not what the character doesn't want or need. A reluctance or an inability to perform an act, or avoidance of the consequences of an act, are difficult to portray convincingly on stage. How, for instance, do you portray not wanting to do something? By not doing it? Where's the action? An inability to act is not a motivation or objective that can be actively pursued.

A positive fatal flaw (that's an oxymoron) like ambition or revenge gives the actor playing Hamlet or Macbeth something to do, something to act. "Ambition"—wanting to achieve something—can be acted. "Indecision"—an inability or failure to achieve something—cannot.

Why else are these plays called *Hamlet, Macbeth, Richard III, Romeo and Juliet, King Lear*? Because, within the context of the plays, these characters appear to have the most to gain and the most to lose. Hamlet, Macbeth, and the other title characters don't just sit around bemoaning their fate. They do something about it. What they do is usually wrong, of course, but that's why it's called a tragedy. Lear needs love, and he spends the whole play searching for it, mostly in all the wrong places. Richard is driven by an overwhelming ambition, and he lets nothing stand in his way to the top. Once there, however, he can't handle the job. Romeo and Juliet . . . well, it's that love thing again, and a remarkable inability to get their collective act together. The reckless passion of youth, a secret marriage, sleeping potions that mimic death. . . Given the circumstances, what did they expect? Tragic heroes may be foolish, duplicitous, ambitious, or reckless, but they are not cowardly or indecisive. They act, and in doing so, provide the impetus for the action of the play.

Examine a selection of classic tragic plays by playwrights of different periods. Review each play for the motivation and intent of the tragic hero—what the character wants and why he wants it. You will find that in great tragic plays the hero's motivation and intent are clearly defined. In lesser plays you will find that this is not necessarily true. We may know what the hero wants, but we may not understand why he wants it. Without understanding why the hero is pursuing a particular course of action, we cannot fully understand the tragic implications of the character's behavior, nor can we fully comprehend the meaning of the play.

Often, lesser plays can be made to seem greater than they are in performance. An imaginative director may impose a motivation for a character that is lacking in the play itself. The actor then endeavors, for better or worse, to enact the role based on the director's fictional motivation. This imposed motivation may or may not be entirely appropriate to the character, however, or to the play itself. Nevertheless, it does give the actor something to play, some compelling reason for doing what he's doing.

Context

Context is the physical, emotional, and intellectual environment in which a movement is performed. It should be readily apparent that the context contributes greatly to the expressive effect of any physical behavior. The meaning of a movement is determined by what is done, how it is done, and in what context it is done.

In the "real" world we may or may not be aware of the entirety of the context in which a movement, activity, or event occurs. We may be unaware of the circumstances, we may not know the people involved, or we may be unfamiliar with the environment. A further consideration is that "there are two sides to every story," often more than two sides, yet we may be aware of only our own perspective on the matter. All perspectives, taken together, form the context.

In a theatrical performance we assume that the audience is aware of every aspect of the context: what the movement is, how, where, when, and why it is performed, and who performed it. The audience knows all the sides of the story. The audience may not know "what happens next," of course, but they know or should know everything they need to know up to that point in the play. It is the responsibility of the director, actors, and designers to insure that the information the audience receives is presented clearly and accurately. The objective for the theatre artists involved in a production is to enlighten, not confuse, them. As in "real" life, false or misleading information often leads to incorrect assumptions and conclusions.

The director, actors, and designers face an interesting challenge—to accommodate the *dual* contexts in which a movement is performed. First there is the context of the play itself—its intrinsic plot, characters, and theme. Second there is the audience's perception of the plot, characters, and theme being presented to them in this particular performance. Reconciling the two contexts has been a major concern of theatre artists since Aristotle first brought it to our attention.

As theatre artists, actors must also be aware of these considerations in physically representing a character. A character's movement is not an isolated event; it exists within a larger context—in the immediate, onstage context of the movement itself, in the context of the play as a whole, and in the context of the overall theatrical production. These considerations must then be reconciled with the audience's perception of the characterization.

Intention and Perception

Expression implies intent. A movement cannot be unintentionally expressive for it would simply be nonexpressive. It would lack expressive content because it lacked expressive intent. Even a movement that is meant to be unexpressive—a blank stare or a "poker face"—is nevertheless expressive in its own right. If it's done on purpose, it's expressive; if it's *not* done on purpose, then it's *not* expressive. This is to differentiate true artistry from the "happy accident."

Purposeful movement like that which takes place on stage, in front of an audience, involves motivation, intent, and expression within a clearly defined context. Part of the actor's challenge in building a character is determining the motivation and intent of each movement and imparting expressive significance to each movement within the play.

Audience members do not expect that every moment of their lives will be filled with expressive movement; but they come to the theatre with just that expectation. The audience assumes, and rightly so, that *every* movement performed on stage has been consciously designed to elicit a specific response, and that any movement that occurs on stage is, or should be, expressive of some aspect of the play as a whole. The true measure of the effectiveness of a particular movement is the audience's perception of that movement. The actor's task is, first, to be *aware* of this process of perception and then to employ the process to the best possible expressive effect.

In the process of perception we extract meaning from the information we receive through our senses and analyze the information within the context of our prior experience. In other words, we cross-reference new information with information already stored in our memory. Even if we have no *direct* prior experience, we probably have one or more related experiences to draw upon. Lacking a frame of reference, we simply remain confused until we have gathered sufficient information to make a reasonable assumption or draw a fairly logical conclusion.

This process is not nearly so difficult as it first appears. We do it all day, every day, for the most part subconsciously. The only time we actually become aware of it is when an anomaly requires the attention and assistance of our conscious mind. We then consciously sort things out and throw the whole process back into the subconscious mind.

Understanding this process does not necessarily ensure acting success, of course. The intention behind a movement and the audience's perception of that movement may be two different things. It is the actor's task to reconcile those two elements—what she means and what the audience thinks she means.

An interesting paradox confronting theatre artists is that all of this must be determined in advance. The director, actors, and designers prepare the production "as if" they know, or can predict with some degree of certainty, what the audience's response will be. After opening night, adjustments can be made to accommodate the audience's *actual* response, of course, but opening night proceeds "as if" the theatre artists actually knew what they were doing. Sometimes the magic works and sometimes it doesn't. That's what makes theatre such a challenge.

In general, if an actor is aware of what he's doing, why he's doing it, how he's doing it, and in what context he's doing it, chances are that the audience will *perceive* it as the actor intends. An actor cannot actually *control* what the audience thinks, but he can move them, lead them, persuade them to follow a certain line of thought through his movement. If a difference arises between the actor's intention and the audience's perception, it is usually a matter of the *degree* of audience response, rather than a total misreading, misinterpretation, or misperception of the actor's intention. A movement may be less effective or expressive than the actor intended, in which case it is simply a matter of modifying it.

This implies, of course, that the actor knows how to modify a movement so that it has the greatest possible effect on the audience. Luckily, actors have directors, teachers, and books to help them enhance their art.

Attributes of Movement and Gestures

The simple movements and gestures we perform naturally, instinctively, and unaffectedly in our daily lives are complicated activities composed of many interdependent elements of mind and body. These movements and gestures become even more complicated when we consciously attempt to reproduce them on stage. As Hamlet once advised, the objective of the art of acting is "to hold a mirror up to nature"—to transform nature into art while at the same time appearing to be enacting nothing more than nature itself.

Every movement and gesture can be analyzed in terms of four distinct, yet highly interdependent attributes that contribute to its overall expressive potential. These attributes are (1) range, (2) frequency, (3) duration, and (4) intensity.

Range is the amount of space an activity occupies or encompasses in its performance relative to the activity itself. A broad sweep of the hand and arm across the body traverses a relatively greater space than raising an eyebrow, yet the sweep of the arm may extend through only a limited or partial range of motion, whereas the movement of the eyebrow may extend throughout the full range of motion.

Two elements of movement that are related to range are direction and level. *Direction* refers to the actual path of the movement in space relative to the body—forward, backward, up, down, sideways, diagonal, straight, or curved. *Level* refers to the position of the body as a whole—standing, sitting, kneeling, jumping, or lying down, for example—at the time the movement is performed.

Frequency is the number of repetitions of an activity within a given timespan. Most often, the significance of the frequency of a movement is related to the *usual* or *expected* frequency of the activity. Any noticeable increase or decrease in the expected frequency is generally indicative of either a physical or emotional change within the individual or a change in the environment affecting the individual.

We normally blink at a frequency of about six to ten times a minute. A bright light, a sudden loud noise, or some other unexpected occurrence will cause an increase in blinking frequency. A person who is anxious, nervous, or apprehensive may blink up to one hundred times a minute. In contrast, a person who is staring at an object or at another person or concentrating intently on a delicate task may blink as few as three or four times a minute.

Duration is the length of time required to perform an activity. The blink of an eye is of relatively short duration. The act of sitting in a chair or walking across a room is of longer duration. Our sense of time is entirely subjective, and duration is relative to both the activity and to the situation. A person may walk slowly across a room or rise abruptly from a chair, thereby increasing or decreasing what would be considered the "normal" or expected duration of the activity.

Two other closely related elements are tempo and rhythm. *Tempo* is the relative speed at which an activity is performed. Like duration, tempo is relative to the expected speed at which a movement is performed. A leisurely tempo will extend a movement's duration, just as a brisk tempo will shorten it.

Tempo and duration are highly interdependent, but the terms are not synonymous. Typing, for example, is a movement normally performed at a relatively brisk tempo, but the actual duration of the activity depends on the time it takes to type a particular document. Some people type faster than others, but the point is not who types the fastest. It is how the typing is done, by whom, and in what context that determines its expressive content.

Rhythm is the regulation of the tempo and duration of a movement in recognizable, ordered sets or in a recurrent pattern. Rhythm is the result of repetition. A nonrecurring movement has no rhythm. A recurring movement or *pattern* of movement takes on its own intrinsic rhythm. A verbal exchange, footsteps across the stage, sipping tea, or any combination of movements may establish a discernible pattern, a rhythm, that is sometimes palpable to an audience. This principle applies equally to a single repeated movement performed by a single character, different movements performed by a single character, a single movement performed by more than one character, or different movements performed by more than one character.

The pattern of movement, in and of itself, holds significance for an audience, and any *change* in that pattern is also significant. For example, a character is walking across the stage in a normal rhythm, when she suddenly stops in her tracks, turns, and runs offstage. In another instance, two characters are engaged in a rhythmic exchange, when one character abruptly stops talking. The audience wants to know why these changes have occurred. Why did one character run away and the other stop talking?

Intensity is related to the apparent expenditure of energy required to perform a particular physical activity or the level of energy purposely imposed on an activity. Movement such as hand-to-hand combat requires a considerable expense of energy. The activity can be made to "look" easy by expert practitioners, but the underlying intensity of the movement is relatively high. Pointing a finger may, of itself, require very little expenditure of energy, but the energetic pointing of a finger infuses the activity with considerably greater intensity.

It is not the apparent size of the movement, or its frequency, range, or duration that determines the intensity of a movement, but the level of energy with which it is performed. It is important to note that the size of a movement may be reduced without a corresponding loss of intensity. Sometimes a reduction in the size of a movement actually *increases* its intensity. The activity itself and the context influence the audience's perception of its intensity.

Just as each movement involves levels or degrees of intensity, it also exhibits observable characteristics related to the intensity with which it is performed. A movement can encompass one or more of these characteristics.

Sustained intensity denotes a smooth and relatively constant flow of movement without noticeable changes in the energy required to sustain the movement or in the direction, speed, or rhythm of the movement.

Rhythmic intensity involves a noticeable fluctuation in the repetition or interior dynamics of a recurring movement. The direction, speed, or intensity of the movement may change, causing an ebb and flow in the energy necessary to sustain the movement.

Suspended intensity characterizes a movement that is held motionless temporarily, but without a noticeable loss of intensity, and then continued.

Collapsed intensity indicates that the energy necessary to maintain an activity dissipates, whether gradually or suddenly. The movement stops because the level of energy is insufficient to sustain it.

These four attributes—frequency, range, duration, and intensity—coexist in every physical activity. They can be separated from one another in the analysis of a movement, but they cannot be separated from one another in the actual physical performance. Raising a finger occupies a specific amount of space (range), occurs a specific number of times (frequency), is performed for a specific length of time (duration), and is performed with a specific expense of energy (intensity). The same characteristics apply to any physical activity, from kicking a football, to chopping vegetables, to stabbing Polonius behind the arras (stabbing Polonius is necessarily limited in frequency, of course).

The motivation, intent, and context of a movement will help determine how an activity is performed; how the activity is perceived by the audience depends on its range, frequency, duration, and intensity and on the interrelationships of these basic attributes. Subtle changes in any one area can enhance or diminish the expressive content of the movement and alter the audience's perception of that movement significantly.

These characteristics of movement are of greatest significance to the audience when one or more is somehow "out of the ordinary" by departing from what might generally be expected within a given context. Altering the expected performance of a movement, even in a subtle way, changes its expressive content entirely. Any departure from the "norm" draws attention to itself, imparts increased significance, and heightens the expressive effect. How each of these attributes is performed and how they interrelate tell us something about the character performing the activity.

> *Choose a simple physical activity such as walking. First, perform the activity in as "normal" a manner as possible. Then repeat the activity several times, each time altering the movement in some way by changing one of more of its attributes. Explore a number of variations and combinations. Notice how the movement changes to accommodate these alterations and how you, as the performer, must accommodate any changes in the movement.*
>
> *If possible, ask someone to observe the exercise and describe her perceptions regarding the movement and the character of the performer after each repetition. Note how perceptions change as the movement changes.*
>
> *The next step is to attempt to re-create one of the observer's perceptions deliberately by performing the movement in a manner intended to elicit that response.*
>
> *The final test is to perform the activity for still another observer to determine if your intentions and the new observer's perceptions are the same—if what you thought you did is what your observer thought you did. If so, you've accomplished your goal. If not, you need to analyze your performance to determine where your intention and your observer's perception differ and then attempt to reconcile these differences.*

Functions of Movements and Gestures

In terms of human interaction, physical behavior has five primary functions: (1) to express emotion; (2) to regulate interpersonal interactions; (3) to present one's personality to others; (4) to convey interpersonal attitudes and relationships, and; (5) to replace or accompany speech. Each type of movement has its own characteristics and its own characteristic ways of being used in human interaction. As with other types of human behavior, certain movements defy neat categorization: some movements fit more than one category and others fulfill some aspects of one category and some aspects of another. Much depends, as we have seen, on context.

To Express Emotion

An audience wants to know what a character is thinking and feeling. Both can be expressed through physical behavior. What the character is thinking is revealed in the actual pursuit of a goal through some particular physical activity. What the character is feeling is revealed in the way a character performs those goal-oriented physical activities, and in the basic expression of the body—of the face, for example, or body posture—and through gestures. In general, large body movements tell the audience what the character is thinking, while small body movements, particularly gestures, tell the audience what the character is feeling.

In every instance, however, emotion comes first. A character must feel before she can think and think before she can act. Likewise, the audience must understand how a character feels in order to understand how she thinks and why she does what she does. Emotion, thought, action—in that order. Taken out of order, the motivation for a character's movement can be misperceived, misunderstood, or misinterpreted.

Any part of the body that is made visible to the audience can express some level of emotion. Certainly there are many, many stories of actors "acting with their backs" (as well as with other parts of their anatomies). The expression of emotion can follow one of two paths: (1) free expression or (2) repressed or concealed expression. In free expression, the individual is at liberty to express his emotions fully and freely. This usually occurs in private, less privately among close friends or relations, or in public under extreme conditions or in heightened emotional situations.

The second, that of repressed or concealed expression, is the one we encounter most often in our daily lives. Due to circumstances usually beyond our control, we can't do what we really want to do or say what we really want to say or express how we really feel. Even if we could, we probably wouldn't. The situation, the circumstance, the people involved, or some combination of these generally inhibit the free expression of our emotions.

We learn through experience that displays of emotion are wholly appropriate in some situations and wholly inappropriate in others. It is not appropriate to laugh out loud in the library or at a funeral, for example, or to express extreme joy at pulling to a straight flush at the poker table. Even if we were to let out a spontaneous whoop of delight in a board meeting or at a formal dinner, we would likely restrain ourselves from any further such display until we could step into a more conducive environment.

In the context of a theatrical performance, repressed, restrained, or temporarily withheld emotion elicits a greater empathetic reaction from an audience than does an immediate outward display. For example, a character in a play who is determined *not* to cry, even in the face of great adversity, is very compelling to an audience, particularly compared to a character who cries at the drop of a hat. A person "busting with joy" holds the attention of the audience until that person finally "bursts." The character and the audience hold onto the emotion until the character finally "lets go." The release is cathartic, both emotionally and physically. Once the character releases the emotion, the audience is also free to cry or shout.

An actor needs to know which of these two emotional paths—free or repressed expression—he is following in order to impart the truest possible representation of the character he is portraying. And because a character on stage is "bigger than life" and not always bound by the dictates of conventional society or decorum, some leeway must be granted in terms of emotional expression. At the same time, it does not serve a characterization to challenge what the audience would consider "normally acceptable behavior" since it might seriously affect the audience's perception of the character's emotional state.

Hamlet berates his mother in the confines of her own bedroom, but he does not chastise her in public. His feigned madness seems to fall well within the bounds of acceptable "mad person" behavior, at least in the Danish court. For the most part, Hamlet behaves himself quite well, except for that unfortunate incident with Polonius behind the arras. It is his only rash act in the play. The rest of the time he is deliberate in his actions and restrained in his emotional expression, except in private circumstances—when alone, with Ophelia, or with his mother. How mad can he be?

An interesting example of the use of movement to convey restrained emotion is what are called *basal hand movements*—the little things we do, often unconsciously, with our hands all the time. In a relaxed state, we might make anywhere from one or two to several nondescript, non-goal-oriented hand movements per minute—what might otherwise be termed "nervous habits" (habitual, yes, but not necessarily nervous). With increased stress comes an increase in these basal hand movements, the number of movements increasing in direct proportion to the level of stress or anxiety—the greater the stress, the greater the increase in the number, frequency, and intensity of the movements. At some point, however, the stress becomes overwhelming and all movement ceases, at least temporarily, until the person can "regroup." What happens next is anybody's guess.

In acting, basal hand movements can be used to help represent a character's emotional state. As a character's hand movements increase in number, frequency, and intensity, the audience will assume, based on their own experience, that the character is experiencing a proportionate increase in stress. If the character doesn't do anything, or if there is no prior basis for comparison regarding what the character normally does, the audience will have no idea what is going on in the character's mind. If the audience has become aware of a character's essential physical rhythms and "standard" basal hand movements then any change in the number, frequency, or intensity of the character's movements, however subtle, will register. The audience will become involved, often subliminally at first, in the character's struggle. As the tension mounts, the audience will become increasingly invested in the character's plight. The character's struggle becomes the audience's struggle. At the moment when the character's movement ceases, the audience will hold its collective breath . . . waiting . . . and waiting . . . for the release.

There is a difference, of course, between engaging the audience's attention and eliciting its empathy, and shamelessly manipulating its emotions. An actor who tries too hard to evoke empathy from an audience or who pushes the audience too far emotionally loses its respect and interest. An audience willingly suspends disbelief and engages in the emotional flow of the play, but if an audience realizes that it is being manipulated emotionally, it will disengage its imagination and its emotions. Being manipulated is *not* part of the bargain.

> *Observe your own behavior (and the behavior of others, if possible) under varying circumstances and in different social situations. Note when you are free to express yourself emotionally and when you must restrain yourself. What are the acceptable levels of emotional expression allowed in each circumstance? What factors influence or determine the level of expression? In what ways and to what extent is your emotional expression affected by the situation, the environment, and the people within the environment? Which of the restraints on expression are self-imposed? For what reason?*

Present-Positive Expression

Nothing about a character is revealed unless and until that character moves. Furthermore, everything a character does can only be conveyed to the audience in positive terms and only in the present. A character on stage can't do "nothing," nor can she not do "something." The audience doesn't see (*cannot* see) what the character doesn't do.

One might argue that a character is doing "nothing" when he doesn't move. On the contrary, the character is standing, or he is sitting, or he is lying down. He may be doing nothing else, but he is doing what he's doing, even if that is standing absolutely still. What the audience sees is whatever the character is doing. The audience also sees only what the character is doing now, at the present time; not what the character did or will do. The audience may have seen what the character did previously, but at the time the audience viewed the action, it was in the present. In time the audience may see what the character does in the future, but, again, the audience will see it as it happens, in the present.

Movement and gestures can express emotional states only in the *present-positive* sense as well. Movements expressing "I am happy," "I am sad," and "I am angry" are all positive affirmations of emotional states. Verbal expression is necessary to convey a negative state of being—"I'm not happy," "I'm not sad," or "I'm not angry." Likewise, movement can indicate only a current emotional state— "I am happy (at this moment). Past and future emotional states can be expressed only in words— "I was sad" or "I will be angry."

The important point to remember is that only present and positive states of being can be expressed solely through the medium of the body, that is, through physical behavior. An actor communicates negative, past, and future emotional states through verbal expression. Certainly voice and body can work together, but only the voice can convey anything other than a present-positive state. The audience may observe that a character's face and body indicate that the character is angry in the present-positive sense, but it is only when the character says, "I will be angry with you if you do such-and-so . . ." that the audience understands that the character might not be angry now, but may be angry in the future.

> *Observe your own behavior and that of others in the present-positive sense. Eliminate all considerations of past, future, and negative behavior, and describe the behavior*

while it is happening. "I'm happy, and I'm walking." It doesn't matter where you're walking from, what destination you hope to reach, how you felt a minute ago, or how you will feel a minute from now. Where you were and what you felt are in the past, and where you're going and how you'll feel are in the future. How you don't *feel is essentially irrelevant. Stay in the present-positive mode—"At this moment, I'm happy, and I'm walking." In the next moment you may trip and fall flat on your face and be embarrassed and annoyed, but for now you are happy and you are walking.*

Directors and acting teachers are inordinately fond of admonishing actors to "*act* in the moment," "*stay* in the moment," or "*be* in the moment." In actuality, you can't not act, stay, or be "in the moment" for the simple reason that there is nowhere else you can be. Everything we do and feel happens now. Our existence is a never-ending succession of "nows," like now . . . and now . . . and now. No matter what you do on stage, you are always and forever acting in the moment. The term refers more appropriately to your continuing awareness of the character's present-positive state of being. Quite simply, there's no other way to do it.

Facial Expession

As we all know, facial expression is an indispensable element of physical communication. The face is capable of making hundreds of distinct movements and of communicating a wide range of emotions. The face is the most reliable indicator of the emotions, and then the body, while verbal expression is the least consistent and credible representation of emotion. We "read" a person's feelings in his face and then reconcile what we "read" with his body and what he is saying. In most human interaction, the face expresses an individual's essential emotional state, whereas the rest of the body communicates only the intensity of the emotion, not necessarily the emotion itself.

This is not to say that the body is incapable of expressing emotion independent of the face. Facial expression and bodily expression are so intertwined in daily interaction, however, that it is difficult for most people to separate them. The presumption of the unity of the body and the face in physical expression is so pervasive that in exercises involving an expressionless (neutral) mask, observers will remember seeing an expression on the performer's "face" that does not and cannot exist in the mask. The observer wants some expression to be there in the face and, in fact, needs to observe something that is related to the expression of the performer's body in order to comprehend the emotional expression of the character as a whole.

In addition to expressing emotion, the face is also capable of projecting the nature of individual personality and personal relationships. Next to speech, it is the principal source of information in interpersonal interactions. According to physiologists, the forty-plus muscles of the face are capable of producing nearly twenty thousand different expressions. Two or three thousand of these expressions convey emotion. That's a lot of expressions. Nevertheless, there are six basic facial expressions from which the other two or three thousand variations are derived: happiness, sadness, fear, anger, surprise, and disgust/contempt. Not all facial expressions are indicative of single emotions, of course. More often, facial expressions are variations in the intensity of these six primary emotions, or combinations of different, simultaneously occurring emotions.

There has been some argument among anthropologists and psychologists over the universality of these six basic facial expressions. Studies have shown that there is a generally high level of agreement among observers, even among individuals from differing cultures and languages, about which facial expression represents which emotion and the relative intensity of the emotion expressed. The same results were obtained whether the expressions were posed, as in still photographs, or spontaneous, as in a filmed record of a subject watching a movie.

There is, however, a lack of agreement on issues beyond the simple determination of the basic emotion represented. What is missing, of course, is the context. The individual in the photograph may be feigning anger, for instance, or she may be truly angry. There is no way for the observer to know for certain without knowing the context.

It may also be argued that the interpretations of an expression in a photograph or on film are simply generalities or possible interpretations. Think of the multitude of interpretations, for example, that may be attributed to a simple smile. (How long have people mused about the enigmatic smile of the *Mona Lisa*?) A smile may represent some level of happiness, for instance, or it may represent any of the following:

flirtation	condescension
annoyance	dismissal
submission	apprehension

mischief	restlessness
pleasure	dissent
familiarity	acquiescence
victory	restraint
inscrutability	confusion

Notice how often people rely on a simple smile to express their emotions and the incredible range of emotions thus expressed. Notice, too, that a smile is the most common facial expression used to conceal a person's true feelings. "That one may smile, and smile, and be a villain . . ." Also, when they are in doubt about a particular situation or about their own feelings or the feelings of others, people often smile. It's the standard "cover up" expression.

Observe, for example, the difference between a spontaneous smile and what might best be termed a "social" smile. A spontaneous smile involves wrinkles around the eyes and the upper part of the face that are not present in a forced or "social" smile. A "social" smile is often asymmetrical, favoring the side of the mouth opposite the dominant hand. (For a right-handed person, the smile will tend to be more pronounced on the left side of the face.) Forced or otherwise non-spontaneous smiles are also likely to appear at inappropriate times during the interaction, to last too long, or to be dropped abruptly. Spontaneous smiles fade gradually rather than suddenly, and they are rarely instantaneous, as are forced, "at the ready" smiles.

In considering the display of emotion, we can divide the face into three areas: (1) upper face—the brow and forehead area; (2) mid-face—the eyes, eyelids, and bridge of the nose; and (3) the lower face—the nose, cheeks, mouth, chin, and jaw. Although it is commonly believed that the "eyes have it" in terms of expressing emotions, there is no one part or area of the face that best demonstrates any single emotion or from which all emotions emanate. In expressing happiness, for example, the most important areas of the face are the eyes/eyelids and mouth/cheeks. For sadness, the eyebrow area and the eyes/eyelids are most important. To convey disgust, the expression of the nose/cheeks/mouth area is paramount. Surprise, however, is expressed in all three areas.

Revisit the preceding list of possible expressions for a simple smile. Notice which involve movement of the lower face only and which require the addition of movement from other areas of the face. "Happiness," for example, requires movement in the upper, middle, and lower face. In contrast, an expression of "condescension" or "inscrutability" involves movement of the area around the mouth, but little in other areas, particularly around the eyes. In fact, if there is no movement in the area around the eyes, we discern the expression as not truly or completely happy: a person can smile, but with "dead" eyes, which we perceive as an expression of some misgivings about the situation, perhaps, or restraint for some other reason.

In terms of audience response, the actual emotion and intensity of positive or "pleasant" expressions are much easier to distinguish than for negative or "unpleasant" expressions. Physical displays of unpleasant or negative emotions must be clear, both in the expression of the emotion itself and in its intensity. The audience must be able to distinguish between expressions of anger, disgust, grief, and sadness. They'll know when you're happy or surprised, but they may not be able to distinguish between your expressions of mild annoyance and an upset stomach.

To test the relative expressive capability of any one area of the face, try to express "happiness" (or any other basic emotion) using only the upper face, midface, or lower face. "Happy" eyes and "surprise" eyes are virtually indistinguishable from one another, but add the midface or lower face to the upper face and the expression becomes unmistakable.

We can exert considerable control over our facial muscles. We can exhibit expressions when desired and inhibit expressions when desired, but not always successfully. Our face might "betray" us on occasion and give away our thoughts or feelings, or be misinterpreted or "misread" by another. We may express exactly how we feel, but at an inappropriate time or in an inappropriate setting. Audiences are extremely empathetic and perceptive in the matter of emotional expression, given the proper frame of reference. An audience is not telepathic, however. You must give the audience something clear, observable, and identifiable to work with.

Contrary to popular belief, the eyes alone are not enough to express emotion. As an experiment, try to express an emotion, any emotion, without using any part of your face or body other than your eyes. It simply cannot be done. You can look up and down, from side to side, even roll your eyes, but simple eye movement is not enough to express emotion. The eyes and eyelids functioning together fare little better. Eyes, eyelids, and eyebrows can express a general, or generic emotion, but only in the context of the face as a whole can the eyes reinforce or contradict emotional information from other parts of the face and body.

The eyes provide information. They do not express emotion. Where a character looks, how a character looks, and at whom or at what a character looks are items of information. It is the physical expression of the body and face accompanying the movement of the eyes that supplies the emotional context.

Expressive Use of the Body

> "What's the matter?" he asks, lightly touching her shoulder. She sighs. "Nothing," she says, quietly, her head down, arms folded limply across her chest, body sagging, weight on her left leg, right foot tracing a small circle on the floor. "Nothing at all," she whispers, wiping away a tear, and pulling away from his touch. "Why do you ask?"

The motivation to move originates in the actor's mind. The impulse progresses from deep within the actor's body to his outer extremities, then out into the space he inhabits, including the actual theatre space, and into the space the audience inhabits. It is there, in the mind of the audience, that the movement finds meaning.

Whether or not an *actor* feels the emotion he represents is entirely inconsequential. What is important is whether or not the *audience* feels it. Many great actors have no compelling need to "feel" the emotion they wish to express. They simply act and let the audience respond to what they do. Acting is not emoting. Acting is appearing to feel or express an emotion by responding physically to an emotion-producing event or situation. The challenge for the actor is to move her body in ways that will evoke an emotional response from the audience, and to know why a certain behavior, a certain movement or gesture, evokes that particular emotional response.

Emotion does not arise spontaneously, out of thin air. It requires a trigger, a motivation, something to set it off. It doesn't just happen, and it certainly doesn't happen just because an actor feels it. An actor can "feel" all he wants, but unless and until he physically projects that feeling to an audience, it will remain a mystery.

Express any emotion—happiness, sadness, anger, surprise, fear, or contempt/disgust—using only the body, not the face. On repetition, vary the intensity of the emotion.

In time, add your face to your expression but without altering the emotion or the intensity of the bodily expression. (We're so accustomed to using the face alone to express emotion that it has a tendency to "take over," to dominate the emotion-expressing mechanisms and abilities of the body as a whole.)

Presenting Individual Personality

It's all an act. Think about it. Much of what we do in our daily lives, particularly what we do in public, is an act. Are you the "real you" when you talk to your boss or your teacher, or to a police officer? Are you the "real you" on a first date? Are you the "real you" at a formal dinner party or at an interview? Are you the "real you" when you meet another person for the first time? Come to think of it, who *is* the "real you" anyway?

It is important at this point to differentiate between a person's character and his personality. *Character* is a person's basic "self"—her essential nature, her intrinsic physical, emotional, and psychological qualities and traits, her temperament, her sense of individual worth, her abilities and capabilities—in other words, who she really is. A person's character may undergo change, but that change is likely to occur slowly, almost imperceptibly, as a person acquires knowledge and experience throughout life. Profound changes in a person's character, like those that occur in plays, may seem to occur rapidly. Remember, however, that a play consists of selected moments of a person's life, and these moments are likely to be those in which a person undergoes the most dramatic change. The audience doesn't observe the weeks, months, or years that have led up to this particular defining moment. *Personality* is a person's projected self—who she appears to be—not necessarily her true character. A person's personality may reflect her character, of course, but the personality projected to others is more likely to be selectively "edited" for a particular audience or circumstance.

Character is innate, essential, fundamental. *Personality* is acting.

Actors need to be aware of the difference between character and personality and be able to differentiate between a character's true self and the personality he projects to other characters during the course of the play. This can be quite a challenge, particularly in a modern play, which includes few monologues that would allow a character to express his true self to the audience. One reason for this is that characters in modern plays spend little time alone. The audience has no opportunity to observe a character when he is alone or to eavesdrop on what he has to say to himself. In addition, characters often talk about each other, but rarely about themselves, certainly not to the same extent that characters in classic plays do. Contrast Richard III's concise, true-character-revealing opening monologue (and his continuing revelations about himself throughout the play) with Willy Loman's terse and often contradictory comments about himself. Willy's remarks are anything but concise or definitive; they are more like subtle clues to his characterization.

How we appear to others is often how we present ourselves to others. How we present ourselves is how we would like to appear. How often, and under what circumstances (if any) do we present ourselves to others as we truly are? Do we really want people to know our true character, or would we prefer to let them believe what they like within the limited context we've presented to them? We all have our little secrets, things we'd prefer that nobody knew, certain aspects of our character that we'd rather not disclose.

Certainly there are occasions when we can just "be ourselves." These are generally informal times spent with close family and friends. Introduce a "stranger" into the mix, however, and notice how things change. Everybody in the room starts to "put on an act." The "acting" may be reflected in subtle changes in physical or verbal behavior or it may consist of totally outrageous attempts to impress, befriend, annoy, or even alienate the unsuspecting stranger.

This behavior is indeed a reflection of ourselves, but it may not be the reflection of our true character that we intend. One vital element of the process is missing—knowledge of the other person. We may not know them well enough to anticipate their responses to our behavior, nor do we know them well enough to interpret their reactions accurately. Nevertheless, we take a chance. We give it our "best shot" and hope that something sticks, preferably something good.

A character in a play, no less than a "real" person, has a public persona (his personality) and a private persona (his true character). A character in a play presents one of these persona to the other characters on stage, depending on who they are and in what circumstances they are interacting. Rarely do those on stage know the true character of any of their fellow characters.

But the audience must know. True character is disclosed to the audience during private moments on stage and through the comparisons the audience makes between the various personae the character presents. The "real" character is not revealed fully at any one point in the play but gradually, throughout the entire course of the play. Only the character herself, the actor portraying her, and the audience know who she truly is.

The debates between Richard Nixon and John F. Kennedy in the 1960 presidential election are a pivotal event in the history of televised politics and a perfect example of the importance of physical behavior in projecting individual personality. According to most political analysts and commentators of the day, Richard Nixon was the better prepared of the two candidates, particularly about foreign policy issues, and he was considered by many to be the more effective debater. For those who listened to the debates on the radio, who heard only the candidates' words, Nixon seemed the apparent "winner."

Those who watched the debates on television, however, experienced an entirely different perception. Though the words that Nixon spoke were the same, those he spoke on television were encumbered by his inability to effectively convey a positive physical sense of himself. Nixon lacked a compelling physical "presence," that quality of confidence, leadership potential, and self-sufficiency that is projected physically to an audience. He looked tense, nervous, and uncomfortable, as if he really didn't want to be there.

In noticeable contrast, John F. Kennedy appeared confident, self-assured, and entirely at ease in front of the camera. Kennedy smiled easily and often. Nixon smiled only rarely, and when he did, his smile seemed forced and insincere. Kennedy's gestures flowed naturally and easily, in harmony with his words and with the expressive intent of his presentation. Nixon's gestures were stiff and occasionally mistimed. At times Nixon's movements seemed to be preplanned, as if he had written in his notes "gesture here," "smile here," or "look sincerely into the camera here." Even Kennedy's makeup appeared superior to Nixon's. He just looked better.

For the most part, Nixon spoke eloquently and forcefully, but his lack of a compelling physical presence and his awkward gestures spoke far more eloquently. Nixon's words may have won the debates, but Kennedy's physical presence propelled him to the presidency.

Observe the physical behavior of politicians and other elected public officials. (It's not always a pleasant task, but it can be very instructive.) Observe the manner in which they

present themselves and ingratiate themselves with their con-
stituents. Note their bearing and posture and the way they
handle themselves physically, particularly in what could be
potentially awkward situations such as entering or exiting a
vehicle (the true test of any politician), or walking onto a
platform. As the person speaks, observe the relationship
between words and movement, the use (or misuse) of ges-
tures, the seemingly ever-ready smile that is tempered only
by the occasional practiced scowl at the mention of the op-
position, or the "thoughtful" pose that is struck in response
to a pointed question from the media. Also notice the re-
markable difference in movement and gestures as employed
by a local politician, a regional politician, and a national
politician.

For many politicians, "image" or personality, rather than
the substance of their ideas, is paramount. It's not what a
politician says, it's how she says it, and how she looks while
she's saying it, that matters. No matter her protestations to
the contrary, the politician is not selling ideas. She's selling
herself. There will be time enough to worry about substan-
tive issues and ideas once she's elected.

Regulating Interpersonal Interactions

Movements that control the back-and-forth, give-and-take nature of conversations between and among individuals are known as *regulators*. Most regulating behavior is performed by the face and eyes. We use our face and eyes sometimes to facilitate and other times to inhibit the flow of communication in our daily interactions with one another. For example, we control the ebb and flow of conversation through facial cues and eye movements. Smiling may indicate that we are open to interaction. Raised eyebrows, often used as a sign of recognition or greeting in the form of the "eyebrow flash," can also indicate an openness to interaction. We may open our mouth in response to what is being said by others or as a signal to the other person that now it's our turn to talk. We may look away when we wish to indicate that we are thinking about what is being said, or to signal a change of subject or an end to the conversation.

The "eyebrow flash" mentioned above is a common greeting ritual throughout the world. Initial eye contact is followed by a slight lifting of the head and widening of the eyes, which is followed almost immediately by a widening of the eyes and a raising of the eyebrows. The greeting most often occurs between acquaintances, but it can also occur between "friendly strangers"—people we pass on the street or encounter in the close proximity of public transportation or an elevator. Between total strangers the full eyebrow flash is usually replaced by a slight up or down nod of the head alone, as an acknowledgement rather than a greeting, particularly when further vocal or physical interaction is not desired.

We also use our faces to accentuate, magnify, minimize, or support our verbal messages. Lowered eyebrows may accompany a sad message. A smile may be used to temper an otherwise negative message—the "sorry" smile or the "oops" smile-and-shrug that accompanies the spilled milk or the crumpled fender.

In addition to supporting our own verbal messages, we often use our face in response to what another person is saying. When a person seeks feedback from someone else, he looks at that person's face and eyes. The listener's facial response allows the speaker to monitor the effect of what he is saying. A dropped jaw, for instance, indicates surprise or dumbfoundedness. Widened eyes and raised eyebrows might denote a nonverbal wow! Inclining the head forward and turning it slightly to either side might imply a silent question, indicate skepticism, or denote anticipation of an expected response. The single raised eyebrow might express doubt, mild surprise, or admonition, depending on the context. These movements convey messages that could be expressed verbally but are communicated through movement alone.

We also use body movement and gestures to regulate interaction, but usually only when facial and eye movements fail to communicate our wishes. Some people just don't get it, or they choose to ignore our messages. We open our mouth to speak, but the other person just keeps talking. We smile, nod, and open our mouth again. She keeps talking. We drop our head back and look off into the distance, nodding again—a bigger movement this time. Still talking. So we raise a finger as if to make a point, first to chest level, then directly in front of our face, as if to say "Look. Look at me. Get a clue. *I* want to talk now." When all else fails, we simply interrupt. After all, we've given fair warning.

> *Observe people in conversation. Note how each person uses his face and eyes to control the interaction, how each responds to what is being said, and how each expresses non-*

verbal "control" messages. Note in what instances movement and gestures are used in combination with and separate from the face and eyes.

Regulating behavior occurs normally and naturally in the course of our daily interactions with one another, but it seems to disappear almost entirely when that interaction takes place on stage. We don't really need regulating behavior on stage, of course, because we already know from the script who is going to speak next, when they're going to speak, and even what they're going to say. While it is true that actors may not need regulating behavior in the real-world sense, if we want the onstage interaction between and among characters to appear "as if" we were speaking and hearing these words for the first time, then regulating behavior needs to be amended to the action of the play so that it appears to arise naturally and spontaneously from the onstage interaction. We may know what's supposed to happen next, but we can still act as if we don't. It's these little things, overlooked by the vast majority of actors and directors, that impart greater depth and believability to a characterization.

Replacing or Accompanying Speech

Quite simply, replacement gestures replace speech and hold a direct verbal translation. They are intentional and intentionally expressive, which is to say that they are used consciously and deliberately to convey information.

The following are examples of replacement gestures:

Come here.	Be quiet.
Look!	Follow me.
After you . . .	I'm hungry.
I'm hot/cold.	That stinks.
I don't know.	Tastes good.
Take it away.	Touchdown!
Have a seat.	Stop.
Turn around.	OK.
Can't hear you.	He's crazy.
What time is it?	Shame on you.
I've got a headache.	I promise.
Take a hike.	

Few gestures are universal, except perhaps a hand to the mouth to indicate food or eating, rubbing the stomach to indicate hunger, or resting the head on the hands to indicate sleep. Gestures like these, which represent common human activities, will likely be widely understood even among diverse cultures. As far as we can determine, however, there is no single facial expression, body position, or gesture representing a concept or feeling that conveys the same meaning in all societies. Even movement and gestures representing such simple concepts as "yes" and "no" differ from culture to culture.

In Greece, for example, shaking the head back and forth means "yes," and nodding means "no"—the exact opposite of the North American interpretation of the same movements. The gesture that represents "come here" in North American culture means "go away" in certain European cultures. There are also different, culturally contextual gestures for "suicide"—a finger (gun) to the head in North America, a fist (holding a knife) to the stomach in Japan, or hands choking the neck on some islands of Indonesia. In our culture we use a gun-to-the-head gesture to represent suicide or "I'm gonna kill myself," but we make a throat-cutting gesture with the finger, thumb, or hand to indicate being killed or being about to be killed by someone else. Other cultures represent being killed by another person with our "gun-to-the-head" gesture or with a hand chop to the back of the neck.

Certain movements and gestures, however, convey a specific meaning within a particular society, culture, or other limited environment. This is to say that most *specific* gestures—those that hold a particular meaning in a particular context—are *culture*-specific. The replacement gestures listed above, for instance, are most appropriate among English-speaking people of North America. Many of the same gestures would be misunderstood (if they held any meaning at all) in non-English-speaking cultures and by those who speak English but are members of European, Middle Eastern, or Asian cultures. Individuals raised in a multicultural environment learn the gestures representative of each culture and use those that are appropriate to each cultural environment.

The well-known mayor of New York, Fiorello La Guardia, was raised in a multicultural neighborhood in a highly multicultural city. As mayor, he moved easily from one neighborhood to the next, "speaking" to the people of each area of the city in their own body "language." People of diverse cultural backgrounds voted for La Guardia because they considered him "one of their own." Mayor La Guardia also spoke more than one language, further endearing him to the populace.

> *Observe a person who speaks more than one language. You will note that each language is accompanied by characteristic movements and gestures and that this is particularly noticeable as the speaker switches from one language to another. Posture, physical attitude, gestures, and facial expressions change with each language. There may be some overlap of movement and gestures, particularly if a person acquired a language later in life, after her characteristic movement patterns had already been well established. Nevertheless, there should still be observable changes and differences in movement and gestures from language to language.*

Unlike verbal behavior, however, replacement gestures are not generally strung together to form phrases and sentences. Although it is possible to carry on a nonverbal "gesture conversation" of some length, replacement gestures are usually employed when normal paths of communication are blocked, inhibited, or otherwise impractical, such as at a loud party, when distance exceeds vocal capability, or at an intimate social gathering when discretion or secrecy is desirable.

> *Observe people in conversation. Note the use of replacement gestures and the manner in which they are employed in conversation. How often were replacement gestures used? In what way(s)? Did you understand what the replacement gestures meant, generally or specifically? What did their use tell you, if anything, about the personality of the person who used them and about the relationship of the people engaged in the conversation?*
>
> *The next time you attend a theatrical performance, note the use of replacement gestures. How were they used, if at all? How might the actors have incorporated replacement gestures to enhance their physical performance? To illuminate the character they are portraying? To define character interactions and character relationships?*

In many theatrical productions, replacement gestures are noticeable by their absence. It's not so much that we miss them or that their absence diminishes the performance to any great extent. It's simply that replacement gestures can add immeasurably to a characterization and impart a greater sense of believability to a performance. After all, this is what real people do every day of their lives. Why shouldn't characters in a play, who are supposed to be real people, do the same things?

Supplemental gestures support or accompany speech and take place concurrently with speech, but they do not have a direct verbal translation. They are totally dependent for their meaning on the verbal contex. *Replacement* gestures may also accompany speech, but the significant difference between a replacement and a supplemental gesture is that a replacement gesture has a direct verbal translation, whereas a supplemental gesture does not. Also, the context of a replacement gesture is incidental to its meaning—the gesture for "come here" means "come here" in almost any context—whereas the context is all important in understanding the meaning of a supplemental gesture.

Although the entire body can be involved in supplemental movements, gestures of the hands, the fingers, and the head are most often employed to accompany speech. The face is generally reserved for emotional expression, while the body reflects the intensity of the emotion as well as the relationship between the individuals engaged in conversation or other interaction. This leaves the actual physical accompaniment to the words to the extremities, primarily the fingers, hands, and arms.

Like replacement gestures, supplemental gestures are also used to communicate, but not as explicitly or deliberately. Supplemental gestures are generally within our awareness, but they may be unintentional, almost reflexive actions that accompany speech. A person may not realize that he is gesturing while he talks and may even be unaware of the extent of his movements. Such a person may be very surprised to watch himself on videotape or film and see himself gesturing wildly as he speaks. In fact, many people are as surprised to see what they look like as they are to hear what they sound like. ("That's not me. I don't look like that. I don't do that. I don't sound like that. Something must be wrong with the machine.")

In our daily lives, the use of supplemental gestures may or may not be intentional and therefore may or may not be expressive. Within the context of a dramatic performance, however, everything a character does is expressive. The actor's choice of gesture, and the range, frequency, duration, and intensity of that gesture, imparts some meaning to the movement that is observed and judged by the audience.

Supplemental gestures serve several different functions in human interaction:

- To *repeat* what is being expressed verbally (such as pointing while giving directions). Try giving the following directions without gesturing in any way: "You go up the street to the next light, make a right, go three blocks and make a left at the stop sign, go two more blocks, and it's on the left side of the street next to the donut shop. You can't miss it."
- To *illustrate,* pantomimically, what is being said, for example, demonstrating the structure of an object physically while describing it verbally. "It was about *this* big, and it was shaped something like *this,* with round, smooth sides, and a little square-shaped thing on the top."
- To *accentuate*, emphasize, or underscore a verbal message without directly repeating or illuminating it. Movements of the head and hands are most often employed in this way. Emphatic hand gestures accompany political speeches, for instance, to "hammer" away at the issues, and "pound" the message into the heads of the electorate.
- To *modify* a verbal message. Gestures of this kind are most often used to lessen the impact or effect of verbal expression. A parent may sharply reprimand a child but accompany the reprimand with an impish sidelong glance, or immediately follow it with a smile or a hug to lessen its severity.
- To *contradict* what is being said. People don't generally contradict themselves on purpose, so this type of movement is usually, but not always, unintentional. A person may say she is open to suggestions or advice, while sitting squarely behind a desk, arms folded, upper body contracted, feet flat on the floor, and legs pressed tightly together. Then she looks at her watch. A person may say that she is glad to meet you but accompany that verbal message with a limp handshake while looking around the room for somebody else to engage in conversation.

As noted previously, we judge the truthfulness of a person's words in relation to the physical action that accompanies them. For the most part, this evaluation takes place subconsciously. If our subconscious is not aroused, we have no reason to doubt a person's words and we believe what he says. When a contradiction arises between what a person says and what a person does, however, our subconscious puts our conscious mind on alert. We consciously compare words and action. The entire body comes under close scrutiny. All possible clues to the truthfulness of the speaker's words are investigated. Except in the case of obvious intentional deception—like sarcasm, in which words and action are considered together on an equal basis—we invariably resolve the conflict in deference to what a person does. The person's words become of secondary importance. We rely on our eyes rather than our ears; we believe what we see rather than what we hear. This is particularly important when observing characters interacting on stage. What a character *does* juxtaposed against what he *says* can reveal a great deal about his relationship to other characters.

This principle applies to the relationships between different movements, as well as to the relationship between physical and verbal behavior. One part of a character's body may express one emotion, and another part a *different* emotion. A character may be smiling pleasantly, for example, but the body is tense, the posture aggressive, and the fists clenched. In these situations, the "negative" emotion—anger, fear, sadness, or disgust—will invariably take precedence over the "positive" emotion—happiness or surprise. It's not that the audience is necessarily looking for the worst in a character, but that negative emotions have a greater intensity, which overshadows all but the most intense positive emotions.

As much as we wish it otherwise, this function of movement and gestures—to reveal contradictions—is unavoidable and inescapable. We can expect that our body will remain constant in representing our true feelings, and that it will betray us if we attempt to be deceitful in our dealings with one another. If we inadvertently raise an eyebrow, touch a finger to our nose, or partially cover our mouth with a half-hearted gesture, the lie is immediately exposed. Certainly, some liars are better than others, just as some actors are better than others. Those who can lie most convincingly with their bodies as well as with their words make the best liars—and the best actors.

Physiologists have observed that those who attempt to deceive but who make no conscious effort to hide their deception are apt to demonstrate one or more of the following physical behaviors: less occurrence and shorter duration of eye contact, fewer and less enthusiastic gestures, more hand-shrug movements (indicating uncertainty), more hand movements to the face, less head movement, and a more formal body position. Also, any failure to perform an activity that ordinarily accompanies verbal communication—a noticeable lack of facial expression or hand gestures, for example—is usually a sign that something is amiss and requires further scrutiny. Any one of these behaviors can indicate deception. Taken together, or in any combination, they virtually cry out "Liar!"

Be aware, however, that a few gestures accompanying speech may also be indicative of social standing. The higher the perceived social class of the individual, the fewer and less expansive will be the gestures that accompany his speech. This is true not only in North

American society and culture but in most societies and cultures, even those that are considered highly demonstrative. As always, it is important to know the context of a gesture before characterizing a person's behavior.

A person adept at deception is likely to be aware of these "betrayal" behaviors and to attempt to compensate for them in some way in order to appear "normal." Still, clues invariably "leak out"—a smile that is too big or held too long, a laugh that is just a little too loud, a subtle shifting of weight from one foot to the other, or a half-formed or half-hearted gesture. Most people are able to control their faces, which leaves the "betrayal" of the deception to other parts of the body.

A person who consciously intends to deceive another pays very close attention to the face of the person he wishes to deceive, watching for clues of possible detection. (In a related example, every teacher knows that the student who spends more time watching the teacher than taking a test is the one most likely to cheat. The other students are simply too involved in the test to be looking at the teacher to see if the teacher is looking at them.) If no evidence that the deception has been uncovered is found, the deceiver feels safe and confident. If the deceiver observes that his deception has been discovered or is in danger of being discovered, he will monitor the behavior of the person he wishes to deceive as well as his own.

In the same way, people in an interview situation become desperately afraid of being betrayed by their movement and gestures. Scores of books have been written about interviewing techniques, advising jobseekers on every possible aspect of their physical behavior—how to shake hands, where and how to sit, how to walk, when and how to gesture, how to use their face and eyes—a remarkable range of physical deceptions. An unskilled interviewer likely will be deceived, unless the deception is noticeably amateurish. A skilled interviewer knows all the "tricks," however, and will be adept at discovering the job applicant's true character, experience, and abilities, in spite of attempts to mislead her.

In acting, the name of the game is deception, although in a positive sense. The actor must nevertheless be constantly aware of the messages he is sending to the audience, whether purposely truthful or purposely deceptive. Through lack of awareness the actor may be misleading the audience, either in that what he is expressing to them or to another character is truth when, in fact, it is not, or that what he is expressing is deceitful when it is meant to be truthful. Confusion or misinterpretation can result. The actor must know the truth of the character, and be able to express it truthfully to the audience.

Observe people in conversation. Choose one of the functions of supplemental movements used to accompany speech (such as "to repeat," "to illustrate," or "to accentuate") and look for that type of movement. Choose a different function and observe conversations for that type of movement. Try to determine if the movements you observe are intentional or unintentional. Note, too, any seeming contradictions between words and movement.

In time, and with continued observation, you will be able to categorize each movement a person makes. You will also become increasingly familiar with the types of movement available to you as an actor and the multitude of ways in which this variety of movements can enhance physical characterization. An added bonus: you will become increasingly adept at detecting deception.

Adapting to the Environment

An interesting category of supplemental movement and gestures called *adaptors* or *adaptive behavior* can be very helpful in developing a physical characterization. The term "adaptor" was chosen by anthropologists and psychologists because children develop a wide range of behaviors in an effort to adapt or respond to their environment such as gestures to accompany or replace emotions or other simple self-assuring or self-controlling activities.

Self-adaptive behavior involves the manipulation of one's own body; it is most often associated with psychological and emotional display. Rubbing one's nose, replacing an errant strand of hair, or straightening one's tie are examples of self-adaptive behavior. These types of behavior usually increase during times of anxiety or stress. Hand-wringing increases, for example, as does self-grooming behavior—loosening the collar, tugging on shirt cuffs, smoothing or rearranging the hair. Other self-reinforcing movements like rocking (whether standing or sitting), foot jiggling, tugging on the ear, or stroking the chin also occur in response to stress-producing stimuli. If the anxiety level is too high, however, an individual is likely to "freeze up," to cease adaptive behavior (or *any* behavior, for that matter). Lack of movement can indicate fear or anger depending on the situation and context. The "flight or fight" mechanism takes over as the person decides how to cope with the stressful situation.

It has been observed that rubbing behavior seems to be reassuring, whereas scratching and picking behavior is often associated with anxiety, nervousness, or hostility that is directed toward oneself or hostility toward another that is redirected toward oneself. Behavior that tends to obscure the eyes is often associated with feelings of guilt, shame, or deception. We know from practical experience that a fist likely represents aggression or hostility. Hand-to-nose gestures frequently denote fear or uncertainty. Fingers to the mouth or lips represent shame, embarrassment, or self-consciousness. Open hand gestures commonly express frustration, confusion, or indecision, particularly when such hand movements are accompanied by shoulder shrugs or other upward movement of the shoulders or arms. These are all generalities taken out of context, but observations of the people around you and of your *own* behavior will serve to support many of them. In context, these behaviors can be very revealing of a person's psychological and emotional state.

Alter-adaptive or *other-adaptive* behavior refers to interpersonal physical activities, things we do to other people and in relation to other people. Picking lint off someone's clothes, fixing someone's tie, or wiping a smudge from someone's face are examples of other-adaptive behaviors toward another individual. Think of any situation in which this kind of behavior might occur and you can appreciate its personality-and-relationship-revealing nature. We won't straighten just anyone's tie, nor do we commonly wipe a smudge from a stranger's face, certainly not without good cause and some degree of trepidation.

These kinds of behavior suggest that "permission," whether explicit or implicit, has been given. "Permission" further denotes the existence of a relationship between the individuals involved. We may not know exactly what the relationship is, but we can get a pretty good idea from the behavior itself and from its context. Mutual grooming is a striking example. The closer the relationship between the individuals involved, the more extensive and intimate is the grooming behavior. Observe the difference in the mutual grooming between working associates (straightening one another's ties before an important meeting, for example) and that between family members and between friends and lovers.

Other-adaptive behavior that does not require permission but nonetheless reveals the nature of the relationship includes giving and taking objects or varying the distance between oneself and someone else. Movement of the feet and legs—tapping a foot, swinging a leg, or shifting weight—are also other-adaptive behaviors and are indicative of emotional state and the nature of a relationship.

Object-adaptive behavior, as the term implies, involves the manipulation of objects, real or imaginary. Rearranging the furniture, touching and using objects, or tapping a pencil are examples of object-adaptive behavior, as are tapping an imaginary pencil or a writing-in-the-air gesture. As with all other adaptive behavior, how a person uses an object or implies the use of an object can be highly revealing of that person's character.

The potential for the expressive use of adaptive behavior in characterization is tremendous. Those "little things" a character does can provide considerable insight and demonstrate the character's relationship to his environment and to other characters.

> *Observe others in conversation and in other daily interactions. Observe the adaptive behaviors. Observe how, when, and in what context these adaptive behaviors occur. Try to determine as much as you can about each individual involved in the interaction in terms of her adaptive behavior, and try to discern the essential nature of the relationship between the individuals.*
>
> *Be aware of your own adaptive behaviors. Which do you perform primarily in private and which in public? There are constraints on public behavior, generally in deference to a social situation, that do not exist in private. How do you modify your freely enacted private behavior for public performance?*

As we have noted, adaptive behavior, like other physical behavior, is often unintentional. We just do it, often without realizing it and without knowing why. We've been doing it so long and so habitually, that those movements and those gestures come naturally to us. When it is brought to our attention, we realize just how much of ourselves we've been "giving away."

How many of these kinds of behavior are used regularly on stage? Not many. How often are they used on stage? Not often. Why not? The capacity of adaptive behavior to reveal character is substantial, yet we rarely see adaptive behavior in a stage performance. Characters rarely touch themselves, each other, or objects on the set. It seems to have been ingrained in most actor's minds from early in their careers that such behavior is "too busy" or "too distracting." "Don't do that. You'll draw focus." Some degree of selectivity, discretion, and subtlety is required, but think how much the depiction of such behavior can add to a characterization, to character relationships, and to the play as a whole.

Types of Movement and Gestures

Every movement or gesture a character makes is (or should be) representative of that character as a whole. There are four basic types of character movement: Basic, Primary, Secondary, and Actions of Reaction.

BASIC

These movements emanate from the basic physical structure of the character and reflect the character's essential physical characteristics—age, height, weight, body shape, physical condition, and so on. Basic movements are fundamental to the character and are character-specific. They are expressive of the physical aspects of the character only, however, not the individual's emotional or psychological aspects. The physical aspects of a character these basic character movements reveal are explicit. They tell the audience what the character looks like. The emotional and psychological aspects, which are more implicit, are revealed through the character's physical behavior. Yes, a character may suffer from some emotional or psychological disorder, but the audience doesn't necessarily know that just from looking at him. The audience may perceive from his basic physical structure or appearance that something about him is odd or different, but only when the character does something is his true emotional and psychological nature revealed.

PRIMARY ACTIONS

Primary actions are purely *functional* and accomplish an immediate goal or objective: rising from a chair, walking across a room, picking up an object, and opening a door are all examples of primary movements. The blocking and other stage business assigned to an actor are also primary actions, that is, unembellished actions that accomplish an immediate and clearly identifiable goal. Like basic actions, primary actions provide information about a character's basic physical capabilities, but they reveal little about a character's inner life.

SECONDARY ACTIONS

Secondary actions are purely *expressive*, and accompany, support, or otherwise embellish a primary action. These actions do not accomplish a particular task on their own (in fact, by their very nature they cannot), but they serve to heighten or augment the effect of a primary action. Primary actions are what a character does to accomplish a particular goal; secondary actions are how a character performs the primary action. For the actor, this is an important distinction. What is done and how it is done are distinct aspects of the same movement. The audience, however, views the activity as unified. It makes assumptions and draws conclusions about a character based on the total behavior they observe.

Secondary actions are highly revealing of character. For example, if a character walks across the room and picks up a book, both walking across the room and picking up a book are functional, goal-oriented, *primary* activities. How the character walks across the room and how she picks up the book are expressive, secondary actions. A character slams a door. She needn't have slammed it simply to close it, but slamming it—a secondary action—imparts an expressive element to the purely functional (and otherwise sufficient) movement of closing the door—a primary action. The secondary action is wholly unnecessary to achieving the goal of closing the door, but how the character performs even this simple physical act speaks volumes about the character's emotional state.

Consider these scenarios:

> **Scenario 1:** A character calmly opens a door and calmly enters a room, calmly walks across the room, calmly picks up a book from the desk, calmly opens the book and looks at it, calmly closes it and, calmly puts it back down on the desk. He then calmly walks back across the room, and calmly leaves the room, calmly closing the door behind him.

> **Scenario 2**: A character bursts through the door and into the room, runs across the room, grabs a book from the desk, tears it open, searches frantically through the pages, slams the book shut, and throws it down on the desk. She then storms out of the room slamming the door behind her.

> **Scenario 3:** A character carefully and quietly opens the door and cautiously enters the room, tip-toes carefully across the room, very carefully picks up a book from the desk, opens it carefully and looks at it, quietly closes the book, and carefully and quietly replaces it on the

desk. He then tip-toes carefully back across the room, and leaves the room slowly and carefully, quietly closing the door behind him.

Scenario #4: A character slowly and quietly opens the door and cautiously enters the room, walks casually across the room, calmly picks up a book from the desk, opens it carefully and looks at it, slams the book shut, and hurls it across the room. She then strides noisily out the door, slamming it behind her.

In each scenario, the primary actions were identical, but the secondary actions were different. The functions of the movement were the same in each scenario, but the expression of the emotional and psychological state of the character was different in each case.

ACTIONS OF REACTION

From the character's point of view, an action of reaction is any spontaneous or involuntary movement in response to some sudden or otherwise unexpected occurrence. Reactions to loud noises, to pain, or to the unexpected actions of another person fall into this category. Spontaneous movement representing emotions, such as facial expressions, are also considered actions of reaction.

From the actor's point of view, however, there is no such thing as an action of reaction. The actor knows what's coming, even if the character doesn't, yet the actor must appear to react spontaneously, even though the reaction is consciously and purposely enacted, and has probably been rehearsed in detail for weeks. Characters have actions of reactions; actors don't.

Like secondary actions, actions of reaction are also highly revealing of character. The audience learns a great deal about a character by how that character reacts to the world around him. Consider this scenario:

Two characters stand on stage. A loud gunshot sounds from offstage. At the shot, one character flinches noticeably and turns to the sound. The other character barely reacts.

One character flinched, and the other didn't. Hmmmmm. Interesting. The audience expects and understands the first character's reaction to the shot. In fact, it was probably the same reaction they had sitting out there in the dark, comfortably watching the play, minding their own business. The second character's reaction is unexpected, however, and intriguing. Either the second character has nerves of steel (or wishes to appear as if he does) or he knew the shot was coming. In any case, the audience learns something they didn't know before.

> *Observe yourself and others in daily activities. Categorize your physical behavior and theirs in relation to the characteristics of movement and gestures noted above—primary and secondary actions and actions of reaction.*
>
> *Explore the scenarios described in this section. Vary the primary and secondary actions in each. Expand the scenarios to include other primary actions, then explore the expressive potential of a variety of secondary actions to accompany the primary actions.*

Consider the difference between language (words) and behavior (action); between motivation (reason or emotional drive) and intent (purpose or objective); between character (true self) and personality (projected self). Consider expression (motivation + intent + action), context (which is everything), and perceptions (yours, the character's, and the audience's). Consider the attributes and functions of movement (body) and gesture (face, hands, arms, and sometimes feet). Consider the factors influencing movement and gesture and the types of movement and gesture. Consider all of the observation exercises. That's quite a lot for an actor to think about, and those are just the basics.

The challenge facing the actor is to convert these theories and observations of movement into practical applications and then to synthesize all the elements of physical behavior into an interesting, compelling, and believable characterization. For that, the actor needs alternatives from which to select the physical behaviors most appropriate to the character that he wishes to portray. That transformation is the subject of the next chapter.

Building a Character 2

Imagine this scene:

> The curtain rises. The lights come up to reveal the set—a living room, circa 1879, Norway. The set is realistic and contains period furniture, props, and decoration. A door upstage right, now closed, leads to the front hall, and outdoors. A door upstage left, partially open, leads to a study, a portion of which can be seen. A curtained window is near the front of the left wall. A small sofa is near the window. Between the window and the door on the left wall is a small bookcase with deluxe edition, leather-bound books. A stove is against the right stage wall, fire in the stove, a rocking chair and two other chairs nearby. Between the stove and the upstage right door is a small table. There is a rug on the floor. Framed etchings hang on the walls.
>
> A character in the play, a woman in period costume, dressed for a winter day, enters from the stage right door. She car-

> ries several wrapped packages, which she
> places on the table near the door. Another char-
> acter in the play, a man, also dressed in period
> costume, enters from the study, pen in hand.

Now imagine *this* scene:

> There is no curtain. The lights come up to reveal
> a nearly bare stage. There is no set as such, and
> no set decorations of any kind. There is one
> small, nondescript table stage right, and one
> straight-backed chair stage left. The stage is
> open to the back wall, and the audience can see
> clearly into the wings on both sides of the stage.
> Lighting instruments hang in plain view over
> the stage area.
>   The first character in the play, a woman
> dressed in modern attire, walks on from right
> stage. She carries a small, plain cardboard box
> which she places on the table. Shortly there-
> after, the second character, a man, enters from
> left stage. He holds a pencil.

What is the difference between the two scenes in terms of the development of individual characterization and character relationships?
Trick question: there is no difference. The play is the same in both instances—*A Doll's House,* by Henrik Ibsen, and the characters are the
same—Nora and Torvald Helmer. To the experienced actor, the bare
stage setting with modern dress and minimal props is certainly more
challenging. The actor can expect no "assistance" from the set and
costumes in providing a ready-made frame of reference in which the
audience can observe the characters. Yet the bare stage and lack of
period set, props, furniture, and costumes are no obstacle to a fully
developed characterization—a minor inconvenience, perhaps, but not
a serious obstacle.

    The inexperienced actor might protest that she will be unable to
work under such "primitive" conditions without what she considers to
be the proper support—the sets, costumes, special lighting and sound
effects, props, and so on. That is the difference between a skilled and
unskilled actor. The skilled actor has the ability to develop a characterization fully from within herself, based on the intrinsic elements of
the play, no matter what her external circumstances may be. All that
is necessary for theatre are "two planks and a passion," and the

planks are optional. Some of the best theatre ever seen has been performed with no planks at all.

Process and Product

Characterization is both a process and a product. It is a *process* in the sense that developing a character begins long before the actor sets foot on the stage and continues through the final curtain on closing night. A character in a play, like each of us, is constantly growing and changing in response to her life experiences—the people, places, things, and situations with which she comes in contact.

Characterization is a *product* in the sense that the characterization is essentially complete and fully formed by the time the audience first sees the character on stage. What remains to be seen is the moment-to-moment development of the character in relation to the development of the play. Every such moment is the result of the character's experiences to that point.

Levels of Characterization

The development of a physical characterization takes place along four distinct but wholly interdependent paths or levels: physical, environmental, psychological, and emotional. In simple terms, the *physical* level establishes what the character looks like. The *environmental* level determines where the character comes from in terms of his social, economic, and cultural background, and in relation to his life's work. The *psychological* level examines the character's thought process and how he processes his thoughts. The *emotional* level addresses how the character feels.

The development of physical characterization is not quite so simple. A character's movement depends on the complex interrelationship of these four levels within the context of the play. An awareness of each of these levels in relation to the basic building blocks of physical expression and the illumination of the play as a whole is essential to an understanding of physical characterization.

The intrinsic physical structure of a character is the point from which all other states are represented. The actor's challenge is, in effect, to represent not only the essential physical state of the character but also the emotional and psychological states of the character, which flow through that basic physical structure. No one level of characterization dominates. All work together to determine the essential elements of the characterization.

PHYSICAL LEVEL

As mentioned in Chapter 1, feeling comes before thought, and thought before action. Each of these processes is presented to the audience through movement. The basic structure of the body and how the body functions will influence how a character's state is portrayed. The imaginary realm between "thought" and "action" is the province of the structure and function of the body, and from this fundamental physical state flows the representation of a character's psychological and emotional states.

The basic question the actor must answer is "What does the character look like?" The actor must determine the external traits of the character, such as age, body shape, and body build, which do not affect the plot or theme of the play directly but form the physical framework for the character's expressive behavior. It is this behavior that affects the dramatic content of the play.

Body types. ■ Plastic surgery and metaphysics notwithstanding, a person cannot escape the body with which he was born. Exercise, diet, makeup, clothing, body carriage, and physical attitude can alter the body's appearance, but its basic physical structure remains relatively constant throughout life.

Body-personality research maintains that there are three major body types: (1) *endomorphic*—round, soft, and fat; (2) *mesomorphic*—muscular, bony, and athletic; and (3) *ectomorphic*—thin and fragile. Research also associates these three body types with certain perceptions of temperament, certain personality traits, and certain kinds of behavior. Remember that these are perceptions of personality traits and general classifications of physical structures.

Particular personality and behavioral characteristics are associated with each body type:

Endomorph (round, soft): Dependent, affable, generous, relaxed, tolerant, sociable, sluggish, affectionate, emotional, cooperative, sympathetic, forgiving.

Mesomorph (muscular, athletic): Dominant, determined, adventurous, confident, outgoing, optimistic, energetic, courageous, aggressive, enthusiastic, argumentative, temperamental.

Ectomorph (thin, fragile): Tense, anxious, meticulous, self-conscious, thoughtful, considerate, shy, suspicious, awkward, tactful, cautious, introspective.

Few people demonstrate the personality and behavioral characteristics associated with one specific body type alone. Most of us are a combination and exhibit an interesting mix of behaviors from all categories. In terms of developing a viable characterization, however, this list is a good place to start.

> *Apply these body shapes and behavioral characteristics to yourself. Which body shape most closely represents your own? Which kinds of behavior apply to you? Are your body type and your behavior consistent with this list? In what ways could you alter your body type to more closely resemble a different one? Naturally, an actor must know her own body type and be aware of her own behavior before she can alter them to project the qualities that are physically and psychologically appropriate for her character.*

Age. ■ Age, like beauty, is often in the eye of the beholder. Individuals are as unique in their aging as they are in other ways. The aging process is affected as much by attitude, level of physical activity, and general health as by chronological age. In fact, psychologists often differentiate between chronological age (actual years on earth), physical age (the disposition of the body in relation to the overall aging process), and mental age (learning ability or mental outlook).

A person's physical behavior represents his attitude about himself and the world around him. An athletic fifty-year-old person can appear, and behave, as if he were several years younger. A sickly thirty-year-old person can likewise appear and act as if he were several years older. Not all eighty-year-olds are resigned to the imminent approach of death or walk with a cane and a faltering step, nor do all seventeen-year-olds have an upbeat mental attitude and walk with a youthful, loping stride. An actor must therefore take into consideration not only the character's actual, chronological age, but his general outlook on life and his physical capabilities.

The age of a character as played is often related to the actual chronological age of the actor. Juliet is rarely played by a thirteen-year-old (somewhere near Juliet's actual age), and few seventy-or-more-year-olds have ventured into the realm of Lear. As long as Juliet is relatively the same age as Romeo, and Mom and Dad Capulet and Montague look old enough to be their parents, all is well. As for Lear, there's always makeup, of course, a fake beard and wig, and a thunder sheet. Hamlet is often played by those who are too old (Edwin Forrest, Edwin Booth, Richard Burton, and Laurence Olivier played Hamlet *well* past their youth), as are most of Shakespeare's other leading characters. No matter. The audience's willing suspension of disbelief includes an implied agreement to overlook sometimes obvious age discrepancies between actor and character.

Much depends, too, on how the character is played. Errol Flynn played swashbuckling heroes, rogues, and pirates until he could swash and buckle no longer. Flynn's exuberance, his youthful good looks, and his remarkable athletic ability enabled him to portray such characters well beyond the supposed limits of his chronological age. Many of these characters became whatever age Flynn appeared to be.

Height. ■ The actual height of an actor is a given, of course, but his onstage height, like his age, is relative. One character may seem taller or shorter than another, not only because of the actual height of the actors in question, but in relation to each character's carriage and demeanor. The relative "stature" of a character in a play has considerable influence on the audience's perception of that character's physical dimensions. A character may dominate the stage physically, but the actor may be only five-foot-two. A tall character may appear to "shrink" in the presence of a shorter, but more dominant or physically imposing character. A shorter character may actually seem to "grow" in the eyes of the audience during the course of the play.

Most of the time, however, a character's height doesn't really matter. Rarely is it relevant, rarely is any reference to height made in the text of a play, and rarely is any mention of it made by the playwright in her description of a character. It happens once in a while, and even in those instances it still might not matter. In *A Streetcar Named Desire*, by Tennessee Williams, the character of Mitch is described by the playwright as six feet, one-and-a-half inches tall. The character of Josie in *A Moon for the Misbegotten* is described by Eugene O'Neill as five feet eleven in her stocking feet. These descriptions give the director and actor a substantial frame of reference in terms of the playwright's conception of a character's overall physical structure. More often than not, however, Mitch will be played by an actor who is *not* six feet, one-and-a-half inches tall, and there is every likelihood that Josie will be played by a woman who is shorter (sometimes *considerably* shorter) than five feet eleven.

For the most part, the audience won't even think about the height of an individual character unless there is a noticeable disproportion in the physical relationship between characters. The audience expects that leading men will be taller than leading ladies, but if they're not, the audience will get over it, unless the leading lady is so much taller than the leading man that the disparity in height distracts from the character's relationship. Even then, this discrepancy in height may be the playwright's intention in order to illustrate some aspect of the play.

For the most part, the height of a character is usually of minor consequence to the plot and theme of a play, and therefore holds little significance in terms of the overall characterization. Judge the relevance of the height of a character (or the relevance of any other physical element of the characterization for that matter) by the importance of that characteristic to the play as a whole. If it's mentioned in the play, it probably matters, at least to some extent. It may not matter very much—that will still have to be determined in relation to the play as a whole—but it matters nonetheless. If the characteristic in question is not mentioned in the play, and seems to hold no relevance to the play as a whole, then it probably doesn't matter.

Posture. ■ "Stand up straight!" "Don't slouch!" "Stomach in! Chest out! Chin up!" Posture has two components: (1) the overall level or degree of tension displayed in the body as a whole, and (2) the position of the body—standing, leaning, sitting, kneeling, lying down—although not all levels of tension are possible in every position.

Posture is described in a number of ways: hunched, stooped, slumped, drooped, slouched, sagging, tired, relaxed, straight, upright, uptight, erect, and over-erect ("at attention"). A particular posture may be intrinsic to the character, part of the character's natural physical structure, and therefore relatively unchanging (such as the "hunched" appearance of the Hunchback of Notre Dame or Richard III). A character's posture may be temporary, and could change or evolve, depending on the situations in which the character finds himself throughout the play. The two components of posture are also relatively independent. Elements of posture can be combined, or they may temper one another. The Hunchback may stand erect, as best he can, and an exhausted soldier may stand "at attention," but in an exhausted sort of way.

> *In a standing position, assume the characteristics you associate with each postural level of tension. As you progress through the list, note how your body changes, often in very subtle ways, from one posture to another. Change your body position from standing to sitting, then kneeling, and then lying down, and again progress through the list of postures. Note in which ways you were able to change or differentiate your posture and in which ways you were not.*
>
> *Assume any one of the postures mentioned above. Try to temper or combine that posture with others from the list.*

Note which postures you were able to combine and which you were not.

Explore the different levels or degrees of the physical representation of each posture on the list. If you discover a new posture or variation, add the new posture to your list for future reference.

Alignment. ■ Alignment is the relationship of the spine to the body as a whole. In a normal aligned body configuration, the spine forms a gentle "S" curve from the base of the neck to the pelvis when viewed from the side. Viewed from the front or back, the spine is relatively straight from neck to pelvis. Misalignment (or curvature of the spine) is generally due to a physical or mental disorder and is a permanent condition corrected only by surgery. An upper-to-lower curvature of the spine—where the upper spine is curved noticeably forward—results in a "hunchbacked" appearance. A side-to-side curvature makes the body appear asymmetrical. Osteoporosis, a degenerative bone disease that often afflicts older persons (particularly women), results in a pronounced curvature of the upper spine. The person appears hunchbacked. In some forms of schizophrenia, the disorder is commonly reflected in a side-to-side misalignment of the body. The body appears to be in conflict with itself or to represent parts of two different people and reflects the person's mental state.

Two examples from the dramatic literature that clearly illustrate the characteristics of *posture* and *alignment* are our old friend Richard III and the character of John Merrick in *The Elephant Man* by Bernard Pomerance. Shakespeare provides no substantive description of Richard in the list of characters other than that he is "Duke of Gloucester, afterwards King Richard III." This briefly describes Richard's station in life at the beginning of the play and offers clues to his future accomplishments, but it tells us absolutely nothing about Richard's physical appearance. Richard does, however, describe himself. On his very first entrance, after a few opening comments to set the scene, Richard assesses his own physical appearance: "rudely stamped . . . curtail'd of this fair proportion . . . deformed, unfinished . . . scarce half made up, and that so lamely and unfashionable that dogs bark at me as I halt by them."

What can we gather from this description that will help us "mold" the physical character of Richard? He says that he is "scarce half made up"; half of his body is deformed. His side-to-side alignment is likely asymmetrical. Accordingly, he walks with a noticeable limp—"as I halt by them"—but no mention is made of crutch or cane. Later in the same scene Richard kneels in front of Lady Anne, so we can assume that the deformity is not seriously debilitating.

Richard is often portrayed with a deformed arm and sometimes with a deformed hand. This could be deduced from another description of himself later in the play: "Behold mine arm is like a blasted sapling, wither'd up." He could be exaggerating his deformity for effect, of course, but there is probably some degree of truth in his statement. Richard makes no specific mention of his hand, although we might infer a problem from the description of his arm.

In spite of his deformities, Richard has a fairly high opinion of himself, which should be reflected by the actor's characterization of his general physical attitude and appearance. In terms of posture, his deformity may cause him to adopt a slightly hunchbacked appearance that favors his deformed side. Margaret, the widow of King Henry VI, calls him a "poisonous, bunch-back'd toad." He may not, in fact, be hunchbacked (or a toad, for that matter), but simply appear to be so because of the misalignment of his body.

The actor playing Richard must decide which side of the character is deformed and proceed from there with the balance of his physical characterization. In Shakespeare's time, left-handed people were considered "sinister" (*sinister* comes from the Latin word for "left" and the Old English word *wynestra*, which translates as "friendlier," but in an ironic sense.) The word in common usage during Shakespeare's time meant "unfavorable," "evil," or "injurious," as it does today. A literal interpretation would suggest that Richard's *right* side (his "good" side) is deformed, whereas his *left* side (his "sinister" or bad side) is fully intact and fully functional—figuratively and literally. This physical alignment and posture (not to mention the "wither'd up" arm thing) may require a considerable adjustment on the part of a right-handed actor. Left-handed actors, already inclined to the "sinister," will have far less difficulty with the physical characterization.

The Elephant Man is based on the life of John Merrick, an actual person whose body was seriously deformed. The playwright offers an admonition to the actor playing Merrick to forego any attempt at a realistic portrayal of the character because it is potentially injurious to the actor's body and distracting to the audience. Early in the play, Frederick Treves, another character who is a surgeon and teacher, describes Merrick's physical appearance in graphic detail, accompanied by slide projections. The playwright suggests that this should suffice to provide the necessary information about the character's physical appearance.

It is assumed, however, that the actor cast in the role of Merrick will make some attempt, however minimal, to suggest Merrick's physical appearance. The actor must decide which of Merrick's many physical afflictions he will portray and to what extent. Merrick's posture and alignment are described specifically in the play; even if they were not, they could easily be deduced from the available information. In addition to his deformities, Merrick also suffers from a disease that has made him lame and he walks with the assistance of a crutch or a cane. Other decisions about Merrick's physical representation will depend on the range and type of movement required of the character over the course of the play. Richard and Merrick are extreme examples of physical adaptation on the part of the actor, but they serve to demonstrate the basic principles of posture and overall physical characterization.

Attitude. ■ Attitude is described as the character's physical bearing or overall physical demeanor. Attitude is related to how the character "carries" herself and how she "presents" herself physically. Some elements of a character's attitude relate solely to the character herself— to her "image" of herself, to her physical demeanor, and to her inherent or intrinsic physical structure. Attitude is also very closely related to the physical relationship between and among characters: a character's posture and alignment may naturally be quite good, but the character may alter her posture or alignment or both in deference to the presence of another character. A character may have a "regal" bearing in one scene—upright, noble, stately, aristocratic-looking, perhaps a little haughty—yet appear to be more like a servant— slightly stooped, deferential, humble, obeisant, and respectful—in another scene or with other characters. The character is the same but her physical appearance reflects a different attitude in different environments.

It might be argued that physical attitude reflects emotional characteristics rather than physical ones. Physical attitude is a representation of the character's emotional or psychological state if the emotional state and the physical representation of that emotional state remain unchanged. The distinction is this: a character's defining emotional state may be one of arrogance, which will be reflected in his physical characterization throughout the play, while another character may only seem to be arrogant in certain situations or in scenes with certain other characters. The character's underlying state may reflect some other emotion that necessitates the appearance of arrogance in selected circumstances.

ENVIRONMENTAL LEVEL

Environmental influences are those factors that place a character within a specific environment and which define or influence her relationship to all the other characters in the play—occupation, education, economic status, profession, social relationships, familial relationships, religious background, and so on. There are two basic environmental concerns: the character's *formative* environment and the character's *present* environment. Each influences the character's physical behavior.

The formative environment. ■ Like every movement, every individual exists in a particular context. These social, cultural, and occupational contexts influence an individual in ways that are represented in that person's physical behavior.

An individual moves in many different social spheres. These are determined by birth or birthright, by culture, by occupation, by relative income, by one's standing in the community, and so on. Each sphere influences a person's behavior within that particular sphere and in relation to other spheres.

When spheres of influence overlap or intersect (or collide), the most conservative, most limited, most restrictive sphere exerts the greatest influence on behavior. Imagine being with friends at a party . . . for the boss . . . at the boss's country club . . . in a very exclusive part of town . . . accompanied by your fiancée . . . and her parents, the King and Queen of Luxembourg. Each social sphere imposes certain expectations as well as greater restrictions.

Everyone is a product of a particular cultural heritage. Some represent only one culture but most represent more than one. Every person reflects, nevertheless, a particular, individual-specific mix of cultures. A person's primary cultural influence is likely to be that into which she was born or in which she has spent the greater part of her life. Secondary cultural influences may arise from places in which a person has lived, people with whom she's come in contact in the course of her life or her own interests, for example, in reading, study, or travel. No matter how few or how many cultural influences affect a person, they are specific to that individual and not likely to be shared with any other person.

Variations in behavior between and among people from different cultures can be quite distinct. The effect of such influences is often reflected in how people greet each other (with a polite "English" handshake or a bone-crushing "Russian bear hug"), how a character holds his knife and fork at dinner ("American style," "European style," or

"Middle Eastern style") or by conversational distance from other people ("Japanese" distance, "Latin American" distance," or "standard North American" distance).

The context in which behavior occurs also adds another level of meaning to the movements. "Fish out of water"-type comedies are constructed around this idea. The comic situations center on a character's inability to adapt to her new cultural environment, her comic faux pas as she tries in vain to "fit in." Each of her failures to adapt to her environment compounds the situation and leads to all sorts of comic possibilities.

As with other such subtle physical behavior, the audience may not know what differentiates one character from another exactly, but it will notice that something is different, something that enhances the characterization, and in time, will discover what that certain "something" is.

Occupational influences are less complex than cultural influences. Everybody has an occupation, something that "occupies" his time. Some are paid and some are not. Some are widely recognized and others are not. Whether a person is paid for his "work" and whether the work fits into a neat, bureaucratically designated category may affect the person's emotional and psychological states, but it does not affect his physical state. What a person does and how a person does it influences physical behavior outside the normal bounds of his occupation.

The movement patterns required in an occupation become habitual over time. Repeated tasks are performed with little conscious effort or thought as the body "learns the routine." What is interesting, however, is that few of the habitual occupational movement patterns that are so much a part of a person's occupational life are relevant to that person's daily life. We carry the trappings of our trade, such as mode of dress and hairstyle, around with us. Think of a surgeon, a lumberjack, or an office worker. Yet specialized skills such as surgery, chopping down a tree, or standing around the water cooler are usually appropriate only in limited and structured environments and situations.

There are, however, residual elements or by-products of occupational movement patterns that can and do relate to daily life. An office clerk may be accustomed to a neat and orderly desk at work and her "home office" may reflect this influence. This same clerk may be accustomed to sitting at a desk in a small cubicle for several hours a day, whereas a landscaper, accustomed to moving around outdoors all day long, may be able to sit in a confined space for only a few minutes at a time. Both clerk and landscaper work with their hands, but each has developed different sets of muscles, different skills and abilities, and different patterns of movement according to the requirements and demands of each particular occupation. Landscapers are not generally required to file and type, nor are clerks required to plant trees.

The present environment. ■ There are as many perceptions of the world around us as there are people. A character in a play is no less influenced by his environment than we are. How a character perceives his environment is of considerable importance to the actor, because it is from this perception that many physical elements of the characterization evolve.

Elements of the onstage environment that most directly influence physical characterization are the setting, the set; the presence (or absence) of other characters; design elements, including props, furniture, lighting, and sound; and the costuming. Each of these elements influences and in some way contributes directly to physical characterization.

The setting of a play includes geographical location, climate, season, temperature, and so on. All of these can affect characterization, some physically and some psychologically. The effects of temperature, for example, are well known to anyone who has stood in subzero weather waiting for a bus or endured a sweltering summer night without air conditioning.

"Stellaaaaaaaaaaaa!!" Some of Tennessee Williams's *A Streetcar Named Desire* is set on a hot and humid late-summer night in New Orleans. To what extent do these elements contribute to Stanley's irritability, his restlessness, or his aggression? How do temperature and humidity affect the other characters? Everybody seems to be perspiring (except Blanche, who "glows"). If enough characters on stage are constantly wiping their brows and fanning themselves, the audience will soon begin to empathize with the characters' plight and may even begin to feel uncomfortably warm. That's what acting is all about—inducing the audience to feel, to react intellectually, emotionally, and physically, to the action of the play. It can be done, and a clear representation of these environmental elements of the play can add immeasurably to the audience's empathetic response to the characters and to their understanding of the play as a whole.

A stage set is designed to reflect the time and place in which the play unfolds, with architecture, furnishings, furniture, and props appropriate to that time and place. The set is also designed to reflect the lives of the people who inhabit it, to serve as a physical representation of their personal history. It reflects their perceptions of their environment, their experiences, their goals, their objectives, their relationships, and so on. The presence of objects—and their absence—reveals something about each of the inhabitants.

The stage set is an artificially constructed environment, however, intended to suggest another environment. The actual space a set occupies is relative to the imaginary space it represents. The actor need not therefore be confined to the actual space; she is free to interpret that space in an imaginative way to suit the purposes of the character, the character's interaction with other characters, and the imaginative environment of the play.

The stage space may be physically confining in a real sense, yet the imaginative space may extend far beyond the walls of the set, perhaps even beyond the walls of the theatre. A set may reveal only one room of a house, for example, yet the action of the play may be enacted beyond the confines of that room. In this case, the actual set suggests only part of the total imaginative environment. If, however, a character were required to live out his life in one small corner of this room, her activity and awareness might very well be confined to the real stage space, in reality and in imagination. It's a matter of the character's perspective.

Implications of the environment for physical characterization. ■ Every interior and exterior space, natural or man-made, reflects the lives of its inhabitants—a house, the lives of the family that resides there; an office, the life of the worker who inhabits it from nine to five. For man-made spaces, the construction materials, the size of the space, the distribution of objects within that space, and the number and characteristics of these objects all have something to say about the person or persons who live or work there.

We try to manipulate our environment to reflect how we'd like other people to perceive us. An executive's office (large desk, plush carpet, and expensive furnishings) is designed to reflect the status of its occupant. In fact, a large office generally serves very little function except to denote the status of its occupant. Never mind that the occupant is an idiot. His office declares to the world that he is someone to be reckoned with.

It's surprising that so little of our environment is the result of our own personal choice. We live and work in environments that are imposed on us, sometimes even against our wishes. Few people, for example, actually want to live in a jail or work in a cold, uninviting, and impersonal factory or office. Nevertheless, that's the environment in which some people find themselves. There are elements within an environment we *can* change and, given an opportunity, we *do* change them. Otherwise, we simply learn to adapt.

Look around you. If this is space you regularly inhabit, many of the objects will be representative of some aspect of your life. Some objects will literally shout your name. (Others may simple spell it out, like your "#1 Dad" or "#1 Mom" coffee mug, your monogrammed towels, or that goofy, personalized hat you got at Disneyland.) Other objects will only suggest your presence, yet most of the things in the room will bear your imprint in some way, even those that may not actually be your personal property. If you have touched an object, moved it, or in any way influenced its placement in this space, it reflects your presence.

The arrangement of objects within a particular environment also provides information about its inhabitants. Look around the space and determine how you would rearrange the objects to accommodate a visit by a perspective employer or other important person. What would you change? What would you hide from view or place in a more prominent location? How would you rearrange the space to accommodate the visit of a friend, the local minister, a known thief, an ex-girlfriend, ex-boyfriend, or ex-spouse? With whom and under what conditions would you abandon this space altogether and seek another space for the visit?

Set and props designers endeavor to reflect not only a play's time and place but also the lives of the characters who inhabit the sets and use the props. That's part of their job. Actors generally take little notice of the set and props in this regard, except to complain when their props are missing or when the left stage door won't open. Actors seem to notice the props and set only when they inhibit their acting or their movement, rather than including them in the development of their characterizations.

Another interesting implication of the relationship between us and our environment: a detective knows that every person (or animal, for that matter) who enters a crime scene brings something to the scene that he leaves behind and takes something else away. It's the detective's job to discover those things that have been left behind and those that have been taken away, and by the process of elimination, to determine who "done it."

Likewise, every character who enters a scene in a play brings something into that environment that one leaves behind and takes something else away. The difference in modus operandi between a criminal and a character in a play is that what the criminal leaves behind and takes away are real, tangible things—drops of blood (the victim's, his own, or both), footprints leading away from the crime scene, a strand of hair, a glove, a body or two—whereas what a character takes away and leaves is more likely to be something of an emotional or psychological nature, such as thoughts, ideas, and emotions. A character brings a rose into a room and forgets her gloves on the way out. The rose and the gloves are important to the characterization, but they are less important to the play as a whole than the string of broken hearts the character leaves in her wake.

Perceptions of the environment. ■ Every day we move through several different environments (even in simply moving from room to room in our own home), and we experience certain reactions in response to each environment, including perceptions of space and time that influence how we relate to each.

Our perception of a particular environment is a function of whether or not we feel comfortable, welcome, and at ease: in general, the greater the perceived formality, the more superficial, hesitant, and conservative the physical behavior; conversely, the less formal a space, the more relaxed the behavior.

In the 1990s, a dining room is generally perceived as a more formal space than the family recreation room. In the 1890s, however, family recreation rooms didn't exist, and a dining room might be considered a less formal setting by virtue of the fact that people commonly dined there (rather than in the family recreation room in front of the wide-screen television). A character in a play set in the 1890s may feel perfectly comfortable in a formal dining room, whereas the actor portraying the character might not. It is the character, however, not the actor, who is attending the formal dinner, and the actor must reflect the character's perception of the setting rather than his own.

Many plays alternate between public and private spaces, and between public and private conversations. Playwrights recognize that characters say and do things in private they would not say or do in public. The contrast between what a person does or says in private and what she does or says in public illuminates that person's character. Think of any of Shakespeare's plays. Characters appear alternately in public and private spaces and often engage in public and private conversations *within* each type of space. A notable example occurs in *Richard III*, where Richard confides to the audience, by means of monologues expressing his private thoughts, that he is a villain. Fair enough. The proof of that, however, is in his public behavior, which supports and reinforces what he has told the audience privately, thereby confirming his villainy.

Privacy affords characters an opportunity for greater intimacy than a meeting in public would allow and helps to reveal individual personalities and true relationships. Lovers may exhibit restrained, even noncommittal behavior in public, but share a passionate and demonstrative relationship in private. Two politicians may appear antagonistic in public, but in a private meeting demonstrate a close, personal friendship.

People can achieve the sense of a private space *within* a public space by behaving *as if* they were in private—moving closer together, sharing intimate if somewhat restrained physical contact, and speaking quietly to one another. A couple holding hands at a table in a crowded restaurant and gazing lovingly into each other's eyes effectively precludes intrusion into this "private" world.

An interesting dramatic situation is that in which a truly private moment is disclosed or exposed in a public forum. The characters find themselves in circumstances that reveal important aspects of their character through their reaction to the disclosure. It doesn't have to be a major revelation: even a minimal disruption of the status quo will suffice.

When we meet a person for the first time, we are apt to be cautious, deliberate, and conservative in our initial interaction. An unfamiliar environment inhibits our responses in the same way. We may not know how to "act" in a given environment, particularly if it is unfamiliar to us. Likewise, finding oneself in an unfamiliar situation, even in a familiar environment, changes the individual's perceptions of that environment. It is one thing to entertain friends in one's home, but it is quite another to entertain an employer, the President of the United States, or "the man who came to dinner."

Notice how often, in both professional and amateur productions, that a character enters a room, apparently for the first time, yet appears perfectly at ease in this unfamiliar environment. Either the character has been there before, thereby revealing important information, or the actor portraying the character has misled us. If a character in a play is expected to be representative of a real person, why then wouldn't that character behave as a real person would? If the character has never been in a room before, the actor must reflect that fact, even if he is intimately familiar with it after several weeks of rehearsal.

Think of Sherlock Holmes entering a room for the first time. Whether it is a crime scene or not, he surveys the room in a deliberate and systematic way and takes the measure of every person in the room. When he is satisfied that he has learned all he can, he makes himself comfortable or simply leaves, having discovered all he needs to know.

> *The next time you have an opportunity, enter a room and*
> *survey it in Holmesian fashion. (You will probably learn*
> *as much about a familiar room as you will an unfamiliar*
> *room.) The purpose of the exercise is to remind yourself to*
> *approach each room anew, as if, like the character in the*
> *play, you were seeing it for the first time. What do you do*
> *when you first enter a room? What do you do once you have*
> *your bearings? You'll discover that much of what you would*
> *do "as the character" is very similar to what you would do*
> *yourself: look around, examine objects in the room, observe*
> *the arrangement of the furniture, scan the titles of the books*
> *on the shelves, touch some objects and refrain from touch-*
> *ing others. Most important, you'll notice things, particularly*
> *those that appeal to you personally or help you understand*
> *the inhabitants of this room.*

Another important factor is an individual's perception of freedom, or the lack thereof, within a particular environment. Is the environment seen as a prison (as Hamlet considers his environment), or is it relatively free of constraints on an individual's movements? The intensity of our perception of constraint is relative to the period of our confinement, our relationship to others with whom we may be confined, and even to the nature of the space itself. Denmark is not a particularly small country, yet it seemed to Hamlet to be far too confining for his personality and his ambitions. We may find ourselves "imprisoned" at a cocktail party with a lot of boring people, but we are relatively free to move about within that particular environment until we can make our "escape" to the real world.

Some people live confined within themselves. By choice or circumstance they are cut off from the outside world and exist solely within their own bodies and within their own minds. Most of us would consider this an unfortunate situation, but it is not our perception that matters. The individual may be perfectly content to live out her life in her own little world, and for the actor, it's the *character's* perspective that counts. The actor's job is to portray that perspective to the audience in the character's physical behavior.

"I could be bounded in a nutshell, and count myself a king of infinite space," exclaims Hamlet. Conversely, we could find ourselves on a huge stage, yet be bounded by the imposed reality of the set or by the totally imaginary limitations within which we are expected to function. A set is real. It is built of real canvas and wood, and it contains real furniture and real objects, but it is not supposed to be reality. It simply represents certain aspects of reality. The reality of the set is contained within the larger reality of the stage and of the theatre building, expanding ever outward to the very limits of our imagination.

It would be interesting to try to discover at what point in the continuum outward from the actor's body reality gives way to imagination. We may have a practical knowledge of the stage, the set, the theatre building, the surrounding neighborhood, and certain other areas of the city, perhaps, but beyond that we can only imagine. We are compelled to rely on our imaginations to "fill in the blanks" of our knowledge, experience, and awareness. "Reality," as we know it, occupies only a small portion of the world around us. The rest of the "real" world is entirely dependent on our imaginations.

It is the actor's belief (or apparent belief) in the imaginative reality of the play that sustains the audience's belief. At the moment the actor ceases to believe, so, too, will the audience. How is it, for instance, that an audience can applaud the reality of a set as the curtain rises and then become totally immersed in the imaginary world of the play only seconds later? How is it that an audience can empathize so completely with a character's death, even to the point of tears, and applaud the living actor moments later in the curtain call? The actor behaves "as if"—as if he is the character, as if the set is reality itself, as if all of this truly matters—and the audience enters into the conspiracy of imagination with the actor.

"Real time" and "stage time" rarely coincide. What seems like real time on stage is not, in the sense that what happens on stage is a selective representation of reality. The art of the playwright is to infuse the two hours of the play with interesting things to watch. This requires that the playwright be very selective. The two hours of a play are a time-condensed collection of playwright-selected events that would normally never occur within the same span of real time.

An actor needs to understand that in relaion to the actual passage of time, her character is changing at an accelerated rate. How much older, for instance, is a character at the end of a play than at the beginning? What physical changes should the character be expected to exhibit (and the actor to represent in the characterization)? How much real time has elapsed in the interim? What must the actor do physically to accommodate these accelerated changes within the real time of the play?

Like time, space is also often condensed on stage. A character may need to look as if he is traversing a considerable expanse, yet he is confined to the actual dimensions of the stage. Characters must reflect the passage of considerable stage time—several hours, days, months, or even years—within the span of a few moments of real time. The challenge to the actor is to portray these "passages" through time and space convincingly and believably.

EMOTIONAL LEVEL

At the emotional level of characterization, the question that arises is not *what* the character feels but *how* the character feels—the mechanism by which the character experiences emotion. We are generally aware of the emotional influences affecting our daily interactions with one another, but we may not be quite so aware of the psychological influences on our behavior. We may know *how* we feel about something, but sometimes we just do things without being able to explain our behavior because we don't know *why* we did it.

We may know that we feel angry, for example, but we may not know why we have chosen a particular way to express that anger. Why do we choose one course of action over another, even when it doesn't matter which course we choose? Why are we content to leave some things unsaid or undone, yet at other times feel compelled to do or say something? Why does a character choose a particular course of action (aside from the fact that it's in the script), when she might do any number of things to achieve the same end? The answers to these questions provide the emotional context for the character's actions.

A character's perception of time and the passage of time is closely related to the character's emotional and psychological makeup. Time is subjective. We all have our own perception of time: one person's "just a few minutes" is another person's "lifetime." Our perception of time changes in relation to our emotional state and to the context in which we experience it. (One wit has suggested that our perception of the passage of time depends on whether we are on the outside or the inside of the bathroom door.) Cultural differences also effect our perception of time: a "New York minute" is appreciably shorter than a "California minute," which is shorter than a "Hawaiian minute," which is shorter still than a "Latin American minute." There are cultures that measure time not in terms of minutes and hours but by the daily passage of the sun, the phases of the moon, the changing positions of the stars, or the seasons of the year.

Everything we do takes time, and each task generally requires a certain *minimum* amount of time for completion. If we try to shorten this requirement—by lessening our effort, rushing through, or "cutting corners"—we will very likely have to repeat the task. (Another wit has remarked, "When will you have the time to do it over if you don't have the time to do it right the first time?") Each task also involves a *maximum* amount of time beyond which its completion may no longer be of consequence. If we take too much time to do something, its accomplishment may be rendered unnecessary. Within this span of "just enough" and "too much" are opportunities to explore a character's experience of time.

A character communicates a sense of time to the audience through the relative urgency of his words and actions. What does the character want? When, meaning how soon, does he want it? Yesterday? today? tomorrow? right this minute? next week? next year? Does the character seem impatient or driven, or does he appear to be relaxed and relatively unconcerned? Does the character subscribe to the philosophy of "time's a-wastin'," "time is money," or "there's plenty of time"? Does he seem to be easily distracted by the trivialities of life, or does he press on, "full speed ahead"?

Does the character enjoy engaging in "small talk" with other characters for the sake of personal relations or social custom, or does she consider it a monumental waste of time? Notice that in most theatrical productions characters rarely interrupt one another, rarely seem impatient with one another, rarely seem to want another character to stop talking. Everyone on stage waits patiently for his turn to speak—as designated in the script. (If only people were so patient, understanding, and accommodating in real life.) Verbal exchanges simply don't happen that way in the real world, as we all know, yet this is invariably how they are depicted on stage. Why is that? Why is this very human (and very compelling) element of personal interaction so often abandoned as soon as the person sets foot on stage? What happened to reality? Instead of the heightened sense of reality, there is a lessened sense of reality. Characters on stage often seem to do less than real people. How can a character be bigger than life if his behavior is lesser than life?

Every character has ideas and feelings about time, the passage of time, the use and misuse of time. The actor's task is to find out what his character thinks about time, incorporate those discoveries into the characterization, and represent them in the character's physical behavior.

Consider the following emotional states:

happy	anxious
sad	restless
angry	nervous
cowardly	depressed
lethargic	belligerent
easygoing	afraid

intense	hurried
patient	paranoid
worried	alienated
jealous	excited

How would you physically represent each state in daily activities? How would each state affect your character's perception of time?

PSYCHOLOGICAL LEVEL

There are two distinct components of the psychological level of characterization: how a character thinks (the *thought process*—the way we acquire information) and how a character analyzes and uses that information (the *process of thought*).

Our *thought process,* the way we accumulate information, conforms to one of two modes: a linear mode or (to borrow from computer lingo) a random access mode. In the *linear* mode, we collect information in a step-by-step process. One item of information leads logically to the next, and the next, and the next. In the *random access* mode, we collect information in a seemingly haphazard, chance, or arbitrary manner. One piece of information does not necessarily lead to another in a logical, step-by-step progression. The mind chooses "one from Column A, one from Column B, maybe two from Column C," and so on, accumulating relevant as well as irrelevant data piecemeal.

The difference between these two modes can be illustrated by the following experiment: walk into a room and look around. Note the manner in which you survey the room. Do your eyes follow a fairly distinct path around the room (linear mode) or do they jump around from item to item (random access mode)? That is your thought process, at least in this particular situation. A change in situation may force a change in thought process, as when you take a mathematics exam (linear mode required) or walk across a busy intersection (random access mode required).

Both modes of information-gathering are equally viable. People are different, that's all, and so are their ways of thinking. The point for the actor is simply to be aware of the difference.

Our process of thought, how we analyze and use information, may or may not reflect the way we gather information. In other words, we may accumulate information in a random manner, but process that information linearly, or vice versa. Look around the room again. Having accumulated some information, note how you actually process that information. Do you try to make sense of the room by attempting to find some logic in the arrangement of objects (linear mode) or do you just "store" the information for future reference (random access mode)? That is your thought process (again, in this particular situation).

The mental process itself may be fast or slow, rigid or flexible, logical or intuitive, reasoned or emotional, and the associations between pieces of information precise or vague. These are all considerations in developing characterizations. How does this character think? How would you portray this? Try starting with how a character might look around a room, or examine objects, or "size up" other characters.

Another important aspect of the psychological level of characterization is the character's basis for *value judgments* regarding the information she receives, and how she processes that information. Some people "judge" the information that they receive, categorizing it as good or bad, valid or invalid, believable or unbelievable, and so on. Others simply accept it as information, filing it away for future reference and assigning no value to it at the present time (value is assigned at some later time by means of a separate thought process).

Again, look around the room. Accumulate some information about it and note whether or not you judge that information or assign a value to it. You observe a painting. Is it a "good" painting or a "bad" painting or "just a painting"? Is the subject matter of the painting something of which you approve, disapprove, or simply accept? Perhaps you consider it a good painting of subject matter of which you disapprove, a bad painting of a subject of which you do approve, or perhaps you have no opinion about the quality of the painting, the subject matter, or both. Perhaps you'll think about it later, after you've accumulated additional information or attended an art appreciation class.

It's very difficult for most people to avoid judging the information they receive. Value judgments are often based on preconceptions, and preconceptions arise from personal experience. The information we receive is tempered by our interpretation of it. Our interpretation is based on our previous experience with the same or a similar object, person, or circumstance. We need that all-important "frame of reference." When we don't have a frame of reference, we become seriously disoriented and confused. Few sighted people could close their eyes and walk through a room, even a familiar room, without bumping into something.

It is for this reason that the concept of stereotypes is so difficult to dispel. The stereotypical character is a frame of reference for us. Our mind categorizes things, even when the categorization is based on limited information. We see something or someone, and in order for our minds to make sense of what we see, we immediately start the categorization process. We cross-reference the new information with information filed away in our memory. We begin with the largest, least restrictive category—"animal," for instance—and work our way from there as additional information is received: four-legged, furred, barks, dog, large dog, Saint Bernard.

Unless and until we receive additional information (or information to the contrary), we will assign that person or things to the largest category in which it fits, in this case, "animal." As we proceed in the categorization process, we also make judgments about the information we receive. "It looks like an animal. I like most animals. Four-legged animal. Furred. Barks. A dog. I like most dogs. Large dog. Saint Bernard. I was bitten by a Saint Bernard once . . . ." This is what you do, and this is what an audience does.

The point of all this? How your character thinks. A good detective studies the criminal mind in order to "think like a criminal," in an effort to understand and anticipate a criminal's behavior. "What's he going to do *next*?" That is the same question a good actor asks of his *character* but with a slightly different emphasis—"What's he going to *do* next?" The actor knows well enough how the character thinks and what the character's actions will be. The actor must decide how he is going to perform those actions to best portray the way the character thinks.

Another aspect of this process concerns the moral and ethical judgments a character makes about her own behavior and the behavior of others. The effect of this aspect of the process of thought on characterization can be substantial. Richard III has no qualms whatsoever about his actions, but Macbeth does. Richard's foolhardiness contributes to his downfall. If he had been more circumspect in his behavior and more moral in his dealings with others, the Battle of Bosworth might never have taken place. Unfortunately, Richard had no conscience. If Macbeth had relied more on his own inherent ethical sense, if he had listened to his conscience (since, unlike Richard, it appears that he actually had one), Birnham Wood would have had no reason to come to Dunsinane, and Macbeth would never have known, or needed to know, the circumstances of Macduff's birth. Nevertheless, Richard was morally bankrupt, and Macbeth ethically compromised. In these two examples, as well as many others in dramatic literature, a character's basis for making value judgments is very important to the characterization and to the course of the play.

A psychologist studies physical behavior in order to understand the workings of a person's mind. In contrast, the actor first studies the workings of the character's mind and then reveals the character's mind to the audience through his physical behavior. The psychologist proceeds from physical behavior to emotional and psychological states, while the actor proceeds from the emotional and psychological states to physical behavior.

Motivation. ■ Our motivations—the emotional basis for our actions—change from moment to moment, day to day, and year to year. Do a character's motivations change? If so, when, why, and how? Do they change suddenly or gradually? What prompts the change? The character's own thought process and behavior? The influence of another character? A change in circumstances? Do the character's motivations alter minimally, moderately, or drastically? Do they change completely or only a little? These questions require answers from the actor about the character he intends to portray.

Intent. ■ Our intentions, like our motivations, also change throughout our daily lives. From time to time we want different things. We pursue different goals, different objectives. Once we have achieved one goal, we replace it with another and embark on a different path toward that new goal. Even if our overall goal remains the same, the steps to it and the interim goals will change with the circumstances of our lives. If one path is blocked, we find a different one, which may necessitate different interim goals.

If our goals are continually thwarted, however, we may feel frustrated, angry, or discouraged. In time we may become desperate. Desperation implies a strong need, and thus a strong impetus to do something, *anything.* Desperate people do desperate (and often very interesting) things, which is why playwrights tend to write about them. As obstacles accumulate, as the path is blocked, the character tries new ways of doing things. Sometimes, however, the character is his own worst enemy. Think of Oedipus, Hamlet, Lear, Tartuffe, and Willy Loman. This type of character (most often observed in tragic plays) does not realize the role he plays in his own difficulties until very near the end of the play, when it's too late.

Generally, a character's motivations and intent remain constant throughout the play, but her minute-by-minute progress toward that goal may change and often does, depending on changing circumstances. The path may also change, resulting in new challenges and obstacles. In other words, when things change, people change to accommodate those changes, and when people change, their behavior changes.

Emotional and psychological disorders. ■ Most major characters in dramas and tragedies (and quite a few in comedies) suffer from an emotional or psychological disorder, and some from physical disorders as well. The mental or physical disorder may be minor or profound, and it may affect a character's behavior to a greater or lesser degree, but there is something physically, emotionally, or psychologically "wrong" with almost every major character in dramatic literature. That's what makes them interesting. From the audience's point of view, "normal" people just aren't very compelling. In fact, they're downright boring.

An actor cannot "play" the disorder. An actor can, however, play the character and represent the effect of the disorder through the character's behavior. What the character actually does should be the actor's major concern, not the clinical description of the disorder the character's behavior represents.

Oddly enough, little of a mental disorder is actually exemplified in behavior. Murderers don't act like murderers but like "normal" people. Their homicidal behavior is selective. Most murderers don't want to be discovered. Those that do suffer from an even more profound disorder. The disorder does not result in a murder (as would be the case with your "standard" homicidal maniac) but is represented by the murder. If the character's disorder arises from a need to be noticed, for example, then the murder is simply a means to that end, not an end in itself.

A villain in a burlesque melodrama is laughable because his behavior is so obvious, so outrageous and unbelievable, unremittingly evil, and so patently false to human nature and human behavior. "Real" people, even "bad" real people, just don't behave that way, certainly not all the time. Insufferably bad people generally have some redeeming social value (as an "example for others," if nothing else), just as insufferably good people have some redeeming antisocial value (even if it's only their self-righteous insufferability). Wholly wonderful and good characters and irredeemably evil and nasty characters are often tiresome because their behavior is so predictable. A hero with endearing, human faults, or a villain with a wicked sense of humor is much more interesting.

Remember, too, that many people suffer from disorders of one kind or another, yet they still manage, somehow, to get through their lives. People grow accustomed to their disorders, learn to compensate for them, and learn to live with them. Richard III suffers from severe physical, emotional, and psychological disorders. Richard is a walking encyclopedia of dysfunction, yet his multiple disorders in no way impede his passage through life and up the ladder of success. In fact,

Richard revels in his dysfunction! He has mastered his disorders and has learned to compensate for them in every possible way. (Richard's multiple disorders actually seem to facilitate his passage through life, bringing him ever closer to Bosworth Field with every halting step.) Richard is the personification of evil, but he is more than that. His self-discipline is astounding. His intentions and motivations are clear, and his belief in himself is unshakable, even in the face of overwhelming opposition. His pursuit of his goals is steadfast and unwavering. His physical deformities are ever present, yet he manages to woo and *win* Lady Anne—the widow of Edward, Prince of Wales, and daughter-in-law of Henry VI, both of whom Richard has killed, and she knows it! Despite his obvious flaws, Richard is a breathtakingly complex and compelling character to watch, and to play.

Play the character in all her inherent behavioral complexities and inconsistencies, and any disorder will take care of itself. As Hamlet re-marked, *"Behavior's* the thing, wherein I'll catch the character of the King." Or words to that effect.

Stereotypes. ■ Actors and directors have been trained from early in their careers to avoid stereotypes and stereotypical characterizations. They have been repeatedly admonished that stereotypes are harmful distortions of the truth. This has been pounded into our brains to such an extent that we rarely, if ever, question the basic premise. By failing to question the premise, however, we fail to recognize the possibility that stereotypes are the result of the distillation of years upon years of human experience, and that a stereotypical characterization may be a more accurate representation of human behavior and may serve a more useful function in human perception than some of us would like to admit. In other words, stereotypes exist for a reason. Actors need to understand that stereotypes do exist, and use that awareness to develop believable characterizations.

As noted earlier, we tend to associate certain personality traits with certain generalized body types—or stereotypes—the "jolly fat person," the "nervous skinny person," the "dumb jock." These stereotypical categorizations may not be accurate in every case, but they exist. The characters in television situation comedies are invariably and almost exclusively stereotypical, yet they are no more or less stereotypical than the stock characters of the *commedia dell'arte.* In fact, the classic characters of the *commedia* and modern television sitcom characters are very much alike—the young lovers, the sensible and understanding best friend, the braggart (academic, athletic, legal, business, or medical), the clever servant, the gluttonous fool, the shrewish wife, the philandering husband, or the meddling mother-in-law. (Many of the plots of sitcoms are straight off the *commedia* shelf.) These characters are instantly recognizable to an audience, even though they may not actually represent any living human being. There is also a quality of "everyman" (or "everywoman") about them—something with which we readily identify. Not all wives are shrewish, of course, nor are all husbands philandering, all servants clever, all mothers-in-law meddlers, or all lawyers braggarts, but there are probably enough of each of them to give some credence to the stereotype.

The important point to remember is that it's not what we personally think about stereotypes and stereotypical behavior or whether or not we reject altogether the notion of stereotypes. What's important is what the audience thinks. The audience responds to stereotypes, even those audience members who may individually reject them. Stereotypes give the audience a frame of reference within which to assess individual personality and behavior. The audience needs basic information, and once they have it, once they have a basic understanding of the character, they can decide for themselves. In many instances, the audience learns about a character by comparing a stereotypical "first impression" with other information revealed throughout the course of the play. In fact, the audience learns more about a character when that character turns out *not* to be the stereotype that the audience first perceived him to be. There is nothing inherently right or wrong about this process. It simply exists. Actors should recognize that it does and work from there.

Certainly actors strive for something more than a stereotypical representation of the characters they endeavor to portray, yet within each character there must be some trait with which the audience can readily identify, some element of the characterization that is "typical." Stereotypical character traits are a "perceptual shorthand," a shortcut to understanding basic personality and patterns of behavior. As we learn more about a character, what we learn either supports or refutes our initial impression. Only through stereotypes, and our responses to them, can we "go against type." If there were no readily identifiable "character," there would be nothing to "act out of."

A character may appear to be one thing but actually be quite another. The jolly fat man may actually be a coldblooded killer. The contrast between our expectations and the reality enhances the effectiveness of the characterization. It causes the audience to think about the character, to wonder how the person they believed the character to be could actually do the things that the character does. The incongruity or outright contradiction between appearance and reality help to make the character more intriguing and, oddly enough, more believable.

The perception of stereotypes exists among the general population, and therefore exists among the general theatre-going population. To assert that this perception should not exist is a matter of personal opinion. To ignore it is ultimately self-defeating. If you want to "break down" stereotypes, by all means do so. Yet to try to change the perception argues for its existence. How can you try to change something if it doesn't exist? And how will you know if the perception changed if you didn't know what it was in the first place? You must meet the audience where they are; then you can take them where you want them to go.

Much of what is discussed in the balance of this chapter is based on stereotypes and stereotypical behavior. Use the information as a point of departure, recognizing its expressive and character-revealing potential and learning to use it effectively. The related challenge for the actor is to manipulate the audience's expected response and use it to her own advantage.

> *Observe one or more television situation comedies (force yourself if you have to). Make of list of stereotypical characters and the characteristics and behavior they represent. Compare stereotypical characters from one program with those of another program. Note the difference, if any, and the development, if any, of individual characters.*
>
> *Ask yourself how long it took you to categorize each character. What characteristics or behavior, or combination of characteristics or behavior "tipped you off" to the type of character being portrayed?*
>
> *Compare and contrast television sitcom characters with those from the dramatic literature, especially from the commedia dell'arte tradition.*

Character types. ■ Few plays are about "normal" people. More often, the characters in plays represent individuals who deviate from the norm, who are "larger than life," or who, for one reason or another, have experienced more of "life's little ups and downs."

The inner psychological and emotional state of an individual is reflected in his physical attitudes and behavior. The relationship between psychological characteristics and behavior is regular and observable, and can be classified into behavioral categories or ascribed to various character types. Character types offer a broad outline of the dominant psychological characteristics often reflected in physical attitudes, expression, and behavior. No person is one type only but combines different types to varying degrees.

The following four basic character types (plus "normal" for comparison) are most readily identifiable among the general population and are often represented in dramatic literature. Within each description are lists of representative psychological traits, physical traits, and examples from dramatic literature. This information should serve as a point of departure, as a foundation on which to build a character, not as a definitive depiction of any one character or character type.

Type: NORMAL
Psychological traits: Natural, flexible, adaptable. Emotionally free and freely expressive. Normal range of emotions, appropriately displayed.
Physical traits: Good body alignment. Expectant, open expression. Spontaneous emotional expression, movement, and gestures.
Examples: Very few in dramatic literature aside from minor or incidental characters.

Type: DEPENDENT
Psychological traits: Feelings of loss, inadequacy, deprivation, helplessness, despair, and inner emptiness. May feel hopelessly downtrodden, with a sometimes overwhelming sense of the futility of life.

Suppresses the expression of feelings. Childlike dependence on others. Needy, clinging. Demonstrates a lack of self-esteem, self-assertion, and aggression. Feels unloved and unworthy of being loved, usually due to lack of love and support as a child, particularly from mother.
Physical traits: Long, thin body. Weak, underdeveloped muscles, particularly in the legs and arms. Sunken chest. Tightly held diaphragm, which causes shallow breathing. Sway back and an inflexible spine. Low overall energy level. Seemingly incapable of sustained physical effort, even in self-defense. Gives up easily. "Unable to stand on his own two feet." Reacts with pained expression to rejection, denial, or defeat.

Emotional pain equals physical pain. The person seems to move as if something "hurts."
Examples: Laura in *The Glass Menagerie*, Mary Tyrone in *Long Day's Journey into Night*, Blanche DuBois in *A Streetcar Named Desire*.

Type: SELF-DEFEATING
Psychological traits: Holds back emotions. Very limited aggression and self-assertion. Grudgingly submissive to others. Rationalizes own behavior and own mistakes, as well as those of others. Reduced feelings of intimacy, love, and tenderness. Dissatisfied with self and place in life, in society, and in environment.
Physical traits: Usually heavy-set and muscular. Thick neck and rounded back, with shoulders slumped down and forward. Tight pelvis, pushed forward. Tight, flat buttocks. Lack of spontaneous expressive movement. Often has a seemingly good-natured smile and a feigned expression of naive innocence and openness. Appears solid, strong, earthbound, but unable to "stand his own ground." Seems overburdened with cares and worries—"carrying the weight of the world on his shoulders." Exhibits physical resignation with a "nothing you can do about it," shrug-of-the-shoulders attitude. Uses rationalizing, whining, and complaining as forms of meek self-assertion.
Examples: George in *Who's Afraid of Virginia Woolf?*, Willie Loman in *Death of a Salesman*, Vladimir in *Waiting for Godot.*

Type: SELF-POSSESSED
Psychological traits: Guarded emotions. Fear of loving or expressing love, tenderness, compassion, or intimacy. Inflexible, narrow-minded attitude. Excessively prideful, self-centered, and narcissistic. Lacks a sense of humor, particularly about self. Afraid to appear weak or submissive. Unable to compromise or "give in." Highly ambitious, competitive, and aggressive.

Compulsive, overly determined to succeed. Motivated by an overriding fear of failure.
Physical traits: Hard, tight muscles. Stiff, straight back. Tight chest. Sustained muscular tension throughout the body. Unbending neck, rigid lower back. Set jaw. Tight diaphragm, restricting breathing. Pelvis retracted in female. Lack of grace and coordination in movement due to tightly held muscles of hips, legs, and shoulders.

Outwardly accessible and sexually aware. Approaches the environment, including other people, directly, and often tactlessly. Not subtle in movement or gestures. Appears outwardly decisive, strong, aggressive, but is actually fearful of much of the world around him.

Examples: Stanley Kowalski in *A Streetcar Named Desire*, Nick in *Who's Afraid of Virginia Woolf?*, Oedipus in *Oedipus Rex*, Julie in *Miss Julie*.

Type: SELF-DENYING

Psychological traits: Strong denial of self, body, and feelings, especially sexual feelings. Feels the need to dominate others, either through force of will, intimidation, or seduction. Cannot admit mistakes or defeat. Rejects criticism, constructive or otherwise. Driven to acquire power and achieve success, usually at the expense of others, but is often unsuccessful.

Physical traits: There are two physical types, dominating and seductive.

Dominating: Physically large and imposing, a strong, well-developed upper body, but underdeveloped lower body. Diaphragm is constricted. Head and pelvis are tightly held. Face appears rigid, distrustful, with suspicious, watchful eyes. Forceful, aggressive, dominant movements and gestures. Tends to monopolize conversations and dominate interactions.

Seductive: Normal-appearing body, but with loose pelvis and flexible, sinuous back. Head held tightly. Tension held in the face. Watchful eyes. Draws attention to self with seductive poses, movement, and gestures.

Examples: *Dominating:* Iago in *Othello*, Richard in *Richard III*, Claudius in *Hamlet*.

Seductive: Martha in *Who's Afraid of Virginia Woolf?*, Hedda in *Hedda Gabler*, Blanche DuBois in *A Streetcar Named Desire* (yes, she can be more than one character type).

Type: SCHIZOID

Psychological traits: Continuing inner turmoil and inner emotional conflict. Dissociation of body and ego from feelings. Seriously repressed emotions. Often exhibits split feelings, such as arrogance/self-loathing or anger/fear. Avoids intimate feelings, intimate contact, and personal interactions. Caught up in own inner world and own inner struggle. Periodic explosive, aggressive expression of built-up emotions.

Physical traits: Narrow body, tight and rigid. Tension in neck, shoulders, pelvis, and legs. Moves stiffly, and not at all gracefully. Pale skin due to poor circulation. Always feels cold.

Body misaligned, asymmetrical—upper-to-lower or side-to-side. Shallow, weak breathing. Blank, unemotional, masklike face. Arms hanging dead and inexpressive at sides. Gestures minimal and restrained. Weight distributed unevenly to the feet and always on one leg/hip or the other. Life-long inner struggle is graphically represented in the body.

Examples: Charlotte Corday in *Marat/Sade.*

The tendency among inexperienced actors is to respond intuitively to the character, to do what "looks" or "feels" right. This may not actually represent the character, however, but rather the personal response of the actor or director to the character. Actors want the characters they portray to be liked by the audience, and they may try to infuse even totally despicable characters with some redeeming qualities that may not in fact be representative of the character. "Likability" or lack of it is only one aspect of a characterization. The overriding consideration is believability. A character on stage must be believable. All other considerations are secondary.

> *Observe people in daily life. Observe their basic physical structure, posture, and movements, and try to determine which character type is appropriate to that person. If a person demonstrates more than one character type, try to determine which type is predominant.*
>
> *Assume the physical traits of the character types described above. Choose one character type, for example, and work your way through the description of the character's physical appearance. Having assumed this character's appearance, attempt to move, gesture, and perform other physical activities in a manner representative of this character.*
>
> *Read one or more of the plays listed above and examine the characters cited as examples of specific character types.*

Styles of facial expression. ■ Facial expression representing emotional states has been discussed in Chapter 1. The topic at hand concerns the manner in which facial expression is used in physical expression, which can be observed, analyzed, and categorized.

Following is a list of the different types of facial expressors (the person doing the expressing):

- The *normal* expressor reacts to the world around him in an appropriate and credible manner. His expression is generally consistent with his emotional environment and emotional state. His expression is not overly expressive or guarded. His facial expression shifts freely over a wide range of emotional display.
- *Ever-ready expressors* are irrepressible and eager to be expressive, no matter how minimal the stimulus may be. This type of person changes expression often and may display an emotion totally inappropriate to the situation. In her eagerness to express something, she quite often expresses the wrong thing.
- Somewhat akin to the "ever-ready" expressor is the *reflector.* This individual seems incredibly empathetic. His facial expression reflects and often magnifies every nuance of expression he observes in others. He seems not to have any emotions of his own, however, but apparently lives vicariously through the emotions of others.
- *Withholders* exhibit the classic "poker face." They purposely show little facial expression and believe that by doing so they reveal little about their emotional state. (If only they were as proficient at "withholding" with their bodies, which tells the trained observer everything she wants to know.)
- *Revealers* are the opposite of withholders. The revealer's face leaves little doubt about his emotional state. For the revealer, there is no emotional middle ground. No expression is tempered or mediated in any way. His expression is one of ultimate joy, sadness, surprise, anger, fear, or disgust.
- The *unwitting expressor* reveals expression or emotions which she does not realize she is expressing. "How did you know what I was thinking?" she asks, totally unaware that her every thought was written on her face.
- In contrast, the *blank expressor* believes that an emotion is being expressed when none actually is: "Couldn't you tell that I was thrilled about it?" Well, no, we couldn't, because there was no expression on his face, nothing to indicate that he had any emotional reaction at all.
- The *substitute expressor* displays a facial expression other than the one she thinks is being displayed, or an expression other than one that may be appropriate to the situation. She may substitute an expression of fear for anger, for instance, or surprise for happiness.

■ *Frozen-face expressors* generally display one dominant expression, which is occasionally—if minimally—tempered by other expressions. The person who smiles through adversity (or through anything else for that matter), who seems to be perpetually surprised by the world around him, or who expresses continual disdain for the human race falls into this category.

> *Observe people in conversation. Classify or categorize each person in terms of their manner, use, or style of facial expression. Next, assume the role of one of the above "expressor types." Engage others in conversation and attempt to sustain the "expressor role" you have chosen. If it seems appropriate to do so, change your role at various times during the course of the conversation, or for subsequent conversations.*
>
> *Note the reaction of those with whom you converse. Those who know you and have conversed with you before may find your facial expressions (or lack thereof) odd, confusing, or even intimidating. Ask them about it and explore their reactions. Those who do not know you may find your expressions strange, but will likely accept that it's "just the way you are."*

Building a Character

Human behavior is about differences. Seldom do we marvel about those things that are the same as we do about differences. We may acknowledge a common bond and experience the sense of security that sameness reinforces among us, but what's really interesting about people is their differences. Differences are also what makes characters in a play interesting to watch. Those among us who dare to be different may be admired or despised, loved or hated, but whatever emotion they engender, they are nonetheless *watched.*

One of the goals of characterization is to represent the universal attributes of a character and at the same time to represent the character's unique and distinguishing aspects—to find ways to differentiate one character from another. The first step toward that goal is to become aware of the many ways in which people differ from one another. The second is to determine which of those differences are most applicable to the character being portrayed. The third is to develop a characterization that capitalizes on those differences. The final step is to convey all that information—*all* the similarities and differences—to the audience in an interesting, compelling, and believable way. If it's not interesting, audience members won't watch. If it's not compelling, they won't care. If it's not believable, they won't watch *or* care.

ACTING METHODS

Much has been written about the many different acting "methods" and philosophies of acting. Despite the overwhelming amount of information available on the subject, there are essentially only three basic approaches or "methods" to developing a characterization.

External to internal. ■ In this method of character development, the actor assumes the physical attributes of the character—the external realities of the character—and endeavors to evoke in herself an emotional state through her physical behavior. She hopes this will be projected to the audience through her movement. A proponent of this approach believes that if you smile, you'll feel happy. If you clench your fist, you'll feel angry. Sir Laurence Olivier believed that if he got the character's nose right—in other words, if he got the character's physical attributes right—he could act the part.

Internal to external. ■ The actor first shapes the internal reality of the character, the character's psychological and emotional base, and then lets the movement flow "from within." The assumption is that the emotional state of the character will be reflected in the actor's movements. If you feel happy, you'll smile. If you feel angry, you'll clench your fist.

A further assumption of *both* approaches is that the audience will necessarily perceive the emotional state of the character through the character's physical behavior.

Balanced approach. ■ Few actors espouse only one method of character development. Most actors, being extremely pragmatic and practical (whether they like to admit it or not), generally use whatever method "works" for them, no matter the current fashion. The actor may not be experienced in more than one method, however, which may seriously limit her choices in developing her character.

Current fashion. ■ The prevailing attitude among many actors, directors, and acting teachers is that if the actor has identified correctly and assimilated the emotional and psychological states of the character he is to enact, then appropriate and characteristic movement must necessarily follow—naturally, instinctively, intuitively, almost magically. In view of advances in the study of human behavior this seems an enlightened approach to actor training. Unfortunately, this popular assumption is based on a myth—an enlightened myth, but a myth nonetheless.

The basic premise of this approach to acting is this: the actor puts herself in the place of the character and asks herself, "If *I* were the character in this situation, what would *I* do?" The proper emphasis of the technique is on the phrase "in this situation," meaning the actual circumstances of the play. The primary goal is to put the actor consciously into the scene and into the character's *mind,* to make the character's objectives the actor's objectives, and thereby to enable the actor to react to the changing circumstances of the play as the character would.

The major flaw in this approach to characterization is that no matter how much an actor may wish it were so, or believe it is so, the actor is not the character. The character is. The truth of the matter, confirmed by studies in human behavior, is that regardless of the actor's emotional or psychological state—no matter how much the actor may think like the character or feel like the character (or think he does)—the actor will necessarily behave like the actor, not like the character. Unless the actor is playing himself (as is the case with most television and film "personalities," which is why some of them are considered such good "actors"), or unless the actor consciously and purposely alters his physical behavior (which is the case with real actors), the actor's body *does not, cannot,* and *will not* move like the character. The actor will move like himself.

The character, not the actor, is in the situation. That makes the balance of the question "What would I do?" highly problematic. In all likelihood, what the actor would do in a particular situation would not be what the character would do in the same situation. (How many actors would poke their eyes out if they discovered that they had killed their dad and married their mom, as Oedipus did? How many would walk out on their husband and children, as Nora did? How many would spend all night arguing with Martha, like George did?) Therefore, how can the *actor,* as herself, decide what the *character* would do? Often, the actor doesn't even have a clue what she would do, never mind what the character would do. You see the problem.

The question is moot: the actor doesn't really have a choice about what the character is going to do, because the playwright has already decided. It's already there, in the script. You want to know what the character would do in a given situation? Just turn the page. What the actor would do and what the actor might decide the character would do are irrelevant. Unless the actor decides to rewrite the play, there is no decision to be made. The character's actions are predetermined, predestined, inevitable, unavoidable, unchangeable, irrefutable, a foregone conclusion—in other words, a "done deal."

Therefore, the question about what a character would do shouldn't even arise. The more important question for the actor is how to do what has already been decided and how to accommodate those decisions in his characterization. The actor must decide what he wants to show to the audience and how he's going to do it.

In the capacity of helping an actor discover practical solutions to these questions, a competent acting teacher can make a substantial and lasting contribution to an actor's development. The role of the acting teacher is not to confine the actor arbitrarily to a single, straight-and-narrow path—one particular acting "method"—but to alert the actor to the many diverse paths available to her, and to help the actor explore those many paths. There's nothing intrinsically wrong with any one path, of course, unless the actor travels one path to the exclusion of all others.

Quite simply, an actor needs more than a single path. An actor needs choices. If an actor has traveled only one path, learned only one way to approach a characterization, when that way doesn't work or is blocked the actor has nowhere to turn. If, however, the actor has many paths to follow and has learned many ways to approach a characterization, he expands his range of choices, greatly expands the depth and range of his characterizations, and enhances his overall acting ability.

The Journey

Every character goes on a journey—a physical, emotional, and intellectual journey of discovery about herself and her environment, including discoveries about her relationships with those she encounters during the course of the play. It is an *imaginary* journey, of course, a journey through space and time that occurs only in the audience's mind. The actor knows objectively that she's not actually going anywhere, but she endeavors for the audience's sake to give the appearance of undertaking the journey.

The actor must maintain his own sense of objectivity throughout the endeavor. If the actor himself gets lost, if he loses his objectivity, he cannot lead the audience. He no longer has any idea of the path he must follow or the destination he hopes to reach. Eventually, of course, the actor and the audience will arrive at the end of the play, but there will have been no journey of discovery along the way. The actor and the audience will have taken a trip to nowhere.

The actor, too, goes on a journey—a physical, emotional, and intellectual journey of discovery about herself within the context of the rehearsal and performance of the play. Seldom do actors pause to observe themselves while they're acting. Actors are generally aware of the audience, the other actors on stage with them, the lights, the set, and all the other elements of the production, but rarely do they actually observe themselves within the context of the production as a whole or notice the role they play in the theatrical endeavor.

In many ways the actor and the character are inseparable from each other, and they are also inseparable from the journey they undertake. The entire production process is a journey, as are each of the many elements of the production, including the acting process.

TEXTUAL ANALYSIS

Character analysis begins with the script, as does every other aspect of the production. An actor need never be at a loss for information about the character he is to portray. Everything an actor needs to know can be found in the script if the actor knows where to look. Sources of information about a character include the playwright, the character himself, and other characters.

A few playwrights (Shaw, O'Neill, and Williams come to mind) tell you everything you ever wanted to know about a character (in Shaw's case, more than you ever wanted to know). Sometimes, however, a playwright doesn't really give you much to go on. Harold Pinter, for example, provides only a cryptic note or two: the character's name (if the character actually has one, other than MAN or WOMAN), the character's age (sometimes, but not always), and a brief description (rarely). After that, you're on your own.

Ancient Greek and Roman playwrights were not very forthcoming, either, nor are most playwrights until very near modern times. (Any character descriptions you find in modern editions of classic plays are usually the work of an editor, not the playwright.) Only in the last hundred years or so have playwrights been inclined to describe their characters with anything more than name and rank and their relationship to other characters.

Most modern playwrights give you something to work with, but no matter how much or how little you're given, anything a playwright has to say about a character is important information. Times change, styles of production change, priorities in casting change. Nevertheless, the playwright's description is what she originally intended for this character. This is the primary source from which all other information about a character is derived.

If possible, find a copy of the original script of the first published edition of the play in question. "Acting" editions often contain stage directions that were not part of the original script, but were transcribed from the prompt script of a particular production of the play. Study the playwright's notes throughout the play as well as introductory notes and stage directions for information relating to every level of characterization, and for insight into the character's personality, motivation, and intent. A simple "he smiles" or "she turns away" can sometimes make all the difference in building a character. Also note any contradictions. You will need to resolve these in relation to information about the character you derive from other sources.

The second source of information about a character is the character himself. At the beginning of *Richard III,* Richard enters alone and speaks directly to the audience in an opening monologue. He describes his physical, emotional, and psychological self in considerable detail, and proclaims "I am determined to prove a villain." We should believe everything he says. In *Othello* Iago says he "hates the Moor." Believe it. In the first scene of *Death of a Salesman,* Willy Loman tells his wife, Linda, that he is deathly tired, is becoming increasingly forgetful, and is preoccupied with strange thoughts. Even though Willy gives us the information indirectly, in a conversation we overhear, we can trust what he says.

Characters never lie to the audience. They may try to deceive other characters, they may even occasionally deceive themselves, but they never lie to the audience. They may not tell the audience everything about themselves, of course, but what they do tell the audience is never a lie. For one thing, it would be futile. The audience sees and hears everything that happens in a play.

Characters are always true to themselves. No matter what they do, they invariably do it "in character." They do what they do and say what they say because of who they are. They cannot be otherwise. Even if they tried to be otherwise, that would be "in character," too.

Characters talk about themselves, about their situation and their environment, and they also talk about each other. Talk is what characters do. They talk about themselves and they talk about other characters. They also occasionally talk to themselves about themselves and other characters. All of this talking usually reveals something useful about the character.

Characters in a play are not always a reliable source of information about other characters, however. Sometimes one character's observations about another are just plain wrong. In cases like these, comments and observations from other characters provide a comparative frame of reference. One character says that another character is such-and-so, but clearly this information contradicts what the playwright says about the character, what the character says about herself, or what we observe from the character's own behavior. By attempting to resolve these contradictions, an actor can derive very useful information. Why, for instance, does the other character say that when the truth is otherwise?

> *Select three plays—one written before 1600, one written between 1600 and 1900, and one written since 1900. Choose one main character in each play and as you read, watch for information about that character in what the playwright says, what the character says about himself, and what other characters say about that character. Look for information on all levels of characterization—physical, environmental, emotional, and psychological. Note any seeming contradictions.*
>
> *Note differences in how information is presented in each play—how much and by whom (the playwright, the character himself, or other characters). You will notice, for instance, that as theatre technology advanced, there is an increasing amount of guidance from the playwright about the technical elements of the play in relation to the characters and more detailed character descriptions (except for Harold Pinter, of course).*

Every play has elements of humor, no matter how serious the theme or how humorless the characters. Why? It's human nature. People want to be happy. They want to affirm life. They need to have hope that all is not lost, all is not desperate, all is not futile. (If it is, what a joke that is on all of us.) Find the humor. It will humanize your character.

Thematic function of the character. ■ Rarely are there extraneous or unnecessary characters in a play. Playwrights are taught, know intuitively, or discover through practical experience that they should use as few characters as possible in telling their story. Every character serves a clearly defined purpose. Every character does something to forward the plot and amplify the play's theme. Otherwise, she wouldn't be in the play.

Why is this particular character in this play? What purpose does he serve? What is his function in relation to the plot and theme of the play? The answers to these questions, which can only be uncovered by a careful reading of the play, indicate the character's *thematic function*—the reason for his character's existence.

It's not always a matter of what a character does or what a character says that is of primary importance. More often it is the effect of what a character does or says that holds the greatest significance. The function of the character can be discovered through the effect the character has on other characters and on the play as a whole. One way to approach this question is to assess what the character does and then ask yourself how the play would change if your character didn't do it. What if the character didn't even appear in the play? How, and to what extent, would the play change?

In *Macbeth*, Ross, Macduff's fellow noblemen and comrade-in-arms, brings Macduff the news of the death of his wife and children, who have been murdered by Macbeth's henchmen. It is important news, and it greatly affects Macduff's emotional state, which in turn influences his subsequent behavior on the battlefield and in personal combat with Macbeth.

Questions arise. Why, for instance, was this news brought to Macduff by Ross and not by a messenger or some other character? What if Ross hadn't delivered the news to Macduff, or what if the news hadn't been delivered at all? In other words, what is the relative importance of the news itself, and, by extension, of the character of Ross, since he's the one who gives Macduff the news? What *else* does Ross do in the play? Does anything else he does have the same level of significance or importance?

Also note the manner in which Ross delivers the news. He is reluctant to tell Macduff what has happened. He hesitates. He dissembles. Finally, after much urging, he reports the murders. The playwright is building suspense, not about the deaths themselves—the audience knows all about that dreadful business already—but about Macduff's reaction to the news. The deaths are important, certainly, but Macduff's reaction to the deaths is *more* important.

Contrast Ross's behavior with that of Seyton, an officer in Macbeth's army, who gives Macbeth the news of the death of Lady Macbeth: no hesitation, no dissembling. He walks up to Macbeth and blurts it right out. The news of Lady Macbeth's death is of considerably less consequence to Macbeth and to the course of the play than is the news of Macduff's wife and children, and it is delivered by a lesser character in the play. Macbeth does get to do his "Tomorrow, and tomorrow, and tomorrow" speech, but it seems a passing thought at best: "Lady Macbeth is dead? Well we all gotta go sometime.

Where's Macduff?" Macbeth is more concerned with other things right now, like the upcoming battle and the impending loss of his kingdom (not to mention his life). Seyton's role in this scene is little more than that of a "glorified messenger." In fact, the next character to enter is a messenger, who tells Macbeth something the audience already suspects: Birnham Wood is, indeed, coming to Dunsinane.

But the really important revelation in the play, that Macduff was "of no woman borne," is spoken not by a messenger or a secondary character, but by Macduff himself. His words have a devastating effect on Macbeth—he realizes he is no longer invincible—and a considerable effect on the outcome of the play: Macbeth is subsequently killed by Macduff.

Every character, major or minor, contributes something to the play, and it is up to the actor to determine what his character's contribution is.

Secondary roles. ■ The general principles of building a character apply equally to secondary characters. Secondary characters are no less important than major characters. In their short time on stage, they allow actors fewer opportunities to supply information to the audience.

This does not imply that a secondary character necessarily requires a less fully developed characterization than a major character. Many actors assume that because they are playing secondary characters, their responsibility to develop a fully formed person is lessened, and that the characterization needn't be as deep. Not so! It's not a matter of how many lines a character speaks or how much time a character spends in front of the audience. A secondary character lives no less a life than a major character. The audience just doesn't see most of it. So, what the audience does see must be overflowing.

It takes only a little research to discover a secondary character's-function in a play and to extract interesting possibilities for characterization. What can an actor tell the audience about her character's life in the few moments she has? Portraying Hamlet is not easy, by any means, but portraying Rosencrantz or Guildenstern is no easier. In some ways, it is more challenging, because the actor must use her considerable skills to build a believable and compelling characterization out of what appear to be bits and pieces of information.

If we were cast in the role of Rosencrantz or Guildenstern, what can we "glean" from the play in which they appear to help us with our characterization? What is the role of these two minor "functionaries" in the play itself? What role did other minor functionaries serve at the time the play was written and in the place where it is set? What is their relationship to the major character(s) in the play? What can we learn about these two guys? First, Rosencrantz and Guildenstern are courtiers. Hmmmm. Well, that's a start. A little historical research should provide a reasonable interpretation of that particular, and sometimes peculiar, function. Delving a little further, we discover from Claudius's remarks to Rosencrantz and Guildenstern that they have been brought up with Hamlet, they are about the same age, they know him well, and they can approach him on a more or less equal footing. Then Gertrude chimes in that Hamlet talks about them all the time, and really, really likes them. She may be laying it on a little thick, but her remarks, following those of Claudius, raise Rosencrantz and Guildenstern above the level of the "standard" courtier and "minor functionary."

Claudius entreats Rosencrantz and Guildenstern to talk with Hamlet, ostensively to find out what's troubling him, but actually to gather information Claudius can use to his own advantage. It is interesting that Gertrude mentions a handsome reward, "As fits a king's remembrance," just for helping out. Gertrude does not trust these two as much as Claudius does. Perhaps she knows them better, or perhaps she's just being prudent, "making sure" the job gets done properly. In any event, Rosencrantz and Guildenstern agree, and off they go. Ever practical, Gertrude sends along a few attendants to make sure that they don't get lost on the way. (It is a big castle, after all.)

Given this information, how then should Rosencrantz and Guildenstern be played physically, at least in this opening scene with Claudius and Gertrude? It seems that they should appear somewhat concerned about their appearance at court, particularly the haste with which they have been summoned. They are aware of the former king's death, which occurred under somewhat suspicious circumstances, as well as the rumors implicating Claudius in old Hamlet's demise. Rosencrantz and Guildenstern may be apprehensive about their own continued well-being. They know young Hamlet well (as we are led to believe), and they have a passing acquaintance with Gertrude (who apparently knows them well enough not to trust them very much), but they probably haven't had much contact with Claudius. They've seen him around, of course, but they don't know him, and, at first glance, the circumstances of their meeting do not bode well. Claudius almost immediately tries to put them at ease, welcoming them to the castle as old friends. This seems to be his "style"— along with smiling a lot, according to Hamlet—and Rosencrantz and Guildenstern likely are not misled. We note, however, that the two were not invited to the king's funeral or to the subsequent wedding

between Claudius and Gertrude, so despite their seemingly close acquaintance with Hamlet, it doesn't seem to warrant special consideration. They have good reason to be suspicious of their appearance at
court and wary of Claudius and Gertrude's intentions.

Initially then, Rosencrantz and Guildenstern would appear physically tense and ill-at-ease, perhaps even a little fatigued from their recent journey, while seeming relaxed and unconcerned, reserved in
their movements and gestures, and properly obsequious to Claudius
and Gertrude. Once the situation with Hamlet is explained to them,
they can relax a little, though not completely, since they are receiving
mixed messages from Claudius and Gertrude, of which they are no
doubt intuitively aware. Ever-smiling Claudius seems a little too casual about the deal, and Gertrude seems a little too desperate. To have
survived this long at court (particularly if they are close friends of
Hamlet, considering the present circumstances) implies that Rosencrantz and Guildenstern are cautious and aware, not the dupes we are
often led to believe they are by the standard shallow characterizations
they often receive from inexperienced and less-than-conscientious
actors.

Rosencrantz and Guildenstern next appear at the end of the
"Though this be madness, yet there is method in 't" scene between
Hamlet and Polonius. It is interesting to note that at his exit, Polonius
says to Rosencrantz and Guildenstern, "You go to seek the Lord Hamlet; there he is." How did Polonius know that Rosencrantz and
Guildenstern came seeking Hamlet? Did he simply assume so, or was
he aware that they were sent for? Does Polonius also know why they
were sent for? Rosencrantz and Guildenstern enter without the attendants, so there is no clue there. Certainly he might have seen them
hanging around the castle with Hamlet on previous occasions, but on
this occasion Polonius does not seem surprised to see them, even
after what might be considered a lengthy absence. (Hamlet has been
away at school, so Rosencrantz and Guildenstern would have no
compelling reason to show up at the castle, unless, of course, they
were "sent for.") No previous mention of them—of which Polonius
would be aware—appears in the play (certainly none in front of the
audience). There is only one occasion, earlier in the same scene,
when Polonius might have seen them in passing if he hadn't been so
preoccupied with the ambassadors from Norway and his own discoveries concerning Hamlet's "lunacy," yet Polonius apparently knows
why they are here. Perhaps he is not quite the doddering old fool he is
often portrayed to be.

Given this interesting line spoken by Polonius, how then would

Rosencrantz and Guildenstern react to his seeming awareness of their "secret mission"? A shared glance between them at his exit would speak volumes to the audience. The lack of a glance would not be missed, of course, but a wonderful opportunity to provide information to the audience would be lost.

How would Polonius's knowledge of their mission at court affect Rosencrantz and Guildenstern's subsequent conversation with Hamlet? Would it not put them on their guard? If Polonius knows what's going on, who else might be party to this intrigue? Might Hamlet not know, too, or at least have his suspicions? Unless they are total idiots, Rosencrantz and Guildenstern must know why they have been sent to question Hamlet (and why they are accompanying the prince to England later in the play), and they must also be aware of the potential hazards of performing their assigned duties. Rosencrantz and Guildenstern must also sense a change in their relationship to Hamlet over the course of the ensuing scene. It is not the easy repartee of childhood friends, but a game of words played in earnest, a battle of wits that might conceivably result in serious consequences for all involved.

"Throw-away" lines and what seem to be unimportant events and situations like these often present unmatched opportunities for deepening characterization—if the actor is aware of them and uses them. How often does such an opportunity as "You go to seek the Lord Hamlet; there he is" slip by unrecognized and unexploited for its potential? There is a wealth of information about Rosencrantz and Guildenstern available for the resourceful, conscientious actor, and a wealth of opportunities for an interesting and compelling characterization. Rosencrantz and Guildenstern have lives, no less than any other character in the play. They, too, go on a journey—a journey that begins with a "hasty sending" to court, and ends in England with their deaths. The audience doesn't see as *much* of their lives as they see of Hamlet's, but their lives are no less important to them or to the play.

As an aside, Tom Stoppard's *Rosencrantz and Guildenstern Are Dead* is a terrific example of a play that turns the common perception of major and minor characters on its head. Stoppard plucks these two minor characters from Shakespeare and makes them major characters in a play of their own. In turn, the major characters of Shakespeare's play—Hamlet, Claudius, Polonius, Gertrude, Ophelia—are relegated to minor roles.

Deciding what really matters. ■ What really matters is always a concern in building a character. What is important to the characterization and what isn't? The character's essential physical, emotional, and psychological attributes are important, but is it of consequence to know (or to imagine), say, what the character had for breakfast? Does the character's breakfast provide any insight into the character or into the play? Is the breakfast ever mentioned? Does it have any effect on the play? (Does the character get indigestion? Does the indigestion influence the character's behavior in any way?)

Overall, it's a matter of priorities. In practical terms, the time allotted for preparing a role is invariably short. If the item under consideration is mentioned in the play, either explicitly or implicitly, if it *affects* the play in any way, or if it substantively affects the characterization or the audience's perception of the character, then it matters. If it's not mentioned in the play, if it doesn't affect the play, or if it doesn't affect the characterization or the audience's perception of the character, then it doesn't matter. If there is already quite enough for an actor to consider in building a character, why further complicate an already complicated process?

Building a character is a highly individual process, as well as a highly selective one. The resulting characterization will be based on the actor's interpretation of the information available to her, tempered by experience and intuition. Naturally, the actor can't possibly represent everything she discovers about a character. There are far too many variables to consider, particularly within the framework of an already-far-too-short rehearsal schedule. The most time-and-energy-efficient approach is to determine which characteristics are most important, which "speak" most directly to the audience, and which lead the audience most clearly and directly to perceive the character as the actor intends.

Theatre is the art of expectation and anticipation. Even if the audience knows "what happens next" or how the play ends, they nevertheless try to "forget" what they know so they can enjoy the journey. Likewise, the characters an audience finds most interesting are those that remain ever-so-slightly mysterious and unpredictable—not so mysterious as to be unfathomable or so unpredictable as to be too much trouble to figure out, but just mysterious enough to keep the audience interested, thinking, and feeling, and just unpredictable enough to keep them guessing.

It is to the actor's advantage to do only what is absolutely necessary to represent the character to the audience. Contrary to popular belief, you don't need to "spell out" the character entirely. A character will be more interesting to an audience who must "fill in the blanks." Simplify. Let members of the audience draw on their own perceptions and experience to define the character for themselves. The character will be all the more believable and real.

The human mind cannot distinguish between what is real and what it imagines to be real. In fact, often what a person imagines to be real can actually seem more real than reality itself. We are frightened by what we imagine to be lurking in the darkness, in the closet, under the bed, in the forest primeval, or beyond the stars. The reality of the situation, once known, is likely to be far less frightening than what we imagined. "Oh, it's only you. Don't scare me like that." Who really scared whom?

Let those in the audience scare themselves. In other words, don't tell the audience everything. Respect the audience's intelligence and imaginative ability; allow them the opportunity to imagine, to ponder, to reflect, and to speculate on their own. "That was interesting. I wonder what it means." "What's he going to do next?" "Oh, I certainly didn't expect that." "I never imagined he would do that."

This is not to sugget that you should enact an incomplete characterization, but that you lead the audience in the direction of the "blanks," the things you already know about the character. Keep the audience involved in the characterization as much as possible. Mystery + Unpredictability + Imagination = Audience Involvement. As an actor, you control at least two out of the three items on your side of the equation. You can evoke a sense of mystery and inject a certain unpredictability into your characterization and you can stimulate the audience's imagination. The audience doesn't even have to meet you halfway to become involved, but you've got to provide some substantial frame of reference. That frame of reference is a solid characterization—interesting, compelling, and believable.

What happens first? ■ On stage, the perceived reality is what happens now, but this present reality has evolved from previous events and will in turn affect the interpretation of future events. The actor must work backward, from the final interpretation of the character to the character's first entrance. In other words, what happens first is actually decided last.

The actor knows what happens at the end of the play. He knows the end of the character's journey. The audience, for the most part, does not. (Members of the audience may know the play, but they will have no idea of each character's journey through the play: every characterization is different.) The audience starts at the beginning of the play, and moves linearly in time through the play, assimilating and accumulating information. The actor must provide that information, but at the same time, he must also be aware of its cumulative effect. By the end of the play, the actor and the audience should share a common interpretation of the character.

This is an interesting idea, but one that is difficult for many actors to grasp. What the actor should understand is that she needs to control as much of the information the audience receives as possible. To do that, the actor must first know what she wants the audience to perceive about her character and then go about providing that information in a careful and systematic way, bit by precious bit, throughout the entire play. It's not a one-shot deal. Actors must realize that it is virtually impossible to provide the audience with a fully-formed character from the character's first entrance. A character is an accumulation of experiences, an accumulation of perceptions, and an accumulation of interpretations of these experiences and perceptions. Until the final curtain, what the audience sees during the course of the play is the development of the character *so far.* Even when a character no longer appears on stage, other characters might still provide information or the character's previously observed behavior might be illuminated by a subsequent turn of events. The characterization is not complete, nor is the character fully formed or fully realized until the play is over.

Charting a Physical Profile

The actor's goal in physical characterization is to create a character whose physical appearance and behavior is specific, expressive, and suggestive of a full and complex life. Every movement and gesture should seem to arise naturally out of the dramatic context. The actor will need to return to the script again and again to search for new answers to recurring questions.

In developing a character, progress from basic patterns of behavior to those that are more complex, gradually "building" the character one behavior at a time, until a living, breathing person emerges. First, determine as much as possible about the character's physical appearance. List these "ideal" characteristics under the appropriate category. Then list the actor's physical characteristics, the "reality." Reconcile the "ideal" with the "real." Determine how best to represent the character's essential physical attributes. A skilled actor finds ways to compensate for any differences between his own physical self and the character's physical self.

For attributes that are not readily apparent or revealed in the text, it is often helpful to extrapolate from available information. Rarely does a character defy all attempts to discover her physical identity. Look for subtle clues in the script—the dialogue, staging notes, even information about the set. If you have no idea what a character is supposed to look like but have determined that she has certain personality traits associated with an ectomorphic body type or exhibits the emotional or psychological traits of a Dependent or Self-Possessed character type, you can refer to the appropriate listing of Body Types or Basic Character Types discussed earlier in the chapter for practical suggestions.

Sometimes even an actor's best efforts prove fruitless. In those instances, make an "educated guess" and refine that guess through the character development process.

> *Actor, know thyself. This is very important. Before you attempt to analyze a character, you must first analyze, describe, and categorize yourself. Work step-by-step through the Physical Appearance Checklist that follows and provide information about yourself in response to each category or question. If you don't know what you look like and how you move, how will you be able to adapt your physical characteristics and behavior to the character?*

Can an actor be expected to remember all these things? No. Are all of them applicable to every character in every situation? No. These explorations of physical behavior are intended as an impetus to further investigations. Incorporating even one of these physical aspects of behavior will enhance any characterization, particularly in situations where nonverbal communication or expression have not been enlisted. In terms of developing a character, nothing is irrelevant or inconsequential.

Physical Appearance Checklist

Age: Determine the character's chronological, physical, and mental age.

Height

Weight

Body Build: Consult the section on *Body Types* in this chapter or deduce it from the character's height-to-weight ratio.

Body Image: Generally speaking, this refers to the character's attitude toward his own body. Does he like or dislike his body? How is this attitude reflected in his behavior? What messages about his body is he giving to others? How does he wish others to perceive his body? How does he wish others to think he feels about his body? It is not always possible to determine this information, but it is an interesting aspect of physical characterization. Good examples of varying body images are Shakespeare's Richard III, Laura in *The Glass Menagerie,* and Blanche in *A Streetcar Named Desire.* Each character has a noticeably different approach to the concept of "body image."

Apparent Strength and Actual Strength: A character may appear weak but actually be quite strong.

Posture

Alignment: This applies to both side-to-side and upper-to-lower body alignment.

Attitude: Describe the overall physical "bearing" of the character, how the character "carries" himself. Use the list of *Basic Character Types* and other information in this chapter as a frame of reference for Posture, Alignment, and Attitude.

Deformities: List them and determine if these deformities can be depicted physically (a limp, for instance) or through the use of makeup (for scars or a broken nose), or if the deformity will require some other artificial device, such as costuming or prosthetics.

Other Noticeable Physical Attributes or Deficiencies: List them and determine how they might best be depicted.

Medical Influences: This category encompasses any noticeable physical effects of disease, broken bones, or other infirmities, as well as any effects of past or present infirmities on present physical behavior—difficulty in breathing, for example, or the inability to move a hand, raise an arm, or stand erect for long periods of time. Also consider the effect of long-term drug use, smoking, or alcoholism on the character's body and physical behavior.

Cultural Background: Determine the character's cultural background and list possible or potential ways it might influence the character's physical behavior.

Current Social Environment: List such things as the relative status of the individual in the community and other pertinent socioeconomic factors that may influence individual physical behavior or occur within a specific environment.

Occupation: Determine the character's occupation and list potential influences on physical behavior.

Facial Expression: Which of the characteristics or types of *Facial Expressors* are represented by this character? Consult the list in this chapter.

Movement: Identify and list characteristic movement patterns and determine the primary and secondary function of each movement as well as the objective(s) of each movement.

Gestures: Determine characteristic gestures, list them, and provide specific objectives, reasons, or expressive intent for each gesture.

Other Character Traits: List any other aspects of the character's physical appearance and any unique characteristic movement(s) or gesture(s).

Character Interaction 3

Character Relationships

Character interactions demonstrate character relationships. If the audience is to understand the relationship between two characters, something must happen between them. It is difficult to determine the relationship if the audience has never observed these characters interacting with each another.

This is not to say that characters must engage in spoken dialogue. Simply being in the same room together can sometimes provide the audience with all the information it needs. Two types of character movement and interaction, eye contact and touching, offer powerful ways to demonstrate character relationships to the audience, but neither requires even one spoken word.

A person's true character is revealed in a crisis, and the crisis in a play is usually the result of personal interaction. A character's objectives are rarely achieved without some kind of personal interaction. The crisis is personified in the individuals involved in the interaction: sooner or later, the hero must confront the villain. If the antagonist and protagonist never interact, then the action of the play is stalled, the true nature of the characters is never revealed, and the theme of the play is obscured.

The two main criteria that affect character interactions are level of involvement and proximity. The level of involvement refers to the perception of the role that individuals play in a particular interaction. Active involvement implies that an individual exerts a direct influence on the situation, on the behavior of other individuals involved, or on the outcome. Passive involvement implies the opposite—that the individual has no direct influence on the situation, its outcome, or the behavior of the people involved. Those who enter into an interaction are considered active participants. Their presence will influence the behavior of the other individuals so engaged and will determine to a greater or lesser extent the outcome of the interaction.

In some instances, however, seemingly passive individuals may be considered active participants, even though they may not engage in the activity themselves. The presence of others may encourage interaction between friends, for example, but inhibit interaction between lovers or enemies. We may not wish someone to overhear our telephone conversation, so we talk quietly or take the call in another room. The presence of others influences our behavior. If was no one within earshot, no accommodation would be necessary.

It might be argued that simply through his presence, anyone could change the outcome of an interaction and the behavior of those involved. Certain individuals may well influence behavior just by being in the same space with others. For example, the school principal enters the classroom and stands at the back, observing the class. He does nothing. He says nothing. He does not interact with the students or the teacher, yet you can be sure that his presence influences the behavior of everyone in the room, students and teacher alike.

On the other hand, some people are just "there," and exert little or no influence on the behavior of those around them. Service workers, servants, and manual laborers (commonly referred to as "the hired help") are usually treated as passive "nonpersons" by those in whose service and in whose presence they toil. If the person's presence influences the behavior, the interaction, *or* the outcome, involvement is *active*. If the person's presence changes nothing, makes no apparent difference, or is of no consequence to the interaction—if the person might as well not even *be* there—then his involvement is *passive*.

Proximity is the relative distance between people. The perception of this distance may reflect the actual physical distance between people, or the psychological or emotional distance between them. How a person perceives and relates to this distance and physically reacts to it are often dependent on the individual's psychological or emotional state. People may feel psychologically "distant" from one another in a small space, for example, or they may feel "close" in a large space.

In contrast, in some situations the physical distance seems to dictate the psychological distance. Close physical proximity may *encourage* interaction between people, even strangers. A crowded cocktail party quite literally bubbles over with lively conversation and frequent physical interactions—touching, hugging, shaking hands, kissing, slaps on the back—albeit of a fairly superficial and emotionally noncommittal nature. Yet you will find "wallflowers" at even the most festive occasions.

In other instances, close physical proximity may inhibit interaction, as might be the case when standing in a crowded elevator, seated next to a stranger on a bus, or pressed next to someone on a crowded subway car. These situations may prompt all manner of "distancing" behavior—reduced eye contact, attempts to "blend into the woodwork," jokes or comments about the forced intimacy, nervous laughter, or awkward (and usually short-lived) attempts at conversation. Yet there are individuals who smile at their fellow passengers, chat amiably with them, and otherwise seem perfectly at ease in what some might consider an uncomfortable if not an unbearable situation.

Note the seemingly contradictory behavior of a group of partygoers who travel silently in the elevator up to the penthouse suite, yet become instant old friends the moment the elevator doors open. Much depends, of course, on the actual context of the interaction—the circumstances, the relationship of the people and their emotional and psychological states, and the nature of the interaction, in addition to the actual physical environment. These elements are interdependent in an individual's overall perception of the experience.

> *In your daily interactions with others, be aware of the level of involvement of those engaged in the activity with you, and that of others who may be present in the environment. How does their presence affect your behavior, if at all? If their presence does affect your behavior, why and how does it affect the interaction? If not, why not? How does your proximity to others affect your interaction with them? Are you more or less likely to interact with someone who is physically close to you or at some distance from you? At what distance do you feel most comfortable interacting with acquaintances? Strangers? Close friends or relatives?*

The influence of the level of involvement and proximity on character interactions and relationships will be discussed in greater detail in the course of this chapter.

Character interaction is also influenced in varying degrees by seven other factors: motivation, emotional and psychological state, environment, and context (all discussed previously), as well as roles, the "rules" governing the interaction, and feedback. For an interaction to occur there must first be a reason, a shared motivation. A shared motivation is essential, but it need not be of monumental significance. "Making small talk" is reason enough.

Personal and shared motivations often coexist within the same interaction. The participants may appear to share a mutual "agenda," but each may in fact be pursuing a personal agenda under the guise of cooperation. Two sides of a business negotiation or "peace talks" between warring factions may share the stated goal of reaching a mutually acceptable agreement, for example, but each side will endeavor to put forward its own particular goals or objectives. The meeting itself is the shared motivation.

Every interaction also takes place in a particular physical setting or environment, each person involved is in a definite emotional and psychological state of mind. The interaction occurs within a specific context that encompasses all of these factors, as well as the intrinsic and extrinsic elements of the play and its production.

Furthermore, each character has her own role to play in the interaction and must ordinarily abide by the rules—the social customs and manners that influence, govern, or control the interaction. If a person decides not to "play by the rules," that in turn defines her role, that of "the rebel who doesn't play by the rules." Finally, each person involved monitors the others for important clues to the effectiveness of her communication, that is, feedback.

ROLES

Interactions often require participants to assume particular "roles" or project certain personality traits. We assume, for example, a general or "generic" role, such as man or woman, child or adult, in nonspecific encounters and interactions. We may assume *specific* roles, such as host, guest, employer, or employee, in other, more specific situations. In many cases, the roles we assume are stereotypical: we behave as we are expected to behave in the context of the interaction. It is important to remember, however, that while a person's behavior or personality may change in deference to the situation, his essential character remains the same.

Stereotypical roles and behavior are apparent in many plays, particularly in what is termed "period" plays. Throughout history, men and women characters were expected to behave in certain socially acceptable ways, and their behavior in plays is based on these stereotypical perceptions of male and female roles. Men were expected to be independent, unemotional, assertive, and logical. Women were expected to be dependent, deferential, emotional, and family-oriented.

Though we may wish it were otherwise, these stereotypical perceptions have changed little through the years.

It is important for the actor to be aware of these stereotypical perceptions and of when and how a character's behavior departs from stereotypical expectations. These are vital keys to characterization. The entire premise of Ibsen's *A Doll's House* is built upon the strong expectations and perceptions the audience develops about Nora's "role" as wife and mother. The audience feels the climax of the play all the more strongly because Nora's actions at the end contradict these stereotypical expectations.

Two components of role-playing and of characterization are the interrelated elements of power and status. The dynamics of most interpersonal relationships, whether between real people or fictional characters, are predicated on the acquisition and use of power, whether real or imagined: who has it and who doesn't, who wants it and how badly, and occasionally, who has it but doesn't seem to want it anymore. Whether or not we like to admit it, most of our daily interactions, even with friends and loved ones, involve the pursuit or exercise of power. To many of us the acquisition and use of status is of no less importance.

Power. ■ Power is the ability to influence, control, dominate, intimidate, or manipulate others physically, emotionally, or intellectually. Once obtained, power is rarely relinquished without a struggle, and the struggle itself is often difficult to avoid. Occasionally, however, power may be temporarily relinquished "for the greater good," as when the general defers to a subordinate's plan of battle, or husband and wife cease hostilities in deference to the well-being of the children. The struggle for power might be suspended for a time by mutual agreement, but the decision to suspend hostilities might also be yet another exercise of power by one or the other of the parties involved.

In earlier times, the struggle for power was resolved by physical combat. People simply "fought it out." In our day, the struggle is more often resolved emotionally or intellectually through a "war of words"—arguments, speeches, campaign ads, commercials, and the like. Quite often, the struggle for power is resolved in court. In some court cases, the actual combatants are not even present; they have delegated their personal power to lawyers and their decision-making power to judges or juries. An interesting war is currently being waged over the control of words themselves, who owns the rights to certain computer software, for instance, or who controls "hyperspace," where the future "war of words" will likely be fought.

Only when an issue of power is not resolved by words is a physical resolution pursued. The physical confrontation is likely to be of short duration, in a limited environment, and with clearly defined parameters. "This is a fair fight between him and me. He insulted my wife (or husband, friend, relative, family, culture, gang, haircut, clothes, dog, or country), and unless he takes it back, I'm going to punch his lights out—right here, right now." Modern civilization turns to physical confrontation only as a last resort, when all other means and manner of "negotiations" have failed. We consider it a failure of the "system" when individuals or countries resort to a physical resolution of their problems and differences in war. Even then, restrictions are often placed on the warring factions—the type, number, and use of weapons and the limitations of the field of battle, for instance. Very often countries not actually involved in the confrontation attempt to control important aspects of the conflict. In many cases, smaller, less powerful countries are simply acting as "proxies" for larger, more powerful interests. It's the price they pay for aligning themselves with the more powerful entities. In earlier times, the fate of countries and the course of civilization were determined by individual, one-on-one, hand-to-hand combat. This is no longer the case. The individual combatant involved in a modern power struggle has little power, if any, over either the outcome of the situation or his own destiny.

Rarely are characters in a play equally matched in terms of actual or perceived power. On first impression, one character appears stronger, more powerful, more influential, more "something" than another. For the play to be interesting, the antagonists should be *fairly* evenly matched or the struggle will seem too one-sided. One character may be physically stronger than another, but be lacking intellectual or emotional strength. Or characters may be well-matched intellectually, but one may lack the practical experience or driving ambition of the other.

Characters continually test one another, "jockeying for position" in the onstage hierarchy. The actor needs to know where, exactly, her character fits in the scheme of things, in the "power hierarchy" of the play. The actor must also know and understand her character's views on the acquisition and use of power, and how the character exercises and responds to power in interactions with other characters. The audience is keenly aware of even the most subtle differences and distinctions in the distribution of power and influence between and among the characters. The audience is very sensitive to the moment-to-moment give-and-take of the power struggle. In fact, the audience revels in the struggle. They become personally involved. They empathize with the characters. They think to themselves, "What would I do in that situation?" They become part of the play. It's part of the actor's responsibility to use her considerable power to influence the audience toward that level of involvement.

Status. ■ Status, one of the physical manifestations of power, is revealed in many ways—attitude, dress, posture, language use, and relationships and interaction with others. These manifestations of power and status can be conveyed to an audience through physical characterization.

Higher status individuals are generally associated with postural relaxation, for example, with more frequent use of expansive gestures and movements, a louder voice, more dress ornamentation with "power symbols" (Swiss watch or French handbag), greater territorial access, greater height (perceived or actual), and a greater concern with the acquisition, use, and control of space.

Compare the following traits of individuals of higher and lower status:

Higher Status	Lower Status
Stands erect	Body slightly hunched or bowed
Body relaxed	Body tense
Good posture	Body asymmetrical, unbalanced
Many gestures	Few gestures, restrained
Large, expansive movements	Small, limited movements
Talks more, and more loudly	Talks less, and more quietly
Often interrupts inferiors	Rarely interrupts superiors
Often invades others' personal space	Always "keeps his distance"
Often touches subordinates	Rarely, if ever, touches superiors

Superiors, those of higher status or those in positions of authority, generally have good posture; they stand tall, with flexed knees and raised chest, their arms held loosely at their sides. The superior initiates and holds eye contact. It is noticeable, imposing, and occasionally intimidating. Superiors signal their superiority by sitting while others stand and standing while others sit, by leaning back in their chairs to survey their subordinates or leaning forward to command their attention and gesturing fluidly and expansively. They also talk more, in a louder voice, and have a tendency to interrupt others who are speaking. In other words, superiors control (or attempt to control) their environment and the people in it in as many ways as possible.

Superiors also tend to invade the personal space of subordinates, putting the subordinates on the defensive. Superiors touch subordinates with a pat on the back (often perceived as patronizing), by resting a hand on the shoulder or grasping the shoulder at arms length (indicating control of the individual so touched), and by squeezing the upper arm (sometimes painfully). The subordinate, in contrast, rarely touches the superior and generally tries to maintain a discreet distance in order to avoid any appearance of confrontation or disrespect.

Subordinates, those of lower status, avoid direct eye contact with superiors, often lowering their heads and looking down. Any eye contact that does occur is usually fleeting and noncommittal. Subordinates' bodies appear tense. They stand in a slightly asymmetrical or unbalanced posture. They lean forward, and often nod in agreement with their superior's statements, whether they actually agree or not. The higher-status individual is "allowed" to put his feet up on the desk, but the lower-status person is expected to sit or stand up straight in the presence of his superior.

Subordinates often employ the "fig leaf" gesture, and thereby appear insecure and self-protective. Other self-protective gestures, like crossing the arms in front of the body, standing at an angle to the other person, or putting actual physical objects or obstacles between oneself and the other may indicate anxiety or an uncomfortable relationship. Through gestures and self-touching behavior, subordinates also indicate that they are nervous or self-conscious.

In terms of interpersonal relationships governed by status, the following "rules" apply: Individuals of dominant or superior status control more territory, are freer to move about, are accorded greater territory and territorial access by others of lesser status, and control more of the preferred space in any given environment.

Status is also revealed by the relative amount of space a person commands around herself, and the distance people maintain in deference to that person. We hold some people in high esteem, and that esteem is reflected in the space we accord them. We grant them the space as a display of respect. People will move close to the Pope, for instance, but they won't touch him. When they've received his blessing, they immediately move away to a respectful distance. In contrast, people will reach out to shake hands with a local politician and remain exactly where they are before and after the encounter.

Celebrities like popular film stars, rock stars, sports stars, or television "personalities" are another matter, however. Rarely are celebrities accorded the space that might be commanded by someone with their apparent status. People want to be close to stars, unless the star is held in high esteem, or their personal life is kept separate and distinct from their public life. People will approach celebrities they think they "know" by personal observation or reputation, but they afford greater deference (and greater distance) to those celebrities with more allusive or mysterious personalities. Sometimes distance is also a matter of bodyguards, security forces, Secret Service agents, and attendant entourages, which discourage close proximity.

It is interesting to observe autograph-seekers in pursuit of their celebrity prey. A determined autograph-seeker will overcome all manner of obstacles in his quest. Yet once he has obtained the autograph, once he has acquired a "piece" of the celebrity, there seems to be no further need for the celebrity himself.

INTERPERSONAL SPACE

An entire field of scientific research is devoted to *proxemics*—the study of space as it relates to interpersonal relationships and personal interaction. According to many studies, our relationship to the space around us and to the people within that space is strongly influenced by our basic character and by our cultural heritage. North Americans and Northern Europeans, for example, have a much more clearly defined sense of "personal space"—the space around us that we consider "ours"—than do people of Mediterranean, Asian, Central American, or Middle Eastern heritage. As a result, North Americans tolerate what we consider impositions on our personal space, such as crowded situations and circumstances of forced intimacy, less than other cultures.

Studies in proxemics demonstrate that we go through our daily lives within clearly defined zones that radiate at varying distances from our bodies. The average North American considers her *private* zone—the space that is most directly related to herself and to her sense of self—to extend out from her body roughly three to four feet in all directions. This zone is the area around our bodies that we consider almost exclusively our own to control and regulate as we choose.

Safely enclosed within the private zone is the *intimate* zone, which ranges from surface contact to about eighteen inches from the body. This zone is reserved strictly for lovers, close family members, and very close friends. Others, particularly strangers, enter the private zone at their own risk and the intimate zone at their own peril. North Americans are very protective of their private and intimate zones and tend to consider any intrusion as potentially confrontational. A stranger who "invades" that sacred, personal territory, even accidentally, may face considerable hostility.

In situations where the private or intimate zone must necessarily be violated—in a crowded elevator, for example—North Americans stare blankly ahead or focus intently on the numbers above the door in order to limit interpersonal contact and to protect their own personal space while at the same time respecting the space of others. In contrast, people of Middle Eastern descent have a very limited personal zone and tolerate quite well what North Americans and Europeans would consider an uncomfortably "crowded" environment.

From four to ten feet from the body is considered the *social* zone. Four to six feet is considered a "safe" distance for informal conversations with acquaintances or "friendly strangers" such as a coworker, a store clerk, or a child's teacher. The space from six to ten feet is generally reserved for more formal encounters, like those between a worker and his boss or an ordinary citizen and someone in authority.

More than ten feet from the body, the *public* zone, feels appropriate to North Americans for wholly impersonal encounters, such as those in public areas—in a waiting room or a hotel lobby, for example—which often require no verbal interaction.

Studies of persons with a history of antisocial behavior indicate that their intimate and personal zones extend far beyond what we would consider comfortable for most "normal" people. Criminals, particularly violent criminals, react strongly to what they consider to be threats to their personal or private territory at distances of several feet, which most people would consider nonthreatening. For some reason, criminals seem to need more "space" than law-abiding citizens. Law enforcement officials use this to their advantage by attempting to control a suspected criminal's personal space. All but a few diehard criminals (or those seriously affected by drugs or alcohol) will succumb to the invasion of their territory by an authority figure, and most will cooperate with an arresting officer, even to the extent of voluntarily forfeiting their personal freedom.

As always, much depends on the context, the situation and the actual or perceived relationship between the persons involved. A stranger appearing within one's personal space and attempting to engage in social interaction is considered rude, whereas a friend or relation appearing within the same zone who does not engage in some form of social interaction is also considered rude. When passing a friend on the street, it's acceptable to wave or give a nod of the head if the distance between you is twelve feet or more. It becomes necessary to *verbalize* the greeting if the distance is somewhat closer than ten or twelve feet. Proper social decorum dictates that if you pass the person within six feet or less, you must engage in brief conversation or have a good reason to avoid doing so, such as children in tow or an armful of packages (or both). Or you might have signaled nonverbally in advance that you are otherwise unable to converse—that "tapping-the-wristwatch-can't-talk-now-gotta-run" gesture. If you wait until the other person is within five or six feet of you to make excuses, however, you must do it verbally and in person, even if only to offer a few words of apology and explanation and continue on your way.

TERRITORIALITY

Territoriality is closely associated with the concept of zones. Both relate to the perception of personal space and the effect of that perception on human interaction. Proxemics is concerned primarily with objective space, the space between people, while territoriality relates to subjective space, the perceived "ownership" of space and the objects (and sometimes people) within it.

We are all familiar with the concept of Mom or Dad's favorite chair, the supervisor's parking space, or a gang's "turf." We also hear sports commentators extol the "home field advantage," another example of territoriality that is practiced by both the players on the field and the spectators.

There are essentially three types of territories, each with its own recognizable characteristics. *Primary* territories are the exclusive domain of one entity—an individual or a clearly designated group of individuals. One's home (group domain) or one's bedroom or private office (individual domain) are examples of primary territories. Primary territories are not shared, but clearly "belong" to the people who inhabit them, as do the objects contained within them.

Secondary territories are those that are most often contained within a primary territory—such as a living room in a home or the lunchroom in an office building—where ownership is not clearly established or maintained, and where space is shared. This also applies to objects within secondary territories, such as a book or magazine, or the television or microwave oven. A person can claim ownership of the television, certainly, but that claim is likely to be disputed, particularly when a conflict in programming arises. There is also the matter of who gets to read the newspaper or magazine first (newspapers and magazines often seem to shift from primary to secondary status after the first reading). Even personal objects can be "up for grabs" if contained within a secondary territory. Without some distinguishing characteristic, such as a name or monogram, a plain coffee cup left unattended in the company lunchroom for a certain period of time is assumed to be common property.

The third category, *public* territories, are those that are available to anyone on a "temporary ownership" basis. Park benches, streets, a spot on the beach, a telephone booth, a seat in a restaurant or on a bus are all examples of public territories. We assume temporary ownership of the territory in question, occupy and defend it, and then abandon it. It's interesting to note, however, how upset people get when a person's right to public territory is not respected or acknowledged. Think of a person who "hogs" the telephone booth for several minutes while others are waiting, takes up two seats on the bus, or drives "like he owns the road," thereby preempting anyone else's right to temporary ownership of the territory. We vigorously defend a territory that isn't even ours, the underlying attitude being "maybe I don't own the street (or park bench, or bus seat, or telephone), but neither does he."

We defend our territory in one of two ways: prevention or reaction. We *prevent* incursions into our territory by "staking a claim" to the space. We place personal objects strategically in the space to advise others of our territory: books or papers on our desk, for example, photographs and awards on the walls of our offices, or a prominent nameplate on the mailbox or the front door of our house. These objects help to define the space as "ours." Often, these attempts to show that we "own the place" are sufficient to dissuade would-be invaders.

If our attempts to define the "ownership" of our territory fail and our territory is "invaded," our reaction may involve the use of body positions, gestures, or, as a final resort, verbal or physical confrontation to dissuade the invader. We may try to "ward off" the invader from a distance with unfriendly glances or facial expressions or by staring intently with no expression or by crossing our arms. If an invasion appears likely, we may shift our bodies, sit or stand more erect in anticipation of a confrontation, "spread out" our arms or legs, or physically place ourselves between the invader and our space. If all else fails and invasion is imminent, we may confront the invader verbally or physically, although research has shown that only about one in ten such invasions results in a verbal exchange, and physical confrontation is rare. Most often, either the invader or the person whose territory is being invaded will move away with little or no verbal or physical exchange. Any verbal interaction (and its physical equivalent, a rude gesture) is more likely to happen after rather than during the event: "There. Are you happy now? You've got the whole place to yourself."

Our reaction to encroachment on our territory depends on a number of factors: Who is doing the encroaching, and what is the nature of our relationship with them? A friendly encroachment is likely to elicit a much less forceful or hostile response than encroachment by a stranger. *Why* did the invader encroach on the territory? Was the encroachment accidental or dileberate? What is the nature of the territory that was encroached upon? (Did someone violate your "inner sanctum," did they mistakenly pick up the wrong briefcase, or pre-empt your parking space in a public lot?) What was the severity of the encroachment? (Were you touched physically, did someone wander into your home uninvited, or were you cut off in traffic?) How long did the encroachment last? (Was it temporary, like someone walking across the corner of your lawn, or did it appear that the person ex-pected to take up permanent residence in your bathroom?) The inten-sity of your reaction to the encroachment will vary in relation to each of these factors.

One consideration for the actor is how this physical interaction with another character will be perceived and interpreted by the audi-ence in terms of the level of physical and emotional involvement, proxemics, and territoriality. In terms of proxemics, for example, an audience composed predominately of North Americans will consider one character's foray into another's intimate zone to impart a special significance to the relationship, whereas the same scene viewed by an audience of Central Americans or Asians will hold no such signifi-cance. The concept of territoriality is a much more universal one, however, and the invasion of one character's primary territory by an-other likely would hold significance in any culture. All such cultural generalizations are based on a broad spectrum of observed behavior and may not be applicable in every situation. The people involved and the context in which the interaction occurs are always the primary factors in determining the significance of interpersonal behavior.

One other consideration: Space is at a premium on a stage set. It is not always possible to maintain the territorial imperatives that exist in daily life. Zones must necessarily be compressed to fit the available space. What is important is that as long as the zones and territorial boundaries remain consistent throughout the play, the audience will likely accept the "condensed" version. It is also possible to subtlely imply greater or lesser distance between characters through blocking and by interposing furniture or other characters in the intervening space. A change in the spatial relationship between characters still implies a change in their personal relationship, however, no matter how condensed the zones and territories may be. Remember, too, that conversational distance and territorial considerations, as well as other perceptions of space, are dynamic elements: As the context and the relationships change, spatial perceptions will also change.

> *Determine your own intimate, private, social, and public "zones," and your primary and secondary territories. In what ways do they coincide with or differ from those discussed in*

*the text? Diliberately but carefully, invade someone else's
primary territory. Note the reaction. Now invade someone's
secondary territory. Note the reaction and compare it to the
"primary territory invasion reaction."*

*Observe the dynamics of life in "public" spaces. How is
temporary territorial "ownership" assumed? How is it designated? How is it defended? How does ownership change?
What factors influence the change?*

In terms of characterization, the actor needs to determine how heavily "invested" a character is in these perceptions of space. How determined is a character in maintaining her personal space, for instance,
or in clearly defining her territories? To what extent is the character
determined to defend her space? Will an incursion into her space
by another character result in passive acceptance or a violent confrontation?

One last consideration: The actor should think of space as a positive rather than a negative element. Space is not simply the distance
between things; it holds expressive potential in its own right. It invites
rather than inhibits dynamic change. A character changes the nature
of space simply by moving through it; he, in turn, is changed by the
space through which he moves.

The Rules

"The Rules" are those unspoken but often explicit standards of behavior that govern public and private interactions. Rules govern conversational distance, physical and emotional display, topics of
conversation, appropriate attitudes and decorum, manners and customs, and so on. The more formal the occasion, the more rules and
the more explicit are the rules. Less formal, however, doesn't necessarily mean fewer rules, only rules that are different and less explicit.
Rules may seem less important in an informal setting, and the consequences of breaking them less drastic, but they exist.

Conversational distance. ■ In the real world, the rules governing conversational distance are the result of a combination of influences,
including the nature of the interaction, the relationship of the individuals, and the on-going physical "negotiation" between them. The distance at which characters converse on stage is imposed by the
director through his blocking. An actor should be aware, however, of
the many factors that can influence the director's choices and be prepared for situations in which he must direct himself.

A number of factors influence variations in conversational distance, and they are interrelated and interdependent: a variation in one affects the others.

Age and sex. ■ Female pairs of equal age generally stand closer together than male pairs, and mixed-sex pairs stand closest of all.

People of the same age stand closer together than people of disparate ages, although the very young and the very old stand fairly close to others, whether of the same or different ages. For younger people, the closeness implies a certain curiosity, an interest in getting to know the other person. For older people the closeness may be the result of diminished hearing acuity or desire to be closer to another person.

Men usually converse in a side-by-side, looking-out-at-the-world-together configuration, whereas women generally converse face to face. Mixed couples seem to prefer face-to-face interaction at varying angles, depending on the actual nature of their relationship. The more intimate the relationship, the more face-to-face interaction.

Culture. ■ Some cultures are considered "high contact": Middle Eastern, Latin American, and Southern European cultures, for example. We would expect that characters representing these cultures would stand closer together than those representing the "low contact" North American, Northern European, or Asian cultures.

In the area of cultural differences between interactants much physical "negotiation" occurs. The person of Latin American background will attempt to move closer to the North American, who will attempt to move farther away. At some point in the conversation, a "happy medium" will be negotiated at a distance that is mutually agreeable, and this distance will be maintained throughout the balance of the conversation, with only minor variations.

Subject matter. ■ Changes in subject matter during a conversation affect the distance between the people involved. "Impersonal" or neutral subjects are discussed at greater distances than "personal" or "intimate" subjects. As the subject changes from "personal" to "impersonal," the distance between the interactants increases. The converse is also true: note how close people stand when a "secret" is being confided, compared to a discussion about the weather or the results of a weekend sports event.

Setting. ■ As one might expect, an "impersonal" setting such as an office or hotel lobby generally implies greater distance between interactants, whereas a more "intimate" setting, a cozy restaurant or a bedroom, implies a closer relationship, and a closer conversational distance. Human beings are highly adaptive creatures, however, and seem to be able to "mold" their environment to suit their personal needs. If privacy is not a concern, a small settee in the corner of a crowded hotel lobby can be the scene of an intimate téte-a-téte. If privacy is an issue, the téte-a-téte will likely occur elsewhere.

People are also influenced by temperature, lighting, ambient noise level, and the available conversational space. People stand farther apart when the temperature is high, but closer together when the lighting is dim, the noise level high, or the space confined.

Other environmental factors, such as familiarity with the space, a sense of freedom within the space, and the relative formality of the space also influence conversational distance. People stand closer together in a familiar, informal space and farther apart in a formal space, even if it is familiar. A person ready to flee the perceived confines of a room will stand farther away from another than a person whose sense of freedom is not compromised by the space.

Nature of the relationship. ■ Strangers converse at greater distances than acquaintances, who converse at greater distances than friends, who converse at greater distances than intimates. No surprise there. The distance between individuals is also a reflection of their relative status by whatever measure that status is determined. People of higher status generally command greater distance between themselves and others, and have more freedom to move around in the space they inhabit. Some people seem to "fill the room" simply by walking into it and are able to move freely throughout the room, slipping in and out of conversations with apparent ease. Others seem to "blend into the woodwork," trying to put as much space as possible between themselves and everyone else. An individual's use of space and her manipulation of the distance between herself and others is a reflection of her status.

Nature of the changing relationship. ■ A changing relationship is any attempt by one of the individuals engaged in conversation to alter the nature of the relationship. When we want to influence another person favorably, or when we seek someone's approval, we move closer to that person. When we are not seeking approval, or when we disdain or dislike the other person, we move farther away. Moving closer to elicit approval can be a risky maneuver, however, particularly if the diminished distance prompts a negative rather than positive response. The other person may view the attempt as confrontational or as an inappropriate step toward intimacy.

Personality disorders. ■ People who suffer from personality disorders exhibit a considerable range of deviations from what is categorized as normal behavior, and these extend to their spatial relationships with others. Those with anxiety disorders, for instance, tend to stand at a greater conversational distance, whereas an obsessive-compulsive person may move in very close to better "control" the conversation and, by extension, the other person.

> *Observe yourself and others in conversation in relation to the factors discussed above. Observe the dynamics of any change in the conversational distance and note the ongoing "negotiations" in the spatial relationship. How do each of these factors affect the distance between those engaged in conversation?*
>
> *Deliberately "change the subject" of the conversation and observe any adjustments in distance. Change the distance between yourself and the other person and notice the reaction. What happens when you close the distance? When you expand the distance? Maintain a constant distance between yourself and the other person, no matter what the other person does to try to change it, and note the reaction.*

Certain characters in every play endeavor to push the limits of acceptable behavior, to question the roles imposed upon them, and generally to make a nuisance of themselves. An actor should try to discover what it is about the behavior or attitude of the character he is portraying that stretches the bounds of societal impositions and restraints. The more trouble a character makes, the more interesting he is. (All the great characters in the dramatic repertoire are troublemakers *par excellence*.)

FEEDBACK

Feedback is essential to most human interactions. In your own experience, you have probably noticed when someone you are engaged in conversation with doesn't seem to care what you think or say or even who you are. He just likes to hear himself talk. Other people seem to be vitally interested in your opinions and ideas. Neither of these is an example of feedback.

The kind of feedback essential to most interactions is the monitoring of behavior that occurs between the participants. One speaks to the other and at the same time monitors the response of the person she is addressing. What the speaker observes will affect her subsequent behavior. She may temper her remarks in some way, explain more fully a point that she wishes to make, modify her position on a certain topic, or even alter her choice of words in response to her perception of behavior of the other person. An interaction is of greatest consequence when significant feedback occurs. Meaningful interaction requires meaningful response.

EYE CONTACT AND TOUCHING

Character relationships are most often defined by means of two distinctly different but highly *character*-revealing and character-*relationship*-revealing behaviors: eye contact and touching. Both eye contact and touching are dependent on the situation, the distance between characters, their individual personalities, the general and specific nature of relationships, physical characteristics, and the task at hand.

What we generally refer to as "eye contact" is one of several different kinds of eye movement. The eyes tell a story about relationships. They don't tell the whole story, but they tell a great deal of the story, particularly in a situation in which the eyes are the only available means of communication.

For the purposes of this analysis, eye contact is a generic term to describe any sort of "looking" behavior by one individual toward another. It is an imprecise term at best, and an oversimplification of a complex physical activity. The term "simple gaze" refers to the looking behavior of one individual that is directed at another. A simple gaze is essentially one-sided—it is not returned—and the term can refer to any type of eye behavior from a casual glance to an intensely focused stare.

A "mutual gaze" refers to eye behavior in which two individuals are actively and intentionally engaged in looking one another in the face, if not the eyes. Two individuals may be looking at one another, but unless their eyes meet or they look one another in the face, theirs is not a mutual gaze but a simple gaze.

A mutual gaze cannot be discerned by an observer at distances greater than three feet. An audience can discern, for instance, whether a character is looking at another character's face, but not whether the character is actually looking into the other character's eyes. At distances greater than ten feet, the audience cannot tell for sure if one character is even looking directly at another character. Since an audience rarely sits closer to the actors than ten feet, and often sits at a much greater distance, it's nearly impossible for audience members to determine where the actor is looking at all, except in the most general terms: left or right, upstage or downstage, up or down. The audience's perspective is actually very limited. This is one reason that guns fired on stage are always pointed at a slight angle away and upstage from the actor being shot. From their perspective, audience members can't really tell if the gun is pointed directly at the other actor or not (the other reason is a safety issue—possible injury to the actor from the muzzle blast, burning gunpowder, and the like).

An excellent illustration of this principle is how we discern whether or not a television or movie actor is reading his lines from a cue card or actually looking at the other actor. In an over-the-shoulder shot from a distance of less than ten feet, we can see what the actor is doing: looking at the other actor or reading the cue card. At distances of greater than ten feet, however, we are unable to distinguish eye contact from cue card contact—unless the actor's eyes are moving from side to side in an obvious reading pattern.

Eye contact and general visual behavior are strong clues to the relationship between characters. The audience observes characters looking or *not* looking at one another and can observe the subtleties of eye movement. The audience sees all, knows all. Even that which is hidden from the other characters is revealed to the audience.

A subtle process of evaluation is going on in the minds of audience members as they observe the characters. In this area the frequency, duration, range, and intensity of visual behavior are most significant. How often two characters look at each other, for how long, in what manner, and with what intensity—these reveal a great deal about the relationship between them. The audience makes its judgement on the basis of the interrelationship of these essential elements.

This analysis is applicable to relationships with every other character on the stage—superior or subordinate, friend or enemy, lover or the object of love (requited or not), major character, minor character, incidental character, or walk-on. How your character looks at them reveals aspects of your character and your character's relationship to the other character. Not looking reveals other aspects of your character and the relationship. The "cause" is unavoidable. The "effect" is inescapable.

A note about blinking. Generally speaking, men blink faster, more often, and more regularly than women. People who are lying—men and women—often try to blink more slowly than normal in an attempt to control excessive blinking that might "give away" the deception. An astute observer will note any departure from normal blinking behavior, however, and be alert to the situation

One person can appear stronger, more powerful, or of higher status than another by minimizing his blinking, particularly during confrontational interactions. The "strong, silent" movie character type can be seen to blink very little, if at all, while the camera is rolling. This unflinching, often expressionless gaze imparts a certain mystique. It is difficult to refrain from blinking on a well-lighted movie or theater set, but the effect might well be worth the effort. A slight squint helps prevent tearing up, as does turning one's head to limit direct light into the eyes.

Certain factors influence *gazing* behavior. The following list is intended to serve as a point of departure in analyzing and exploring your character's visual behavior patterns.

Factors influencing *increased* gazing behavior:

You are physically distant from the other person.
You are discussing uncomplicated or impersonal topics.
There is nowhere else to look.
You are interested in the other person's reactions to your words or your behavior.
You are interested in the other person—you like or love the other person, and you are looking for reciprocal visual activity.
You are of a lower status than the other person, in which case you may be looking for reinforcement, acceptance, validation, or some other form of positive feedback.
You are trying to dominate or influence the other person.
You are from a culture that values visual contact in human interactions, as in most parts of North America.
You are an extrovert, or wish to appear so.
You want or need to be liked or accepted by the other person— you are "looking for acceptance."
You are dependent on the other person—for love, for food, or for a job.
You are listening rather than talking.
You are female.

Factors influencing *decreased* gazing behavior:

You are physically close to the other person.
You are discussing difficult, complicated, or intimate topics.
You have other objects, people, or background to look at.
You are not interested in the other person.
You are talking rather than listening.
You are not interested in the other person's reactions to you, your words, or your physical activity.

You perceive yourself as of higher status or of greater importance than the other person.

You are from a culture that does not encourage visual contact during human interaction (an Asian culture, for example).

You are an introvert, or wish to appear so.

You don't want or need to be liked or accepted by the other person, or wish to appear so.

You are detached or distracted from the conversation.

You have a mental disorder.

You are embarrassed, ashamed, sorrowful, submissive, trying to hide something, or attempting to be deceitful.

You are male.

Your character's personality and the dramatic context will determine the expressive content of your visual behavior. You may, for example, wish to look more often at an intimate friend instead of less, even if you are in close proximity to one another, a situation that would normally limit or inhibit gazing behavior. Then again, you may be uncomfortable with your friend in such a situation and wish to "distance" yourself from him by averting your gaze and avoiding eye contact. These are things that you will have to decide for your character.

People communicate with their eyes in situations that otherwise require silence. Observe how lovers look at each other in the company of others, revealing their intimacy to all the world whether they actually intend to or not. Note the hierarchy revealed by eye contact at any meeting or official gathering. Eye contact will reveal the relative status and level of influence of every person in the room and uncover hidden alliances. Bring people together in any situation and it will be almost impossible for them to conceal their relationships from an attentive observer.

Be aware that visual behavior is culture bound. In some cultures it is considered rude to stare or to look directly at another person while speaking to her. In others, the reverse may be true—lack of eye contact may categorize the individual as untrustworthy, dishonest, or deceitful. What is perceived as an innocent, flirtatious "come hither" look in one culture may well lead to incarceration for solicitation in another. Cultural context is everything.

Actors are often admonished by acting teachers and directors to "look the other actor in the eye" while engaged in onstage dialogue. How often does this occur in real life? Only on stage do people never become distracted, never avoid eye contact, never look anywhere but in the other person's eyes. For many different reasons, however, characters might not look at one another.

In fact, depending on the situation and the characters involved, "looking the other actor in the eye" might be wholly inappropriate and might mislead the audience. What if your character is not the type of person who looks other people in the eye when he talks to them? Doing so would imply a relationship that may not exist and impose a false element on both characters.

Eye contact must be appropriate to the character, not imposed solely in deference to some preconceived notion of "correct acting." Acting is not real but it must *appear* real. Constant eye contact between characters on stage is not only not real, it doesn't look real. Real people don't do that. If real people don't do that, then characters in a play, who are supposed to represent real people, shouldn't do it either.

Touching, like eye contact, is a vital aspect of human relationships and human interactions. The act of touching or being touched can have a profound impact on our response to a person or a situation. In some instances, touch may be the most effective means of communicating with another person. A touch might inspire confidence, love, or trust, it might elicit suspicion, fear, or hostility. The meaning we attach to touching varies according to who does the touching, what part of the body is touched, how long the touch lasts, the frequency of the touch, the intensity of the touch, the nature of the touch itself, and the context in which the touch occurs.

Touching behavior also varies greatly according to age, sex, and the nature of the relationship. A mother may touch her daughter more often and in more areas of the body than she touches her son. Acquaintances, as opposed to close friends, will likely limit their touching to very limited areas of the body, and will touch each other only on social occasions and only in a socially acceptable manner—a handshake upon meeting, for example, or a noncommittal pat on the shoulder on the way to the punch bowl. Young lovers seem to exhibit very little restraint, either in terms of the areas of the body touched, or the environment in which they do their touching. More mature couples, no less in love, will mutually agree to refrain from public displays of affection and reserve their most intimate behavior for a more "appropriate" time and place.

In North America, we generally avoid touching one another in our daily lives—even members of the same family, intimate friends, and long-married couples refrain from touching—so observing the act of touching on stage gives a heightened sense of reality to relationships and enhances the "bigger than life" aspect of a dramatic presentation. The audience feels the touch. People intuitively understand its intent and meaning. They respond empathetically to the physical contact that they observe on stage. For people who rarely touch others in their daily lives or scrupulously avoid being touched themselves, touching is a big deal, a major event, and actors and directors can use this perception to advantage in performance.

Touching encompasses a wide range of physical activities, which are grouped in five distinct categories: professional, social, friendly, intimate, and sexual.

1. Professional. ■ This type involves only the touching required to accomplish a particular objective or to perform some specific "professional" service—a doctor giving a physical examination, for example, or a tennis instructor demonstrating a forehand shot. Professional touching is without meaning other than accomplishing the function it serves, and it is performed in a relatively cold, impersonal, unemotional, and businesslike manner. The person being touched is treated more like an object than a person or individual. This allows the touching to take place without imposing any other message or meaning on the relationship (like one of intimacy, for example), and keeps any personal feelings or emotions that may exist from interfering with the task at hand.

2. Social. ■ A handshake on meeting another person is the best example of social behavior. The handshake can be little more than the expression of a long-standing social custom, or it may imply a deeper relationship. In social touching, the other person is perceived as a person, but little involvement is intended or perceived by the interactants. Social touching is "expected" behavior. The activity is essential to affirm, or reaffirm, a social custom and conform to standard rules of conduct. In some circumstances, a kiss on the lips is considered normal social behavior, even between strangers, while some social customs dictate a kiss on both cheeks, an embrace, or a hearty thump on the back. Customs and context dictate acceptable touching behavior and help define its meaning.

3. Friendly. ■ Friendly touching is intended as an expression of friendship. It can also be an offer of friendship to a person who may appear to be in need of a friend—someone who is emotionally upset, for example—who may otherwise be a total stranger. In the case of a person in need of friendship, touching expresses an emotional bond, no matter how tenuous or momentary that bond may be.

4. Intimate. ■ The person being touched is the object of one's expression of intimacy or love. An emotional attachment or bond between the individuals is apparent. This type of touching behavior is highly person-specific—the message expressed by the touch is intended for that person alone.

5. *Sexual.* ■ On the most basic level, sexual touching is solely the expression of physical attraction. Certainly, something more than an expression of physical attraction may be intended or conveyed, but no other expression is required. The touching may include expressions of intimacy, or it may be dispassionate, impersonal, and unemotional.

These types of touching behavior are mutually exclusive; they do not occur in combination between the same individuals in the same context. Professional touching may evolve into intimate touching, but they remain completely different types of touching and therefore cannot coexist. The touching is either intimate, for example, or it is professional, not both. There is no such thing as intimate-professional touching. A doctor may be in love with his patient, but the professional doctor-patient relationship is distinct from the intimate relationship, and there is a distinct difference in the touching behavior appropriate to each type. There is also a noticeable difference between the professional touch a doctor uses in the examination of her patient, and the friendly "you-can-put-your-clothes-back-on" pat on the hand or shoulder that lets the patient know when the examination—the professional touching—is completed.

It would seem that the categories of touching behavior are based on the intention of the person doing the touching, but this is not the case. It is rather the perception of the person being touched, the person who reacts to the touching, that defines the category. The effect, not the intent, defines the meaning.

An audience can usually discern the intent of the person doing the touching, and also clearly observe the effect of the touching by the reaction of the person being touched: the person being touched may perceive the touching behavior in a completely different way from how it was intended, or misinterpret the touching. Simply because a touch is intended as professional, social, friendly, intimate, or sexual, does not mean that it will necessarily be perceived or received that way.

Touching is also an interactive process in which both individuals play a part. One person may seem passive, but having been touched or approached to be touched, the person becomes an active participant in the process, willingly or otherwise. The dynamics of touching are such that one person cannot touch another without eliciting some kind of reaction. Even no response holds some meaning to the individuals involved, and is representative—to the individuals and to the audience—of the relationship between them.

Consider these scenarios:

- She reaches across the table and gently places her hand on his. At first he does not respond. Then he slowly slides his hand away.
- She reaches across the table and gently places her hand on his. At first he does not respond. Then he gently places his other hand on hers.
- She reaches across the table and gently places her hand on his. At first he does not respond. Then he grasps her hand fervently, nearly crushing her fingers.
- She reaches across the table and gently places her hand on his. At first he does not respond. Then he lifts her hand from his and brusquely pushes it aside.
- She reaches across the table and gently places her hand on his. At first he does not respond. Then he slaps it playfully.
- She reaches across the table and gently places her hand on his. At first he does not respond. Then he takes her hand in both of his and caresses and kisses it.
- She reaches across the table and gently places her hand on his. He does not respond.

In each scenario, the reaction to the touching behavior defines the effect and categorizes the nature of the touch.

> *Watch how other people touch. Keep a checklist, like the one below, of the different types of touching behavior you observe. Which type occurs most often and which least often? In what situations are different types of touching most likely to occur?*
>
> *Explore the various types of touching behavior, and consider their suitability in different situations and with different individuals.*

The following list summarizes various touching behaviors and the area(s) of the body toward which each touch is most often directed. Use this list as a guide in developing your characterization.

Patting: shoulder, back, head, hand
Slapping: face, back, hand, buttocks

Punching: shoulder, upper arm, chest
Pinching: cheek, upper arm, buttocks
Stroking: hair, face, hand, thigh
Shaking: hand, shoulders
Kissing: mouth, cheek, face, hand
Licking: fingers, face
Holding: hand, arm, knee
Guiding: hand, arm, shoulder
Embracing: shoulder, upper body
Linking: arms
Laying-on: hands to head, shoulder
Kicking: legs, buttocks
Pushing: shoulders, arms, chest, back
Poking: chest, shoulder, arm, thigh
Grooming: hair, face
Tickling: anywhere, depending on the individual

Although touching can be an expressive, character-revealing activity, you will notice that in many theatrical productions the actors rarely touch one another, except in the most functional and script-fulfilling ways. Actors and directors simply fail to capitalize on the remarkable expressive potential that touching affords them in the development of characterization, character interaction, and dramatic action. A touch can strengthen one relationship and shatter another, incite a person to violence, or provide the impetus for an ill-fated love affair. Words alone are often insufficient. The intricacies of some relationships can only be brought fully to light through touch.

Touching behavior may be directed at another person, but it may also be directed at oneself. Self-touching may include: shielding or protecting actions intended to reduce or inhibit sensory input or output, such as putting a hand over mouth, eyes, or ears; cleaning, preening, and self-management activities, such as scratching, picking, or rubbing oneself; self intimacies, such as hugging or stroking oneself or holding one's own hand.

Psychologists agree that there seems to be a link between the lack of social contact or a withdrawal from interaction with others and increased self-touching behavior. Acutely depressed individuals, for example, show a preponderance of body-focused hand movements. Highly narcissistic individuals show a marked tendency toward self-touching, sometimes to the exclusion of others from their awareness and perception, even to the extent of total withdrawal from interaction with others.

The deliberate avoidance of touching can also provide clues to a character's emotional or psychological state and relationship with others. Lovers who are intimate in private may avoid any contact whatsoever in public. One person may refuse to shake the other's hand on meeting or perform such a pitifully deficient rendition of hand-shaking that no one who sees it will have any doubt about the relationship between the individuals.

> *Observe the many ways that people touch themselves and others. Note the range and variations of touching behavior. Observe the ways that people avoid touching one another. Note the lengths to which some people will go to avoid being touched or to avoid touching someone else, particularly a stranger.*
> *Try to determine, as best you can, the nature of a touch, and the nature of the relationship the touch represents.*

The embrace. ■ The embrace is an interesting interpersonal physical phenomenon. It can denote the most intimate of relationships or a most impersonal one. The embrace between lovers is distinct in manner and intent from that of two close friends parting, two people of passing acquaintance meeting, or the spontaneous display of two unaquainted spectators who happen to be seated next to each other at a football game.

In a full embrace, the two parties are pressed close together frontally, the sides of their heads in contact or very close together and their arms wrapped around one another's bodies. All manner of variations are possible on this basic position—the relationship of parts of the body, the intensity and duration of the embrace, and whether or not the embrace actually occurs or is pointedly avoided, for example.

Whether or not two characters embrace in a play is generally a matter for the director. Nevertheless, as an actor you should decide for yourself on your character's intent toward another character, as well as the potential expressive content of the embrace (or lack or avoidance of the embrace) in terms of audience perception. You might also consider whether or not an embrace is the best way of expressing or revealing your character and your character's relationship to another. A simple, uncomplicated kiss or the touch of a hand might be more appropriate.

> *Observe how people embrace one another and how they move in and out of the embrace. Try to determine the nature of the relationship between them. You will find that every element holds meaning and reveals some aspect of the per-*

sonality of each individual and the relationship between them.

There are cultural differences in the use of the embrace, just as there are differences in many other aspects of touching behavior. Resources are available, most notably books and articles written for people (particularly those in business) who travel in foreign countries and wish to avoid insulting or alienating their hosts by inappropriate behavior. One culture's wave "hello" or "thumbs up" can be another culture's insult. A socially acceptable embrace in one culture can be an invitation to disaster in another. References such as these can also be a good source of information on protocol, dining customs, and the relationship between the sexes, which are always problematic, even within one's own culture.

Courtship behavior. ■ The pursuit of love (or of a lover) is a fascinating component of many plays, and the courtship ritual a fundamental aspect of the dramatic action. In many ways, the courtship ritual can define the relationship between characters more clearly than any other means.

The courtship process follows a fairly structured and ritualized path. The steps to intimacy, with allowances for slight cultural variations are (1) eye to body; (2) eye to eye; (3) voice to voice; (4) hand to hand; (5) arm to shoulder; (6) arm to waist; (7) hand to head; (8) mouth to mouth; (9) hand to body, and; (10) mouth to body. All but one (#3) of these steps to intimacy is physical, and in some instances that step may be "skipped" entirely. These steps generally follow the same order, except in socially formalized body contact, such as a handshake, embrace, or other socially acceptable meeting behavior. The progression may be interrupted or broken off at any time and by either party. One person may not "make the next move," for instance, or the other may discourage or forbid it.

Couples seem to know and understand these steps to physical intimacy almost instinctively. They go through the motions of courtship, but they often have no conscious understanding of what they're doing or why they're doing it. It is a rare individual, however, who is totally oblivious to the process, and unless both individuals are unaware of the natural order of things, the more knowledgeable will make it clear just what the proper progression should be.

In our culture, men and women are considered "fast" or "slow" (advanced or inept) according to whether or not they follow the prescribed order of steps on the road to intimacy. If someone skips a step or takes it out of the proper sequence, that person is considered "fast."

If a person ignores the signal to move on to the next step, or takes action to avoid or prevent the next step, he is considered "slow."

Consider these steps in terms of characterization and character relationships. Where in the "natural order of things" is the physical relationship between two characters taken up? Are the characters at step 1 at the beginning of the play, or have they already progressed to step 4 or 5? At any particular point in the play, where are the characters? Might you consider the characters "fast" or "slow" in terms of the context and the condensed timeframe of the play itself? How might the actual relationship be portrayed to the audience using these ten steps as a general frame of reference?

Readiness for courtship is signaled through a wide range of physical behaviors, such as physical preparation, preening behavior, positional cues, and actions of appeal or invitation. Physical preparation involves the appearance of high muscle tone, generally achieved through reduced food consumption, increased exercise, and a more active role in the development and maintenance of one's physical health. The increase in exercise and the emphasis on proper diet and nutrition also result in improved posture, reduced eye bagginess and jowl sag, less slouching and shoulder hunching, and decreased belly sag. What, for instance, is the stereotypical response of older males to the presence of a young and attractive female? They stand up straight, suck in their stomachs, and thrust out their chests, as if this alone would make up for years of nutritional neglect and overall physical decline. (Psychologists note that increased concern about one's physical appearance might signal a romantic involvement outside an ongoing relationship. How might such an observation be used in characterization?)

Preening behavior involves such actions as stroking or rearranging the hair, touching up makeup, glancing repeatedly in the mirror, rearranging clothes—opening buttons, adjusting suitcoats, tugging at socks or hose, and readjusting ties. Although not all self-touching behavior is preening behavior, all preening behavior is self-touching behavior.

Positional cues involve arranging the body and organizing the physical space around oneself to allow maximum opportunity for courtship. Examples include arranging the seating so that it suggests openness to one person and not to others, arranging the body to inhibit or limit others from joining the interaction, opening oneself to interaction by positioning oneself in someone's line of sight or movement, interrupting an ongoing conversation, or physically imposing oneself on someone whether subtly or blatantly, depending on one's level of interest (or desperation).

Actions of appeal or invitation include flirtatious glances, re-peated or lengthy gaze-holding, rolling the pelvis, crossing the legs to expose a thigh, muscle flexing, posing, exhibiting the waist or the palm of the hand, and other movements that accentuate certain parts of the body. People who share similar physical attitudes also seem to share a common interaction posture, whereas incongruent posture may reflect attitudinal distance.

These "readiness for courtship" behaviors can occur separately or together, depending on the individual and on the nature of the relationship. Audiences are very sensitive to this behavior, since its variations demonstrate one of humankind's primary motivations—continuing the human race. The development of any one behavior greatly enhances any characterization and the audience's under-standing of character relationships.

Character Interaction Analysis

Character interaction involves much more than the director's block-ing. Physical interaction can be very complex. Much of what the audi-ence believes about characters and relationships will be based on the comparison (and reconciliation, in some cases) of physical behavior to verbal behavior. If there is a discrepancy between what a character says and what a character does, the audience will invariably believe what the character does.

In developing the physical level of characterization, an actor must know two things about an interaction between characters: the context and the participants.

The context of the interaction is the present context—where the characters find themselves at the exact moment of their interaction. The present context includes the physical environment and the emo-tional environment. The actor must know where the character is po-sitioned in the immediate physical environment of the scene and what environmental influences are likely to be felt by each character. Are the characters alone, for instance, or does the scene take place on a set that is crowded with other characters? Is the scene indoors or out-doors, and what effect, if any, does location have on the interaction? What about the decor, the furniture, the props, and all other elements of the physical setting of the scene? What about the temperature of the space and similar subtle influences? Each of these elements af-fects an interaction as it affects individual characters.

The emotional environment of the interaction is the present emotional environment. What is the emotional relationship, if any, between the characters? How is your character relating to the other character right now? What is the immediate emotional environment of the interaction? This is what the audience observes; and it is the only way that the audience can observe it—at the moment it is happening. If the audience has already observed these characters interacting, these observations will join earlier impressions. If the audience has not seen these characters interact before, this will be a first opportunity to observe and judge the characters' relationship. Either way, the audience's understanding of the relationship is derived from the cumulative process of "present moments." The information may relate to a past or future relationship, but the audience learns about it now, in the present, and extrapolates to form an opinion.

The participants are the characters directly involved in the interaction at any given moment. During the course of a scene, a character may interact with several other characters, but while the physical environment may be the same, the emotional environment will be different because of the individuals involved. Each interaction is therefore different. An actor should have a "plan of acting" for interactions between his character and with each of the other characters.

In Shakespeare, a character may interact with another of equal status, higher status, or lower status, with one with whom he has an emotional relationship and another with whom he does not, with one who is dead, perhaps, with one he loves, another he likes, and another he despises, detests, and abhors—sometimes all within the same scene, occasionally within the span of eight lines. The living person represented in the play would know how to differentiate among these relationships physically and emotionally. So, too, should the actor.

The following basic "building blocks" apply in some degree to every physical interaction between individuals in real life and between characters on stage. Only after a character's death are these characteristics rendered inapplicable, since even the act of dying involves all of them.

Body position: The character's physical orientation in space. What is the character's overall physical position? Is the character standing, leaning (against a mantelpiece, for instance), sitting, kneeling, squatting, or lying down? In general, the director determines a character's body position.

Posture: What is the character's posture in relation to the other character and the interaction? Does the character's posture change? If so, how, to what extent, and with what effect? Posture is usually determined by the actor, with the director's guidance and feedback.

Body orientation: This is the relationship of the body of one character to the body of another. As the character, you will be concerned with your own character's orientation, but you should also be aware of the other character's body position in relation to yours. Is your character facing the other character straight on, face-to-face, at a slight angle, from a profile position? Is your back to the other character? Would you consider your orientation to the other character "closed" (facing) or "open" (turned away)? Note changes in physical orientation during interaction.

The position of a character's feet can tell the story of a relationship. The feet point toward people the character likes, respects, or admires, and away from those she dislikes or disdains, even when her upper body and facial expression denotes openness, friendliness, or cordiality. Body orientation is usually the director's decision, at least at the start of the interaction. Changes are generally determined by the actor with the director's guidance.

Placement: Placement is the relationship of the bodies of two characters in space. Is your character directly in line with the other character, facing one another or side to side, for instance, on the same stage level, or displaced upstage or downstage, or to the right or left? If body orientation is the relationship of one character to another, regardless of where the other character is, body placement is the relationship of the characters to one another in space. Body placement is usually determined by the director through the blocking of the play.

Distance: What is the relative distance between your character and another character? You might think of this in terms of the "zones" discussed in Chapter 2. Where (in terms of your character's zones) is this interaction taking place? Within your character's "intimate," "personal," or "social" zone? Is this interaction taking place within your character's intimate zone—but with a character with whom your character is not intimate? It makes a difference. The distance between characters is determined by the director.

Mirroring: To what extent is your character "mirroring" the body positions or movements of the other character? To what extent is the other character mirroring your body positions and movements? Even though you are not necessarily analyzing the other character's movement, it helps to be aware of the possible effects your movement will have. Although the director generally determines the extent of mirroring between characters, mirroring movements may arise naturally from within the actors themselves, through their characters, and during their interactions with one another.

Eye behavior: Eye behavior relates specifically to character interaction and to the revelation of relationships between characters. Eye behavior is within the purview of the actor. Few directors actively monitor it, and appear to notice very little about it except when it is lacking. They will admonish the actor to "look the other actor in the eye," but it may not always be appropriate to the character.

Gestures: An actor must determine not only the specific gestures used by your characters, but the frequency, range, intensity, and duration of those that express character interaction. Your character may repeat a particular gesture throughout the play, but it will change as the character interacts with other characters in different situations. Your character may be physically expansive in the company of one character and physically restrained or intimidated in the presence of another. These attitudes will be reflected in specific gestures and overall movement.

Gestures are usually handled by the actor, except when an actor does not know what to do with his hands. In such cases, the director may make suggestions.

Touching behavior: Is there any touching? If so, what is its nature and extent? Is touch initiated, received, or both? Is touch encouraged, discouraged, welcomed, sought, avoided, offered and withdrawn, or withheld? Is touching utilized to get the other character's attention, as a gesture of love or caring, to intimidate or control, or simply to comply with social convention? What is the frequency of the touch? The intensity and duration? Where is your character touched by others? Where do you touch other characters?

Touching falls within the responsibilities of both actor and director. The director usually determines when and where one character touches another in terms of the needs of the play, and the actor generally determines how to touch, in terms of the other character.

Physical contact: Physical contact consists of those moments or extended periods of physical interaction other than touching: holding hands, embracing, kissing, hitting, pushing, falling down, fighting, or simply brushing past another character. The director usually determines the nature and intensity of the physical contact between characters, while the subtleties of physical contact

are left to the actors. Although actors ought to be able to perform these actions quite naturally and comfortably, much more
is involved than a simple transfer of skills from one context to
another. Physical contact on stage can be quite different in form
and function from the same contact in daily life. Embracing and
kissing, for example, cannot occur spontaneously on stage but
must be enacted for the audience. Fighting on stage bears little
resemblance to a "real" fight but must be made to appear real.
This requires a certain "adjustment" of its essential physical
elements and a regard for the set, furniture, props, costumes,
and other actors on stage, none of which would ordinarily inhibit the action of a "real" fight.

Emotional display: "Display" does not refer to the actual, bodily representation or expression of emotion, but to an emotion's overall
intensity. In some instances emotions will be restrained; in others, emotions will be given full and free expression.

The physical relationship between characters is rarely static. Character interaction reflects a changing, dynamic relationship. Something is
happening almost all the time. Only on stage do people stand absolutely motionless, staring at one another for long periods of time.
It's just not real. People just don't do that. In real life, people are constantly in motion, even in their sleep. It is almost impossible for them
to remain completely still for any length of time. Inaction is all the
more noticeable since so much of the world around us is in constant
motion.

An actor should not be moving constantly, searching for something to do on stage. An actor should seek to fill his time on stage with
meaningful, character-revealing and relationship-revealing movement.

Movement for Period Plays

4

irectors, designers, and actors speak of "period" plays—plays representing distant times or unfamiliar cultures. In fact, every play is a "period" play. Some are simply more immediate or more familiar. People change. So do periods, so do cultures, so does playwriting, and as a reflection and a record of all these changes, so do modes of theatrical production.

More important than the actual historical period, however, is what directors and designers refer to as the *world of the play.* Every play proposes its own particular interpretation of reality and exists within its own particular self-contained "world." This world is composed of intrinsic and extrinsic elements. The intrinsic elements include the script—the words, language, structure, and form—the particular time or period in which the play is set, the place or setting, and the situation or specific circumstances. The extrinsic elements are those that are imposed on these intrinsic elements—the sets, costumes, props, and lighting, the style of presentation, and other aspects of the physical production.

Every play, whether modern or "period," challenges all involved to explore its broader historical context. What social, political, and economic factors influenced the playwright and the first production? Was the play written to be performed or simply read? The actor needs to be aware of these and other factors that could affect how he interprets his role and portrays his character. The "period" of the play is only one of the considerations of which the director, designers, and the acting company need to be aware.

It is likely that the theatre artists associated with a production will research each play thoroughly, so that the set, props, costumes, choreography, music, direction, the overall "look" and "sound" of the production (the extrinsic elements) conform to the period and the other intrinsic elements of the play. It's their job. It's also the actor's job.

What an Actor Needs to Know Before Acting in a Play

PLAYWRIGHT

Who is he, and when and where did he live? What is known about his life and the social, political, and economic circumstances in which he worked? How did he come to write this play? What relevance does this background information have for the play itself? What is the play-wright's reputation? Did he write any other plays? other forms of writing? Where does this play fit within the overall body of his work?

Playwrights write plays for different reasons. Some write to entertain. Others write to teach, to argue a philosophical issue, to confront (or even alienate) the audience, or to advocate a particular political agenda. Some plays reflect only one of these motivations, whereas others may encompass all of them. How can an actor begin to develop a characterization without knowing more about the playwright and what she is trying to say? Many actors attempt to do just that. They jump into a play without knowing anything about it.

TITLE

What does the title of the play mean? Is there an allusion of some kind (literary or otherwise) contained or implied (for example, *A Doll's House, Cat on a Hot Tin Roof, The Mousetrap, Who's Afraid of Virginia Woolf?*)? Does the play have a subtitle? Shaw's *Misalliance* is subtitled *A Debate in One Sitting*, and Shakespeare's *Twelfth Night* is subtitled *What You Will*. Are there subtitles to different acts or scenes? Was there a previous title or subtitle for the play that is not widely known or no longer in use? (*The Exorcism*, the subtitle of the third act of *Who's Afraid of Virginia Woolf?*, was the original title of the entire play.)

Do any of these titles, subtitles, or previous titles have particular relevance to the play?

"PERIOD"

When was the play written? When does the action of the play take place? Are either of these significant to the plot, characters, and theme of the play? Is there any relationship between when the play was written and when it is set? (Consider, too, that the play may actually be performed in yet a different period.)

SETTING

Where does the action of the play take place? At what time of year? How are these significant to the play's plot, characters, and theme? What local, regional, national, or international events might be important to the play?

LANGUAGE

Examine the playwright's choice of words, use of language, and recurrent grammatical structures. Is the play in verse or prose? Translated from another language? (If so, is this a good translation?)

All these things influence physical characterization. Unless an actor knows why she does something, what she does is of little consequence. Acting is purposeful doing. No purpose, no acting—and no reason to act.

STYLE

The terms "world of the play" and "style" are often used synonymously, even interchangeably, yet they do not refer to the same thing. When we say that a playwright writes in a certain "style," we mean that he organizes the intrinsic elements of the play, its component parts, in a characteristic way; he uses particular words in a particular order within a particular grammatical structure and dramatic form. We might say his style is unique (clearly distinguishable and identifiable as his work) or we might say his style is "derivative" (based on somebody else's work). Shakespeare's style was distinctive and is clearly identifiable as his. Subsequent playwrights may write in a "Shakespearean style," or in one reminiscent of Shakespeare's, just as some plays are referred to as "Shavian," "Chekhovian," "Pinteresque," or "Brechtian." If we know, for example, how Shaw or Chekhov wrote, we can recognize the similarities and differences, and classify or categorize other plays accordingly.

The production of a play involves sets, costumes, and props that embody the artistic vision of the designers and artisans who plan and construct them. The director organizes the elements of the play according to her own sense of priorities—which aspects of the production to emphasize and which to downplay, for instance—and in a style she considers appropriate to the play.

The "world of the play" is determined by the intrinsic elements of the play itself and by the extrinsic elements of the production. "Style" encompasses not only the world of the play but also each distinct element of the play and the manner in which each element is presented to the audience.

In some productions, such as modern-dress presentations of Shakespeare's plays, the world of the play is altered to conform to the style of the production. The intrinsic elements of the play (such as dialogue) remain unchanged for the most part, but the extrinsic elements (set, costumes, props, and so on) are made to conform to a different historical period. Sometimes the transposition works and sometimes it doesn't, but in either case, the overriding concern of the production team is that the elements of the production remain stylistically unified and consistent.

PRESENTATION STYLES

There are essentially two styles of theatrical presentation: representational and presentational. At any time, a production may reflect either or both. For a play presented in a *representational* style, the action is entirely stage-centered: nothing from beyond the stage set (or outside the world of the play) intrudes on the characters or the action. The actors perform as if the play were real and true-to-life and in playing the characters are oblivious to anything that does not happen on stage. The audience does not participate in the play, nor is it even acknowledged; it simply observes the action from a distance through the imaginary "fourth wall" of the stage set.

In a *presentational* style of production, the production as a whole proceeds within an awareness of a world beyond the world of the play. The actor knows an audience is out there in the darkened theater, and "presents" certain elements of the play directly to them. Members of the audience also know (and are frequently reminded) that they are watching a play—neither reality nor a true-to-life "representation" of reality.

In a *representational* (stage-centered) production, the audience is essentially excluded: audience members just sit still, mind their own business, and watch. In a presentational (audience-centered) production, the audience is acknowledged as an integral part of the presentation.

Acting styles. ■ Acting styles are likewise either presentational or representational. The acting style is imposed by the necessities of the production (or, more often, by the dictates of the director).

The actor may also be called upon to portray his character in a realistic or nonrealistic manner. The nonrealistic, non-true-to-life approach to characterization is often referred to as "stylized" acting, yet the nonrealistic portrayal is no more a matter of style than the realistic portrayal. The difference in the characterization is a matter of emphasis, not one of stylized or nonstylized acting.

In a *realistic* portrayal, the actor attempts to re-create the natural world in her characterization. The character behaves believably, in a manner consistent with the audience's perception of reality and intended to elicit an empathetic response to the character as a real person.

In a *nonrealistic* portrayal, the actor has no intention of re-creating the natural order of things. The actor may emphasize angular movements, for instance, or prolonged vowel sounds, or rapid, repetitive gestures in order to represent an unreal character in an unreal world. The audience may empathize with the character but knows, without a doubt, that the character does not represent a real person. Taken as a whole, these elements of a nonrealistic characterization are a style of acting but not "stylized" acting.

No two actors approach the same role in exactly the same way. Each actor is unique in mind and body and brings those distinctive qualities to a role. How an actor chooses to embody a character defines her own personal acting "style." We don't want to get too caught up in this "style" business. Theorists and practitioners have debated the meaning of the word for centuries. Essentially, "style" is how you do something, whether it's a big something or a little something, one something or a whole lot of somethings put together.

DIRECTOR'S CONCEPT

The director is responsible for the artistic unity of the theatrical production. His responsibility is to insure that all the elements work together in a unified theatrical experience. This unity is based on what is termed the director's *concept* for the production, which is derived from the director's assessment of the major intrinsic elements of the play (plot, character, theme, language, period, and so on) combined with the director's determination of the extrinsic elements (staging, lighting, set design, costume design, and so on). The director's concept is the overall objective for the production, one that is shared by everyone associated with it, and so needs to be comprehensive enough to encompass every aspect of the production.

The director usually expresss the concept to the designers in terms of a visual metaphor, an image that represents the world of the play—"a topsy-turvy carnival atmosphere" or "an old, faded family portrait." The designers use this metaphor to bring the play to life through the physical elements of the production.

Directors rarely tell the actors what a play's concept is, at least not in so many words. An actor needs to know what the director's concept is, however, and should ask the director to explain her concept. The director may not be aware that she even has a concept until she starts talking. (She may not even know that she needs one until you ask about it.) Asking the question may prompt the director into defining, developing, or refining her concept (all of these are good things). If the director is unable or unwilling to share her concept, the actor will need to try to discover it for herself. What the director says, particularly when she is talking in terms of "This is what I want the audience to feel . . . ," or "This is what I want to say in this scene . . . ," or "This is how I want this scene to look . . ." provides important clues to the director's overall vision for the production. Another source of information is the designers. Since they're designing the production, they usually have *some* idea of what they're doing and why.

Some directors don't have a clue. Some are blissfully unaware that they even need a concept, and others proceed through the rehearsal process hoping one will appear to them magically in a dream or by means of divine inspiration—and sometime before opening night. If the director has no concept, then it falls to the actor to make something up. Seriously. It gives the actor something to work with, and until the director imposes his own (or finally gets one), the actor is pretty much on his own. Study the play. Look at the staging and at the sets and costumes (or the designs). Try to determine the logic of the vision that governs the artistic and technical elements of the production.

Period Movement

The following discussion of distant historical periods is based to a considerable extent on the "best guess" of theatre historians about the style of movement representative of each period and the style of presentation that most directly influenced physical characterization. In many cases, even into the last century, the historical record is contradictory or incomplete. Observations on ancient Greek and Roman drama, for instance, are highly conjectural. Debate continues regarding the use of masks in Greek tragedy and comedy, the technical elements of the production of Medieval drama, and the exact nature of the physical interplay among characters of the *commedia dell'arte*. More reliable information is available for the later periods of theatrical history, particularly after the Middle Ages, when more complete records were kept, more records have survived, and the information is less contradictory. The information on any period is only a general frame of reference for building a character, rather than a definitive set of rules.

In every instance, the play itself should be the measure of the interpretive and analytical resources devoted to it. Consider each play first on its own merits and then in relation to other plays within the same historical period. Most plays fit neatly into a given period or "movement," and are closely identified with other plays within the same category. A few plays, however, defy such neat categorization: Georg Büchner wrote expressionistic plays like *Woyzeck* and *Danton's Death* nearly a hundred years before the Expressionist movement.

The following overview of the movement of each major period of theatrical history includes a brief listing of representative plays of that period that are most often produced in educational and regional theatres in North America.

THE ANCIENT GREEK PERIOD

The period when Greek drama flourished extends from the sixth century B.C. to the first century B.C., when Greece was conquered by Rome. The period is divided into two parts: the Classic period (from 500–336 B.C.) and the Hellenistic period (beginning with the reign of Alexander the Great in 336 B.C.). The majority of plays that have come down to us are from the Classic period, including the great tragic plays of Sophocles, Aeschylus, and Euripides, and the comedies of Aristophanes. The Hellenistic period is noted primarily for advances in theatre architecture and for the development of what is termed "New Comedy"—situation-based plays with recognizable stock characters—represented in the plays of Menander.

The style of production in Greek tragedies was almost exclusively presentational—audience-centered, rather than stage-centered, with little attempt to represent characters and events realistically. The the-

atre of ancient Greece developed from religious rituals, and the presentation of Greek tragedies was part of a religious festival rather than
a purely theatrical event. The stories of the tragic plays—ancient
myths and legends—were well-known to the audience. The tragedy
was simply "acted out" as a means of moral or religious instruction for
the audience. The playwrights emphasized the theme of the play
rather than plot or characterization. It was not entertainment but a religious lesson, and the actors and audience knew it.

In general, since the characters represented in Greek tragedies—
gods and persons of high social and political standing, like kings and
queens—are invariably "bigger-than-life" and heroic in stature, the
actor should carry himself with as much authority, dignity, and self-
restraint as possible, projecting a strong, controlled physical presence. Movement is slow, stately, measured, sometimes rhythmic and
repetitive, and generally restricted to the upper body. Gestures are expansive, clear, direct, and flowing. Much depends on the costuming,
of course, and whether or not the actor is masked. A thick, heavily
embroidered tunic; *cothurni* (heavy boots with thick soles); and *onkus*
(an elaborate headdress), as well as a mask can severely inhibit all but
the most restrained movements and gestures.

Lucian of Samosta, writing in the second century A.D., took a
rather dim view of the physical presentation of tragedy:

> In forming our opinion of tragedy, let us first
> consider its external presentation—the hideous
> and appalling spectacle of the actor. His high
> boots raise him up entirely out of proportion.
> His head is hidden under a huge mask. His huge
> mouth gapes at the audience as if he would
> swallow them up. To say nothing of his chest
> and stomach pads which he wears to give him-
> self an artificial corpulence, lest his deficiency in
> this respect emphasize his disproportionate
> height. And in the midst of all this is the actor,
> shouting away.

If audiences in the fifth century B.C. found the presentation "hideous
and appalling," no one mentioned it. Aristotle does not mention the
actual presentation of plays in his *Poetics* except to say that it doesn't
really matter all that much; he limits his criticism of acting to remarks
about the occasional inappropriate movement or gesture. No matter
what we (or Lucian) think, Greek plays were presented according to
the theatrical conventions of the day, which were familiar to the audi-

ence and accepted without question: it wasn't what the actors looked like or what they did that mattered but what they said. The lesson of the play was contained in the words.

The physical action of a Greek tragedy is minimal and restrained, and is intended to accomplish a single goal. Physical contact between characters, who generally stand at a distance from one another, is rare. In fact, physical interaction between characters is most often "reported" by another character, rather than acted in front of the audience. The audience observes the results of physical action—particularly violent action (a dead body, for example, or Oedipus's bleeding eyes)—rather than the physical act itself. (The report of offstage action is usually very graphic, however, and leaves little to the imagination.) Characters remain relatively immobile on stage, letting the force of their words and their large gestures carry the emotional impact of the play.

Occasionally movements such as running, falling to the ground, or wielding a weapon are implied in the text. Props are minimal—a staff, scepter, torch, or a weapon, at most—although a god might carry props emblematic of his station in life. It should be noted, too, that in the original productions of the Greek plays, actors were expected to play more than one role, changing masks to effect the changes between characters, and men played female roles—a situation imposed by social and religious customs that continued in the established theatre in Europe until the Restoration in 1660. (An exception to the all-male casts were traveling troupes of actors who performed throughout Europe from the Middle Ages through the seventeenth century.) Although these ancient Greek plays are seldom enacted today by an all-male cast, the modern actor needs to be aware of the prevailing order of things during the period when these plays were first presented to appreciate the inherent challenges they pose to the actor.

Greek tragedy exemplifies deeply held beliefs, strong emotions, and exalted passions. Plays by Euripides, particularly, explore the broad range of human feeling, although confined within a somewhat restrictive dramatic structure. A character's motivations and intent are usually unambiguous and uncomplicated (much like the plays themselves), but this is not to say that the characterization is necessarily superficial. The characters in Greek tragedies are idealized, often one-dimensional, and distinguished by a "tragic flaw" that precipitates their eventual downfall, but they are not completely mindless. (You didn't get to be a king by being an idiot, as was the case in other countries, notably Great Britain and France.) The playwrights fashioned their characters to represent the frailties to which all humans (and some gods) are subject, and to demonstrate the consequences of those frailties when confronting forces beyond the individual's control.

In contrast to Greek tragedies, physical action in Greek comedies was energetic, expansive, precise, and bold, drawing on the expressive capabilities of the entire body. Considerable athletic prowess was required of the actors, along with skill in dance, juggling, mime, and acrobatics. There was extensive use of comic business and physical contact between characters. Singing and dancing served as transitions between scenes, and dialogue was punctuated with slapstick and comic acrobatics. The actors were free to move about the stage and to address one another (or attack one another) in close proximity.

Although masks representing stock characters, animals, birds, and insects may have been used (and therefore restricted movement to some degree), costuming for the comedies was based on the conventional dress of the period and permitted greater freedom of movement. The actors wore simple tunics and long cloaks, which were "color-coded" to the characters: old men wore white, and young men wore red or purple (depending on their rank); young woman wore white, as did priestesses; old women wore green or light blue; "parasites" (social climbers, hangers-on, busybodies, and troublemakers) wore a black or a gray cloak; slaves wore a short white cloak.

Emotion in Greek comedy is exaggerated, superficial, and fleeting. Motivation for action is minimal and often whimsical because depth of character simply does not exist. Characters are single-minded—often obsessively so—and occasionally fantastic rather than realistic. (In his plays, Aristophanes turned to animals, birds, and insects to satirize human characteristics.) The theme of Greek comedy is subservient to plot, often farcical, and secondary to the stereotypical characters and situations.

If Greek tragedy is distant, restrained, moralistic, and democratic, Greek comedy is immediate, chaotic, down-to-earth, and anarchic. Greek tragedy exemplified a moral lesson. Some Greek comedies made an attempt at social commentary, while others were more satirical, but most were devised simply to entertain.

Representative plays. ■ Tragedies: *Agamemnon* and *Prometheus* (Aeschylus), *Oedipus the King* and *Antigone* (Sophocles), *Medea, Electra,* and *The Trojan Women* (Euripides). Comedies: *The Birds, The Frogs,* and *Lysistrata* (Aristophanes), and The *Grouch* (Menander), the only example of New Comedy to survive in its entirety. Productions of ancient Greek drama are generally limited to college and university theatres and public television. Productions of *Antigone, Medea,* and

Lysistrata can be seen on regional stages, however, and occasionally, as in a recent production of *Medea,* on the Broadway stage.

THE ROMAN PERIOD

The greater part of Roman dramatic activity occurred between the third century B.C. and the end of the first century A.D., from the height of the Roman Republic (509–27 B.C.) through the early years of the Roman Empire (27 B.C. to around 476 A.D.). Note that the organized performance of tragedies and comedies comprised only a small part of Roman theatrical activity. During the period of the Republic, public performances were dominated by variety entertainments, including athletic events, acrobatics, trained animals, music, dance, and mime. During the Empire, dramatic productions were all but abandoned in deference to more extravagant and increasingly lurid public displays. Even Seneca's scenes of violence, carnage, destruction, and horror could hardly compete with the real-life violence on view daily at the Coliseum (with special evening performances featuring human pyrotechnics).

Most of the characteristics of Greek tragedy and comedy can also be ascribed to Roman tragedy and comedy, for the simple reason that the Romans appropriated much (if not most) of their formal dramatic tradition and theatrical technique from the Greeks. In contrast to Greek drama, however, Roman drama was not associated in any way with religion or religious rituals or festivals. There were no lessons to be learned. Roman plays were offered strictly for entertainment.

Movement in Roman comedies was broad, acrobatic, and often violent. Running, hitting, and falling down were predominant physical activities, and the "running slave" was a stock character (no doubt because the stage of a Roman theatre could be more than a hundred feet wide!). Movement in the tragedies was broad and violent. In theme, character, and action, Roman drama was anything but subtle.

Roman comedy, which consisted almost exclusively of outrageous farces, employed one-dimensional stock characters, who were single-minded in motivation and purpose and crude in manner and behavior. The predominant feature of Roman comedies was action, not theme or depth of characterization.

Representative plays. ■ Tragedies: *Thyestes, The Phoenician Women, Agamemnon* (Seneca). Seneca wrote plays based on Greek tragedies, changing the names of the Greek gods to Roman ones, as appropriate, to protect the innocent and to disguise (not very effectively) the source of his plots and themes. Seneca did not shy away from onstage violence as the Greeks did, however, although his plays were otherwise highly reminiscent of the Greek theatrical tradition—five acts divided by choral interludes, elaborate speeches, a unified plot, and one-dimensional, single-minded characters. Nevertheless, if somewhat bloody and emotionally overwrought, Seneca's plays were well crafted and influenced Renaissance drama, serving as models for Thomas Kyd, Christopher Marlowe, and William Shakespeare, among others. (Seneca was also Emperor Nero's tutor and seems to have had a remarkable influence on the young emperor's approach to life.)

Comedies: *The Menaechmi, The Braggart Warrior, Amphitryon* (Plautus). *Phormia* and *The Brothers* (Terence). Terence wrote comedies of more substance and consequence than did his predecessor, Plautus. Terence's plays involved themes and characters of slightly more depth than those in most Roman comedies. It was his intention to instruct the audience as well as entertain them.

Aside from *The Menaechmi,* few other Roman plays are ever produced, even in educational theatre settings. The tragedies are thought to be too bloody and too awkward to produce (or too bloody, period), and the comedies are considered inferior to the Greek plays on which they are based.

THE MEDIEVAL PERIOD

The medieval period, or the Middle Ages, extends over nearly a thousand years, from the fall of Rome (around 476 A.D.) until about 1500. From the fall of Rome until 1300, Europe was dominated by the Catholic Church, which opposed theatrical productions of any kind. Organized theatrical activity diminished to a considerable extent, although it can be assumed that popular entertainments like acrobats, singers, jugglers, and animal acts continued, in spite of religious opposition.

By the tenth century, the performance of *mystery* plays (stories from the Bible), *miracle* plays (lives of the saints), and *morality* plays (allegorical dramas), all sanctioned by the Church and intended to instruct the peasant population in the Church's teachings, had risen in popularity. With a decline in the influence of the Church after 1300, and a growing interest in secular activities, nonreligious forms of drama evolved from these religious presentations. As the plays themselves became more secularized, performance "migrated" from the interior of the church to the church steps, and then into the streets.

One aspect of the performance of these plays is particularly important and influences few other forms of drama to such an extent: the occupation or trade of the characters. In the medieval period, a person's trade, how he earned his livelihood, was the focus of his existence from an early age. Children were apprenticed to skilled artisans or master tradepersons, lived with them, and learned the skills of their trade; when they had mastered the skills, they left the master and embarked on their own.

Characters in medieval plays are carpenters, stonemasons, tailors, cobblers, farmers, goldsmiths, and members of the clergy, particularly monks. Even when the occupation is not specifically stated, it can often be discerned from the text. Occupation defines to a great extent how a character views the world, how he thinks, and what is important to him in the overall scheme of things. The character's trade also defines his social, economic, and political status in the hierarchy of the medieval world. The plots of medieval plays are generally straightforward and uncomplicated, and the characters go about sorting out their lives. The few emotional scenes (and an occasional monologue) serve to reveal the character in ways that otherwise might go unnoticed.

Movement in medieval plays is simple, direct, and uncomplicated, as befits their simple plots and uncomplicated characters. The acting style is generally realistic, even though the actor may be called upon to portray a one-dimensional allegorical character in less than realistic circumstances—where devils, angels, and deities appear—such as an ascent into heaven or an occasional foray into hell. For the most part, these characters should be portrayed in a true-to-life way through appropriate realistic movement and gestures that draw on the details of everyday life, particularly the character's occupation or trade.

Representative plays. ■ *Everyman, Pierre Patelin, The Second Shepherd's Play, Abraham and Isaac* (all by anonymous, a popular writer of the period), and *The Iron Pot* (Hans Sachs). Although these plays are often read, they are seldom produced. Productions of *Everyman* occur occasionally, but for the most part medieval plays are used as training exercises and as introductions to the period and the characteristic style of presentation. Occasionally, some of these miracle, mystery, and morality plays are produced in smaller European towns and villages as part of a local or regional religious pageant.

Transition to the Renaissance

The Renaissance emerged during the last two hundred or so years of the medieval period. Italy was first to reflect this cultural shift, producing the first important innovations in the Renaissance theatre, including the "Neoclassical Ideal"—*verisimilitude,* faithfulness to reality and the appearance of truth—the development of opera, innovative scenic practices, advances in theatre architecture, and a remarkable contribution to theatrical tradition—the *commedia dell'arte.*

The *commedia dell'arte* flourished first in Italy and then throughout Europe, from approximately 1600 until 1750. The performance style of the *commedia* draws heavily on the traditions of Ancient Greek and Roman comedy, particularly the use of stock characters, topical subject matter, improvised dialogue based on a brief scenario, and a highly physical style of performance. The stock characters of Greek and Roman comedy included the young lovers, the meddling father, the old miser, the pedantic scholar, doctor, or lawyer, the braggart soldier, and comic servants, who were clever, dull, lustful, lazy, or gluttonous. The stock characters of the *commedia* were essentially the same. The plots of the Greek and Roman comedies involved lovers' follies and foibles, mistaken identities, and other innocent deceptions, as well as political intrigues, abuses of office, legal and medical malpractice, and misanthropy. These are also the favorite plots of the *commedia.* As in the Greek and Roman comedy tradition, there is no "lesson" to be learned. The *commedia* performance is intended solely for the entertainment of the audience.

The overriding focus in the *commedia* is the stock characters, who are essentially one-dimensional, instantly recognizable, and stereotypical. Each character possesses readily identifiable physical traits, movement patterns and gestures, and totally predictable behavior. Capitano, for example, the braggart soldier, wore an exaggerated version of a military uniform (with miles of gold braid), a sword, and an oversized plumed hat. Nose in the air, he strutted back and forth across the stage, gestured broadly, and waved his plumed hat incessantly. Dottore, the pedantic scholar, wore a long academic gown and cap, carried a large book he consulted continually, spoke in fractured Latin, and wandered around the stage mumbling to himself and making "thoughtful" gestures.

Commedia characters are generally classified into three types: lovers, masters, and servants. The *lovers* are the "straight" characters, young, intelligent, good-looking, witty, and wise beyond their years. They wore costumes in the fashion of the day but did not wear masks. The *masters* and *servants* are "exaggerated" characters. Three types of masters prevailed: Capitano, the braggart, cowardly soldier; Pantalone, a foolish, middle-aged or elderly merchant who often tries to pass himself off as a younger man, particularly when he is in pursuit of a young woman, and; Dottore, a Doctor of Medicine or Law who likes to show off his learning by spouting Latin words or phrases, but who is easily duped by other characters. The servant characters, or *zanni,* are the backbone of the *commedia.* They keep the plays moving through various intrigues involving the other characters. The most notable *zanni* is Harlequin, a clever, cunning fellow, usually an accomplished acrobat and dancer, who can be found at the center of any intrigue.

A staple of the *commedia* is what is termed *lazzi,* or comic stage business: slipping on a banana peel, hitting another character in the back of the head with a long board, and other familiar types of comic business, comic acrobatics, and comic fights. *Lazzi* and other comic byplay were developed by the actors within the bare scenario of the improvised play. Although some scholars assert that *lazzi* occurred spontaneously during the course of a play, it is more likely that the *lazzi* were rigorously rehearsed (since they sometimes involved dangerous physical stunts and acrobatics) and their insertion into the plays was predetermined.

Here a few typical *lazzi* from the *commedia,* most of which will seem familiar to contemporary audiences because of their repeated use in silent films and television situation comedies:

- *The Statue.* A character, usually a servant, assumes the pose of a statue. She eavesdrops on private conversations and plays tricks on the other characters when their backs are turned.
- *Hands Behind the Back.* A servant hides behind his master, places his arms around his master, and makes hand gestures for him. The servant sometimes slaps the master, pinches his nose, or makes rude hand gestures to other characters.
- *Somersault with Wine.* A character executes a backward somersault or other acrobatic turn while holding a bottle of wine without spilling a drop.
- *The Innocent Bystander.* Two characters threaten to fight one another. A third character tries to separate the other two and ends up being beaten by both of them.
- *The Chair.* A chair is pulled away from another character just as he is about to sit in it.
- *Eating the Fly.* A character snatches an imaginary fly from the air, studies it for a moment, and devours it.
- *Eating the Cherries.* While one character is speaking, another character takes imaginary cherries out of his hat, eats them, and throws the "pits" at the other character.
- *The False Arm.* Wearing a false arm, a character allows herself to be apprehended, only to escape, leaving the false arm behind in the hands of her apprehender.

- *The Chase.* One character chases another, but both characters remain stationary on stage, miming running, and making threatening gestures at one another.
- *The Script.* A character tells a joke that gets no response from the audience. He tells the joke again but more slowly this time. Again receiving no response, the character consults the script and either retells the joke in a slightly different way or rips out that page of the script and tosses it away.
- *Nightfall.* Using candles, lanterns, or torches, the characters behave as if night has fallen and they are in total darkness. This allows unlimited opportunity for mistaken identities, tripping over furniture (and each other), and other comic business.

Movement of the characters in the *commedia* is fluid, inventive, often acrobatic, energetic, precise, and quick. There is never a dull moment in a *commedia* performance. Considerable physical contact occurs between the characters, particularly the servants, and between the servants and their masters, usually at the master's expense. Gestures are broad but controlled. The style of acting alternates between representational, in scenes with the lovers and the more realistic characters in the play, and presentational, particularly in the scenes involving the servants and the more stereotypic characters.

Masks alter the performer's physical appearance, of course, and depending on the type of mask and its construction, they may affect the performer's physical capabilities. A full-face mask is more physically inhibiting than a half-mask, which is more inhibiting than no mask at all. As mentioned earlier, the young lovers usually wear no mask. The more active comic characters, like the servants, who must tumble about the stage and perform other highly physical stage business, may wear no mask or only a half-mask. Characters like the miserly old man or the braggart soldier may wear a full-face mask. It seems odd that the actors of the *commedia* would wear masks that obscured their faces (and seriously inhibited facial expression), but it was more important that the characters be instantly recognizable.

On the plus side, masks clearly and quickly identify each character and heighten the comic effect of mistaken identities, one of the favorite story lines. The use of masks in a particular production will likely rest with the director in consultation with the costume designer. If masks are used, the actors would be wise to begin rehearsing with them as early as possible.

Representative plays. ■ Representative plays of the early Renaissance period are an original comedy in the Roman style, *La Mandragola*

(*The Mandrake*), by Niccolo Machiavelli (yes, that Machiavelli), and *Achilles,* by Antonio Laschi, considered the first Renaissance tragedy. *The Mandrake* is occasionally performed at universities or regional theatres. Despite its claim to early Renaissance fame, *Achilles* has yet to experience its own rebirth.

Various collections of *commedia dell'arte* scenarios are available (about 700 known *commedia* scenarios or outlines exist; refer to the list of Further Reading at the end of the book). Plays are occasionally presented in the *commedia* style, yet few companies undertake productions of actual *commedia* scenarios. Most actors simply lack the training in improvisation, physical comedy, and the other skills *commedia* requires.

THE TUDOR PERIOD

The Tudor Period in England encompasses the time from Henry VII's assumption of the throne in 1485 to Elizabeth I's rise to power in 1558, from the end of the Middle Ages to the early years of the Renaissance (technically, the Tudor period extended from 1485 until the death of Elizabeth I in 1603, the last of the Tudor line descended from Henry VII).

Early Tudor drama was essentially a continuation of medieval practices and conventions. Plays and imitations of plays by Terence and Plautus were popular fare. Biblical plays were also enacted, as were works of the period, most notable of which are *Ralph Roister Doister* (based on a play by Plautus), and *Gammer Gurton's Needle* (a curious combination of medieval farce and Roman comedy).

The late Tudor period might better be termed the *early* Elizabethan period, since many of the plays considered part of the Tudor period were written after Elizabeth ascended to the throne. Nevertheless, there are distinct differences between the Tudor and Elizabethan periods in terms of the content of the plays, the styles of playwriting, and the production techniques.

The first true English tragedy, *The Tragedy of Gorbuduc,* by Thomas Sackville and Thomas Norton, was produced in 1561. Queen Elizabeth herself was said to have been present at the first performance. *Gorbuduc* effectively "bridges the gap" between the Tudor and Elizabethan playwriting styles. The story, based on English legend, is presented in the Senecan tradition—five acts, much blood and gore (reported, however, rather than enacted in front of the audience), and the deaths of all the main characters—tempered by the growing influence of humanistic thought and the neoclassical ideal of verisimilitude, or truthfulness to life.

Major playwrights of the later Tudor period include Thomas Kyd and Christopher Marlowe, who specialized in serious drama, and John Lyly and Robert Greene, who wrote comedies. The influence of Seneca is apparent in many of the plays of the period, which emphasized well-crafted, suspenseful plots, stage violence (often considerable), a juxtaposition of serious scenes with short, comic ones, poetry and poetic imagery, and the soliloquy. *The Spanish Tragedy,* by Thomas Kyd, is a notable example of a classic "revenge play" in which all of these elements are melded together to produce considerable emotional impact. Marlowe's *Doctor Faustus,* strongly influenced by the medieval morality play, exemplifies two other important themes in plays of the period, the concept of self-determination and the influence of the supernatural, juxtaposed in the same play. In *Doctor Faustus,* individual choice is the focus of the play. Faustus makes his own decision to sell his soul to the devil. He is not manipulated by overwhelming forces outside of himself, as he might be in a Greek, Roman, or medieval play, but makes a conscious, individual choice based on his own motivations and intentions. As a result, he must be held personally accountable for his choices and suffer the consequences for his actions.

Movement in Tudor plays, although fairly realistic, particularly in terms of manners and social customs, is to a great extent dependent on costuming. As in every other country in Northern Europe, actors wore contemporary clothing in the fashion of the day. Clothing was extravagant in style and elaborate in detail. Movement in Tudor drama requires a strong sense of period fashion, manners and customs, and the limitations imposed by period costumes.

Men wore some variation on the fitted tunic with puffed sleeves (gathered at the wrists or trailing to the ground), padded breeches, stockings, and pointed shoes. Men strode rather than walked because of their thick breeches, and moved about forcefully in order to show off their legs and general physique. When they bowed, they assumed "third position," knees and toes turned out, back leg bent, back heel slightly off the floor, and front leg extended.

Women were encumbered by tight, formfitting bodices with pinched waists, and full, heavy skirts that required energetic leg action in walking. In curtsying, a lady lifted the front of her skirt slightly to allow her to bend nearly to the floor and return to a standing position smoothly and gracefully. She walked with a stiff, straight upper body, and held her head up to balance her sometimes elaborate wig and headdress. She turned from the waist and tried to keep her skirt aligned with her shoulders (not an easy task considering the bulky skirt).

Gestures were smooth and controlled, not overly broad or grandiose, in keeping with the realistic tone of the plays themselves. The occasional, over-the-top graphic violence was simply an aspect of the times. Emotional and psychological motivations could be complex, therefore physical characterization must represent inner conflict as well as the character's relationships to her environment and to other characters.

Representative plays. ■ Early Tudor Period: *Gammer Gurton's Needle, Ralph Roister Doister* (both anonymous), and *The Tragedy of Gorbuduc* (Sackville and Norton). These plays are seldom produced except as actor training exercises or curiosity pieces. Everybody reads *Gorbuduc,* but nobody ever produces it (in spite of considerable violence and other sensational aspects, it is a deadly dull play). Late Tudor-Early Elizabethan Period: *Doctor Faustus* (Marlowe) and *The Spanish Tragedy* (Kyd). *Doctor Faustus* is a favorite of university theatres but is rarely seen in any other context. *The Spanish Tragedy* has too much blood and gore for modern theatergoing sensibilities. (We seem to prefer abstract television and movie violence, but Tudor audiences had no such qualms.)

THE ELIZABETHAN AND JACOBEAN PERIODS

It is remarkable that so many major playwrights emerged during the half-century reign of Elizabeth I and that so many advances were made in the dramatic arts. Shakespeare was not the only Elizabethan playwright, of course. In fact, upwards of ten of his plays, including *Macbeth, Othello,* and *King Lear,* were written after Elizabeth, during the reign of James I (1603–1625). Other important playwrights include Ben Jonson, Thomas Middleton, John Marston, Francis Beaumont, and John Fletcher (Shakespeare collaborated with Fletcher on two of his later plays, *Henry VIII* and *The Two Noble Kinsmen*) and later, John Webster and Cyril Tourneur. Shakespeare's work dominates the period, however, and defines the times.

After the death of Queen Elizabeth, the focus of playwriting shifted from complex questions about man's essential nature and beliefs to simple stories about characters caught in interesting, exciting, and often sensational situations. Serious plays ended happily, and tragic situations were resolved easily, often through a last-minute revelation about one of the main characters. The acting style seems to have remained the same.

To speak of "acting Shakespeare" as a fundamental approach to his work or as a particular *style* of acting associated with his plays is sheer folly. *The Tempest, Hamlet, Macbeth,* and *Henry VI, Part 1* are very different works (even completely different genres), set in various historical periods and widely diverse locations, and emotionally and psychologically divergent in terms of character development and character relationships. Yet these plays are "lumped together" under the heading "Shakespeare," to which the term "acting Shakespeare" is applied, as if there were a universally applicable acting technique for Shakespeare's work. Nonsense. Each of Shakespeare's plays must be examined (and respected) on an individual basis.

The characters in Shakespeare's plays represent living, breathing human beings. Shakespeare's characters are overflowing with life, emotionally and psychologically complex, full of contradictions, and imbued with human qualities. Yet, for some reason, actors tend to "act" Shakespeare's characters out of existence. They become icons, pieces of moving sculpture abstracted from reality and devoid of life.

The solution: Play the character. Be who the character is, do what the character does, and let Mr. Shakespeare take care of the rest. His characters' words needn't be infused with meaning and shouted from the mountaintops. They speak quite eloquently and forcefully on their own. His characters' motivations, even when complex, are direct, universal, and persuasive. Their movements and gestures need not be made larger than life because the characters are already larger than life. The actor needn't impose anything on the character. They are entirely self-sufficient. They speak for themselves. The actor needs only to get out of the way and let the inherent qualities of the character pour out through his body.

Certainly there are common elements throughout Shakespeare's canon that can form the foundation for a physical characterization appropriate to the period in which the play was written, the period in which the play is set, and the period in which the play is performed. Conflicts concerning manners and customs invariably arise and must be resolved.

Which should supersede the other—Hamlet's relationship to Ophelia in terms of the perspective of Shakespeare's time, the perspective of Denmark several centuries earlier, or the perspective of the modern audience viewing the play? Can these be balanced in some way, or must only one perspective prevail? A further complication is that Shakespeare was an Elizabethan, and his plays reflect the attitude and mores of the Elizabethan period, but they are not about the Elizabethan period. (*Henry VIII* comes closest, but barely, since Elizabeth is born at the end of the play.) To what extent did Shakespeare temper the Elizabethan view of the world with a particular historical perspective in each of his plays?

Our purpose is not to answer these intriguing questions, but to pose them. It is important for actors to realize that there is considerably more to "acting Shakespeare" than having a role in a Shakespeare play. The style of the production and the individual play will determine how characters are played. A production of *Julius Caesar*, for example, might be set in Roman times, Elizabethan times, or modern times (representing Roman, Elizabethan, or modern sensibilities). In *The Taming of The Shrew*, Katherine's last speech about her relationship to Petruchio runs counter to some modern sensibilities. The intrinsic elements of the play itself, such as the text, remain unchanged (or relatively so), yet the external environment imposed on the play—its extrinsic elements—will affect the actor's approach to a character.

There *are* guidelines to appropriate movement in plays of the Elizabethan period or set in the Elizabethan period. In general, movement in Elizabethan plays was graceful, precise, and assertive for men and women alike. Actors moved from place to place on stage with little wasted motion. In serious plays movement was highly selective, controlled, and restrained, particularly among the upper classes and royalty. In comedies movement was natural, spontaneous, and inventive. Gestures were fluid and energetic, not broad but slightly exaggerated for the audience's benefit. Contemporary actors hoping to perform Shakespeare should be prepared to sing, dance, tumble, wrestle, fence, and fight—in addition to the usual requirements of learning their lines and not tripping over the furniture.

Shakespeare's theatre, "The Globe," and other theatres of the day were not large, as is sometimes imagined, but fairly intimate. The Globe held about three thousand spectators, but no audience member was much more than sixty feet from the stage, and some stood within a few feet of the actors. Therefore, contrary to the stiff, formal, rhetorical, declamatory, and bombastic style of acting that is assumed to be "Elizabethan" or "Shakespearean," the actors did not have to overly project their voices or exaggerate their gestures.

The action in Elizabethan plays moved quickly, expedited by the design of the stage and the nature of the staging. The stage was relatively bare, and scene changes were minimal—a throne here, a table there—and incorporated into the dialogue. The actors in one scene exited on on side of the stage while the actors in the next scene entered from the opposite side. The Elizabethan audience expected the play to keep moving, and if it didn't, they let their feelings be known—loudly and rudely. There are more than forty changes of scene in *Antony and Cleopatra*, for example, and the actors could ill-afford to make the audience wait for even one. The "two hours traffic of our stage" mentioned in the prologue to *Romeo and Juliet* may have been an exaggeration (it takes longer than that for most people to read the play), but the action progresses swiftly and without intermission. (The five acts that are common to modern editions of Shakespeare's plays were imposed on the printed editions at a later date.)

The Elizabethan attitude toward movement and toward the body was that the physical representation of the character—his attitude, posture, and alignment as well as his movements and gestures— reflected the character's inner state. Richard III may have been a nasty so-and-so, but he was a remarkably cheerful nasty so-and-so nearly to the end (he didn't get really serious until the nightmares on the eve of the Battle of Bosworth). Richard's physical demeanor should reflect this seeming contradiction in his character, as well as the many other contradictions of his body and mind noted previously. Hamlet, in contrast, is not nearly as nasty, but neither is he very cheerful. He is witty, yes, but ironically so, and otherwise not much fun. Prospero is magical, but, like Hamlet, he's terribly serious most of the time. Prince Hal undergoes quite a transformation through the course of three plays, as does Falstaff. The Elizabethan audience would expect to see these transformations expressed in the physical demeanor of the character as well as in his words an actions.

Read Hamlet's advice to the Players, Act III, scene 2. "Suit the action to the word, the word to the action." That just about covers it. Shakespeare was an actor and a producer as well as a playwright. He knew what he was talking about.

Costuming for Elizabethan productions is no less a concern for the actor than for Tudor productions. The costumes were of the type of clothing worn at court and in the upper levels of society. In fact, many of the costumes were "hand-me-downs" from upper-class and royal patrons, or purchased from their servants when one of their masters died. For any costume that had to be constructed, the best materials were used. Remember that audience members were not far from the stage, so the quality of the costumes was important.

The costumes were sumptuous (as might be expected, given their original owners), but heavy and unwieldy, seriously restricting the actor's movement. Men were constrained to wear a tight doublet, a stiff ruff around the neck, breeches of varying length and design and occasionally heavily padded, stockings, shoes or boots, a long-sleeved coat padded at the shoulders and tightly cuffed at the wrists, and variations thereof. A plumed hat generally completed the ensemble.

Women fared no better. Their attire consisted of an immense bell-shaped skirt with a farthingale (hoops) worn underneath, a long bodice that fit tightly from the neck to below the waist, a stomacher (stiff waist front), long, tight sleeves with a stiff roll at the top (occasionally with even longer over-sleeves), a stiff ruff at the nape of the neck, and a cap or headdress. Ladies sometimes carried a fan, more often in the comedies than in serious plays. The expansive skirt made walking, sitting, and turning difficult, and made sudden changes in direction virtually impossible. A lady's arms could not hang naturally from her shoulders; to accommodate the full skirt they were held away from the body, placed on top of the skirt, or clasped or posed at the waist. Women glided almost magically across the stage, with upper body and head held erect. They didn't have much choice: the costume effectively precluded any other body position or manner of movement.

Remember that until the Restoration, women's roles were played by men and boys. A young apprentice actor generally played Juliet, for example, a slightly older boy or young man might enact Lady Macbeth, and an older male might portray any of the older female characters. Note, too, that in most of Shakespeare's tragedies and histories there is little intimate physical contact between male and female characters—not much embracing and even less kissing. In *Romeo and Juliet,* for example, very few kisses between the lovers are explicit or implicit in the script, six at most, and half of those occur while one or the other of the star-crossed lovers is dead or believed dead. Shakespeare's comedies do involve physical interaction, but it is generally of a superficial nature. The comedies also introduce the interesting phenomenon of a female character enacted by a male, who undertakes to disguise herself as a man—a man playing a woman playing a man. Orlando (actually a man) falls for the fair Rosalind (played by a boy) and practices his wooing technique with Ganymede (who is actually Rosalind, *played* by a boy, in *disguise* as a boy). An interesting challenge to the actor.

Elizabethan staging ■

- ■ *Fencing.* Elizabethan stage fighting, particular fencing, was very skillful. The audience knew good swordplay when they saw it, and they expected to see it on stage. Actors took part in swordplay in close quarters (space on stage was limited) with a heavy rapier in one hand and a dagger in the other. The rapier was used for thrusting and cutting (rarely for the roundhouse attacks often seen in movies and on stage). The dagger was used for short, quick thrusts to the eye or ribcage of the opponent, and for deflecting the blows of the opponent's rapier and dagger.

Fencing action was energetic, intense, and realistic—which is to say, brutal. The Elizabethan audience expected action, and the bloodier the better.

■ *The Bow.* The formal bow in use during the Elizabethan period is performed as follows: Starting with the feet apart, the gentleman moves either foot approximately ten to twelve inches to the rear of the other, turning the rear foot outward. The rear leg should be slightly bent. The gentleman now removes his hat, if it is appropriate to do so, and drops his hat-holding hand to the side or toward the rear. The other hand falls to his side, palm toward the person being addressed. (If he does not remove the hat, the gentleman drops both hands to his sides, palms toward the person being addressed.) The gentleman then drops his head toward his chest, and bends his upper body slightly forward. He recovers from the bow by reversing the order of these movements.

An *informal* bow dispenses with the one-leg-behind-the-other movement. The gentleman simply removes his hat, carries it to his side or somewhat to the rear, and bends his head and upper body slightly forward. The informal bow is appropriate in addressing persons of equal or lower rank or status (the lower status person bows first). The formal bow is appropriate in addressing persons of higher status, nobility, and royalty.

■ *The Curtsy.* The formal curtsy is performed as follows: The lady rests her hands, palms up, on her skirt. If she uses a fan, she holds it in one or both hands. If the fan is connected by a cord to her wrist, the lady may hold it or let it fall gently to the skirt, to be retrieved at the conclusion of the curtsy. The lady places one foot several inches behind the other, the distance dictated by balance and decorum. She then bends both legs and inclines her body forward. How far forward depends on the person being addressed: if it's a person of equal status, the lady bends her knees only a few inches and inclines her head only slightly; if it's the Queen, the lady falls nearly prostrate at her feet, both legs bent to the maximum, head near the floor, and arms outstretched toward the Queen.

An *informal* curtsy is performed with the feet only a slight distance apart. The head is lowered only a little and the knees are bent just a few inches. The informal version is often used *en passant* ("just passing through") as a quick acknowledgment, and for entering and exiting a room in which others are assembled. At an impending exit, for example, the lady crosses to the door, turns to face those assembled, offers a sprightly informal curtsy (almost a bounce), turns to the door, and leaves the room. Remember that the Elizabethan costume severely restricts any high-speed maneuvering. If the actor plans ahead, however, she can accomplish her "curtsy and exit" or curtsy *en passant* in one nearly continuous motion. The trick is to keep the movement flowing and the skirt moving.

- *Dumb Show.* The dumb show is not pantomime as such, but silent acting. The performers are appropriately costumed, props are used, and the scene is enacted, often on a fairly realistic set. The only thing missing is words. The acting is often slow, exaggerated, and exceedingly precise, which is intended to differentiate the dumb show from the "real" acting of the balance of the production and to make sure the audience "gets it."

Hamlet goes to great pains to insure that the play-within-a-play, *The Murder of Gonzago,* contains the exact circumstances of his father's murder. Hamlet believes that he can elicit a guilty response from Claudius if the murder enacted by the Players is close enough to the real event to cause Claudius to "blench" (whatever "blenching" is). The dumb show is first performed as a prologue enacting old Hamlet's murder and the other circumstances surrounding Claudius and Gertrude, which is followed by the *scripted* play of *The Murder of Gonzago.* Hamlet was right, of course. Claudius does indeed "blench," which sets the entire cast of characters on a course to near-total destruction. Be careful what you wish for.

The dumb show in *Hamlet* is one of the more famous examples of the form, but dumb shows occur in many earlier and later plays. They were a staple of court entertainment and street theatre alike during Elizabethan times. The fact that modern actors rarely enact a dumb show should not be reason for dismay; rather, it should alert the actor to the need for historical research and conscientious preparation, including training in mime and dance.

Dumb shows are rarely presentational. The action is invariably stage-centered, even in a comic version. Certainly a character can react to the onstage action in a presentational manner, but in practice, the lack of the spoken word seriously inhibits any substantive exchange between performer and audience. The audience simply watches. On the positive side, the presentation is direct: nothing comes between the audience and the performance. The audience doesn't have to be able to hear and understand words; they need only see the action. Even from a distance, the audience's perception and understanding of the dumb show are based solely on the clarity of the movement. The performance of a dumb show requires the actor to demonstrate a heightened sense of physical expression. Time and space are condensed, sometimes to a considerable extent, so movement must be selective and precise in order to impart as much meaning as possible within the fixed time frame and limited space.

Representative plays. ■ Any play by Shakespeare, *Volpone* and *Sejanus* (Jonson), *The Jew of Malta* (Marlowe), *The Duchess of Malfi* (Webster), *The Revenger's Tragedy* (Tourneur), and *The Maid's Tragedy* (Fletcher and Beaumont). Shakespeare's plays are performed at every level, from elementary schools to national theatres. *Volpone, The Jew of Malta,* and *The Duchess of Malfi* are performed occasionally, usually at university and regional theatres.

THE FRENCH NEOCLASSICAL PERIOD

The seventeenth century in France was the period of Pierre Corneille, Jean Racine, and Molière (Jean-Baptiste Poquelin), three of France's greatest playwrights, the time of Louis XIII, Cardinal Richelieu, and Louis XIV. It was also the age of the "neoclassical ideal," which reaffirmed the unities of time (the events of the play occur within twenty-four hours), place (one location), and action (a single, unified plot) as represented in ancient Greek drama. The ideal reinforced adherence to the concept of *verisimilitude* (true-to-life drama), and added the characteristically French notion of *decorum* (doing what's right).

Corneille violated most of these ideals in *Le Cid,* which compresses the action (including a war and events which occurred over many years) into five acts and twenty-four hours, confines the four distant locations of the actual events to one town, and tries to make sense of multiple plot lines, thereby straining the three unities and verisimilitude, all at the same time. Corneille further offended decorum (as well as Cardinal Richelieu and the French Academy, whose duty it was to pass judgment on these sorts of things) by having the lead characters, Rodrigue and Chimène, agree to marry, even though Rodrigue killed Chimène's father only twenty-four hours earlier. The French academy was not thrilled and wrote a judgment that alternately praised and condemned the play. Disheartened by the reaction, Corneille stopped writing for four years.

In general, Corneille's plays contain simple, almost one-dimensional characters but complex plots. They represent the single-mindedness of purpose and indomitable will of a protagonist caught in a complicated series of external events and confronted with increasingly formidable obstacles, who refuses to compromise his principles and ultimately chooses death over dishonor. The protagonist experiences no internal struggle, no self-doubt or fear, but moves inexorably toward his destiny.

In contrast, Racine's plays have uncomplicated, straightforward plot lines, centering instead on the internal struggles of individual characters. In *Phèdre* and *Iphigénie,* for example, the action and theme of the play evolve from the emotional and psychological turmoil of the main character. Racine's characters are passionate and intense. Their departure from established order and decorum and their inability to reconcile their inner selves with the world around them leads to their downfall.

Molière is the established genius of French comic playwriting. Many of his stock characters and comic situations are based on the traditions of the *commedia dell'arte* (in fact, when Molière and his company were given a theatre in Paris, they shared their performance space with the Fiorilli-Locatelli *commedia* troupe). His plays are highly satirical. Molière wished to draw attention to the pretensions of French society, and at the same time, to urge reforms in the prevailing social and economic order.

Like earlier playwrights (Sophocles and Shakespeare, for example), Molière was also an actor and a producer. He understood acting as well as he understood playwriting. He had a keen sense of what would "play" to an audience and how far he could press his ideas while retaining the interest of the audience.

The mode of performance of neoclassical tragedies and dramas was almost exclusively presentational. The movement in tragedy was restrained, slow, elegant, graceful, and somewhat larger than life. Movement of the characters reflected grand passions grandly portrayed. The focus was the upper body, particularly facial expression, and gestures. Realistic movement around the stage was limited by a small acting area and extremely poor lighting conditions. Characters rarely interacted physically with one another. In the original presentation of these plays, the actors stood in a semicircle center stage, facing the audience, and declaimed their lines, "acting out" the emotional state of the character through selective, stereotypical movement and gestures.

The characters in neoclassical tragedies are driven by one overriding passion that influences everything they say or do. The overall theme of tragic plays is the triumph of reason over emotion, yet it is the triumph of emotion over reason that motivates the characters and drives the plays forward.

Whereas movement in the tragic plays was constrained and characteristically stereotypical, movement in the comedies, particularly in those reminiscent of the *commedia,* was highly inventive, energetic, and quick (although perhaps not as zany as that of the *commedia*). In the plays that owed less to the *commedia* than to Molière's own genius, characters moved in an elegant and controlled manner. They also moved around the stage more freely than in the tragedies, and often interacted physically with other characters. Occasionally, they danced and sang.

For men the focus of individual movement was on a virile yet graceful stride, fluid and expansive gestures, and elaborate finger movements—the manipulation of a handkerchief, cane, or snuffbox. Female characters seemed to glide about the stage, curtsying a great deal, waving their fans, and fluttering their handkerchiefs. Both sexes usually held their hands up and away from the body, free to gesture or manipulate props, and to emphasize the lace cuffs adorning the wrist. Props, particularly personal items like a handkerchief or fan, were handled with a stylish, even ostentatious flair.

The male bow consisted of a slight step back with one foot, knee bent, the right hand placed over the heart, and a slight bend forward from the waist. A hat, if worn, might be swept to the side or backward during the bow for a more elaborate show of respect (or simply for a more elaborate show). The curtsy was essentially the same as that used during Elizabethan times, but performed more energetically and stylishly. Bows and curtsies were frequent, and often employed for comic effect. Female servants, particularly, seemed always to be bouncing around the stage, curtsying from one character or comic situation to another.

Characters in the more refined comedies rarely simply "stood" or "sat." Whether standing or sitting, they invariably "posed," as if for a painting (the camera not yet having been invented). Movement and gestures were self-conscious in the sense that the characters were constantly aware of their physical presence, of their appearance, and of the "message" they wished to convey to others through their behavior and comportment. Rarely did a character move without a purpose, that purpose usually being to impress others.

Leone di Somi provided us with what might be called the neoclassical version of Hamlet's "Advice to the Players":

> The actor must always be nimble of body, and
> his limbs must not be unbending and stiff. He
> must keep his feet still while he is speaking, and
> move them with grace when it is appropriate to
> do so; he must hold his head in a natural way,
> so that it will not appear that it is secured to his
> neck with nails. And he must let his arms and

his hands (when it is necessary to gesture with them) go where nature guides them, and he must not do, as so many do, who, wishing to gesture too much, do not seem to know what to do with them. For example, if a woman in a certain scene has placed her hand at her side, or if a young man has put his hand on his sword, neither one must remain in that position forever; but when he has ended his speech which requires such a position, he must abandon that position and find another one more suitable to the speech that follows; and when he does not find another or more fitting gestures, or when he does not need to assume a certain posture, he should let his arms and his hands be loose and relaxed, and not hold them raised or inflexible, as if they were attached to his body with sticks. He must always maintain a greater or lesser level of dignity, as the situation requires of the person being represented. He must avoid like a curse a certain manner of acting, which for lack of a better word I call pedantic, similar to the recitation of school children before their teacher. And he must, above all, make an effort (changing the tone of his voice and accompanying these changes with the appropriate gestures) that what he says be spoken with effectiveness and seem to be nothing more than a familiar discourse which occurs spontaneously.

Costumes underwent frequent change, in accordance with the changes in popular fashions—although less so for the tragedies and dramas than for the comedies, which reflected fashion trends more directly.

In general, French women abandoned the immense skirts and farthingales and the tightly corseted bodices of earlier periods, and adopted a looser skirt with a high waist, made of soft, flowing fabrics. Instead of wearing the exaggerated headdresses of earlier periods, they lavished more attention on the unadorned head: hair was "frizzed" and curled and arranged to frame the face. Ribbons were very popular to adorn both hair and dress.

The costume of French men also underwent a noticeable change. Breeches were no longer padded and stiff, but hung loosely around

the leg, usually split at the side from knee to thigh to display a decorative lining. Doublets were shortened to the waist, and were berib-
boned, designed to reveal a contrasting lining, or both. A stiffened
lace collar adorned the man's neck from shoulder to shoulder, fram-
ing his face and shoulder-length hair.

Fashions continued to evolve throughout the period. For women
the waistline went up and down, the neckline varied from high-neck,
to V-neck, to extremely revealing, and corsets went in and out of fashion (as, apparently, did waistlines). Men's clothing became increasingly decorative and ornate. By mid-century, lace and ribbons all but
obscured the clothes beneath them, and curly, flowing, shoulder-
length wigs adorned the more fashionable heads. A skirt was added
over the man's frilled breeches, and a cape or long waistcoat and
plumed hat completed the effect.

To the modern actor, the costume of the period might pose problems, particularly the lady's revealing dress and the gentleman's wig
and skirt. For the most part, however, these changes unburdened the
actors of the day considerably, and allowed them to perform more realistically (and with considerably less effort) than they had been able
to do for many years.

Molière's plays range in style from highly presentational (like
Scapin and *The Imaginary Invalid*) to highly representational (like *The
Misanthrope* and *Tartuffe*). In the plays reminiscent of the *commedia*,
one-dimensional, audience-centered characterizations prevail. The
characters are usually driven by one overriding emotional need,
which they pursue single-mindedly, often obsessively. In the more so-
phisticated and socially relevant plays, however, the characters are
much more complex. Although many of Molière's characters closely
resemble stereotypes and represent specific aspects of societal behavior, they are nonetheless multidimensional, emotionally developed
and intellectually adept individuals who are motivated by a wide
range of needs and desires.

One element that differentiates Molière characters from those of
other major playwrights is that his characters rarely evolve or change.
Their essential character—who they really are—is the same at the end
of the play as at the beginning. Molière's characters go on a journey,
yes, but they don't necessarily arrive anywhere. They may come to a
realization about some aspect of their lives, they may make some discoveries about themselves, but it doesn't alter their fundamental nature or their view of the world around them. Tartuffe is still a
hypocrite. Alceste is still crabby. Harpagon is still miserly. Scapin is
still a scoundrel. Molière's characters reflect his own rather pes-

simistic view of human nature: try as he might, man cannot escape his fundamentally flawed nature.

Characters like Tartuffe and Alceste require a conscientious approach, and one that resists easy answers to difficult and complex questions. The actor should recognize that although these characters may appear ludicrous or ridiculous to her and to the audience, they pursue their goals in deadly earnest. They are serious about who they are, what they do, and what they hope to achieve. It is important that they not be portrayed in a sardonic, superficial, or stereotypical fashion. We know they are ridiculous; *they* don't. The actor should not impose anything on the character that is not apparent from or inherent in the script: Tartuffe is serious about his conquests. Alceste is serious about his views of mankind. Harpagon is serious about his money. Serious, too, should be the actor's approach to characterization.

Representative plays. ■ Tragedies: *Phèdre, Bérénice, Iphigénie* (Racine), *Le Cid, The Death of Pompey,* and *Horace* (Corneille). Comedies: Any play by Molière, notably *Tartuffe* (the most often produced of Molière's plays), *The Imaginary Invalid, The Misanthrope,* and *The Miser.* (Molière wrote one tragedy, *Don Garcie,* which he never published. It was not a success. A resourceful man, Molière later appropriated some of the best verse in *Don Garcie* for *The Misanthrope.*) Molière's plays, particularly those listed above, are very popular at the university theatre level. Unfortunately, most university level actors lack the skill and training necessary to sustain the subtle, stylish nuances and complex character relationships, and they lack training in the movement of the period, a skill that is essential to a successful performance. Molière's plays occasionally surface as part of a regional theatre's offering, most often as a vehicle for the costume designer, a dubious honor often accorded well-known Restoration plays as well.

THE RESTORATION

The performance of plays was suppressed in England by Oliver Cromwell from 1642 until the restoration of Charles II to the throne in 1660. During the Restoration period, from 1660 until approximately 1710, a particular type of comedy, the *comedy of manners,* became the predominant form of theatrical entertainment. This is not to say that the performance of tragedy disappeared entirely from the English stage during that time. Plays categorized as "Heroic Tragedy," the predominant characteristics of which were excessive emotionalism and rhymed couplets, were performed occasionally. John Dryden's play,

All for Love, is one such example. In the play, Antony and Cleopatra love passionately, rhyme incessantly, and suffer terribly (whether for their passionate love or for their incessant rhymes is an arguable point). The comedies proved to be more durable and stageworthy than the tragedies and much more appealing to audiences.

A Restoration comedy typically involves a credibility-straining variety of love entanglements, sexual infidelities, and intrigues, yet manages to convey a realistic portrayal of the customs and manners of the day. Dialogue is witty and sexually suggestive. In the world of the play (which represented to a remarkable degree the world of the audience), immoral behavior was tolerated, but self-importance was not. The "fop," a dandified pretender, the "bore," and the cuckolded elderly husband with a beautiful young wife were the primary targets of ridicule and abuse. In fact, it is a rare Restoration play, indeed, that does not include a cuckolded husband.

Costumes in the Restoration period closely resembled the actual fashion of the day. From the top down, men's costume consisted of a large, wide-brimmed, usually plumed hat, a long curly wig that fell past the shoulders, a heavy, square-cut, knee-length coat with wide cuffs, a fitted waistcoat nearly as long as the coat, a ruffled shirt with lace at the cuffs, breeches, stockings, high-heeled shoes or over-the-calf boots, and bows—lots and lots of ribbon and bows and on every available surface.

Women wore a gown with puffed sleeves, a bell-shaped skirt, and a form-fitting bodice that emphasized the breasts, and a mantilla or other headdress with a veil. Outdoors, they would add a long, hooded cloak to the ensemble. Both men and woman affected beauty marks, eye patches, false noses, powder, rouge, and lipstick, and the men might also wear a fake beard or mustache.

Most of the characters in Restoration comedies are remarkably one-dimensional, and their existence is totally subservient to the plot. The characters exist solely to engage one another in rapid, witty repartee, and to manipulate one another into compromising situations, usually of a sexual nature. A few characters of substance with intelligence and a functioning moral compass appear in the better plays of William Congreve, Oliver Goldsmith, and Richard Sheridan, but these characters are few and far between indeed.

Still, the actor undertaking a role in a Restoration comedy should look below the surface of the character for any redeeming social qualities or moral values. More often than not, none exist, but it's worth the actor's time to investigate the possibility, just in case. It would be a major accomplishment for an actor to invest a Restoration character with substance and depth.

The style of performance of Restoration comedy is almost exclusively presentational. Everybody (actors and audience alike) *knew* this was a play. The characters are one-dimensional abstractions of social stereotypes. The movement is affected, artificial, and exaggerated. This is not to say that the movement is unrealistic, however, since it does reflect the realistic, everyday movement of the people being satirized. Gestures are broad, excessively stylish, and highly conventionalized, almost to the point of broad pantomime. The actor pointed to his head to indicate thought or reasoning, placed a hand on his heart to indicate love or longing, threw his hands up in front of his face, palms forward, to indicate fear or surprise, and so on.

Nevertheless, movement in Restoration comedies is graceful and elegant. Characters move around the stage in clearly defined patterns, often following a curved path. Posing is common, particularly by the fops, and posturing and other forms of physical "one-upsmanship" were often employed by other characters. Men swaggered, strutted, or minced about the stage, depending on their essential character, accentuating their leg movements and musculature. They held their hands up and away from their bodies, and often carried long, ornate walking sticks on which they displayed their hands, lace shirt cuffs, or handkerchiefs. Men bowed and women curtsied in the prevailing French manner (see the Neoclassical Period), and the bows and curtsies were directed to the audience as well as to other characters, thereby reinforcing the presentational performance style.

Gestures were mannered but precise. Note the following excerpt from a contemporary Restoration text on theatre history, purportedly written by Thomas Betterton, one of the period's leading actors:

> The head ought not to be lifted too high and stretched out extravagantly, but an exception to this will come for the player who is to act a person of such a character.
>
> The head ought always to be turned on the same side to which the actions of the rest of the body are directed, except when they are employed to express our aversion to things; for these things we reject with the right hand, at the same time turning the head away to the left.
>
> You must lift up or cast down your eyes according to the nature of things you speak of. When a man speaks in anger, his imagination is inflamed, and kindles a sort of fire in his eyes, and this fire of the eyes will easily strike those of

the audience which are continually fixed upon yours; and by a strange sympathetic infection, it will set them on fire, too, with the very same passion.

In the lifting up of the hands, you ought not to raise them above your eyes; nor must they be very little lower. Your arms you should not stretch out sideways above half a foot from the trunk of the body. You must never let your hands hang down, as if lame or dead. Your hands must always be in view of your eyes, and so corresponding with the motions of the head, eyes, and body that the spectators may see their concurrence.

If any action comes to be used by only one hand, that should be the right hand, it being indecent to make a gesture with the left hand alone. You must be sure, as you begin your action with what you say, so you must end it when you have done speaking. The movement or gestures of your hand must always be agreeable to the nature of the words that you speak.

Aside from the apparent artificiality of the motivation it presupposes, this is the Restoration version of Hamlet's "Suit the action to the word, the word to the action."

Restoration staging ■

- *Kissing the Lady's Hand.* How often this is done, and how poorly. The custom of kissing a lady's hand became fashionable in the English court in the late 1600s (well after the contagion of the plague, one hopes) and continued though the next few centuries. Gentlemen kissed ladies' hands at every possible opportunity, but always upon meeting her and departing from her. The custom was imported from the Italian and French courts where the practice was common, even during the time of plagues (the connection between physical contact and disease apparently went unnoticed, social custom overriding the concern for a particularly nasty form of death).

It is important to point out that the hand of a young, unmarried woman is never kissed. A brief handshake and a slight bow will suffice, thank you very much. The hand of an older lady or married woman may be kissed if it is offered for that purpose. Again, a handshake (if the hand is offered) or a bow (if not), or both will do. The fashion, except in Italy, was to bend over the lady's hand without actually kissing it. The Italians, in contrast, were passionate about actual physical contact between the man's lips and the lady's hand. It was universally considered an insult to touch the nose to the lady's hand, however, whether actually kissing it or not.

The following instructions for kissing a lady's hand are from *Manners: A Handbook of Social Customs,* by Elizabeth Marbury, published in 1888 (somewhat later than the Restoration, but nevertheless appropriate to the period):

> Always kiss the right hand. Never touch the hand to your lips, but keep it somewhat distant. Bend the hand a little, do not keep it straight. When raising the arm and bringing the hand toward the mouth, keep your wrist and hand curved inward. Bring the Lady's index finger nearest the mouth.

The index finger was chosen because it was the favored ring finger at the time (the Pope and other heads of state continue to wear rings on their index fingers to this day). One further note: the lady was likely wearing gloves, so familiarities like blowing or breathing heavily on the hand would go unnoticed and therefore unrewarded.

It takes a little practice to perform the hand kissing smoothly and elegantly. The important points to remember: wait until the hand is offered; no actual kissing of the hand (except in Italy or when playing an Italian character); no touching of the nose to the hand (an insult under any circumstances); no kissing of *unmarried* young ladies (on the hand or anywhere else for that matter), especially in public, and no taking of "liberties" with the lady's hand.

Ladies had their own instructions for hand kissing when meeting the queen. (Men would follow the instructions above in meeting the queen, as in meeting any other lady, if the queen offered her hand to be kissed. Otherwise a respectful bow or polite handshake with a slight bow—again, if the hand was offered—would be in order.)

> The Lady advances and bows (curtsies) very low, extending her right hand, palm downwards, and the Queen places her hand upon it, which the Lady kisses.

Again, the lips never touch the queen's hand, of course, nor does the nose (unless, of course, you wish to lose it, along with the rest of your head). And definitely no heavy breathing.

- *Snuff.* The taking of snuff was common throughout Europe, and widely practiced by both men and women. Snuff—a mixture of powdered tobacco, dried herbs, and occasionally drugs—was used for its mildly intoxicating or invigorating effect, to make one sneeze to clear the nasal passages, and, most important, to draw attention to oneself. As such, the taking of snuff found widespread use on stage, since characters in plays emulated the attitudes and behavior of society, particularly the foibles and follies of the upper classes.

The technique for taking snuff: The small ornate snuffbox is removed from the waistcoat pocket, from one's sleeve or cuff, or from one's evening bag with appropriate fanfare. The snuffbox is held up and away from the body in the fingertips of one hand, and tapped on the top with the fingertips of the other hand to cause any particles on the inside of the lid to fall into the box. The box is opened with a small flourish, a pinch of snuff taken between the thumb and middle finger, and then applied directly to the nostrils—first the left nostril, palm inward, then the right, palm outward—or placed on the back of the hand, and inhaled vigorously. (Sneezing generally follows, so a handkerchief should be kept close at hand.) The snuffbox is snapped shut with a flourish, and returned from whence it came. One final ostentatious display of snapping the handkerchief at the cuffs or front of the body to remove errant particles of snuff from one's clothing completes the artful performance. The entire procedure is executed in high style to achieve the greatest possible affect on the "audience."

- *The Fan.* While the taking of snuff was an affectation adopted by both men and women, the use of the fan was the province of women alone. A fan was an important part of a lady's wardrobe, serving as an enhancement of her eyes and face, protection from a too-penetrating gaze, and a subtle means of communication. An elaborate "language of the fan" evolved, which allowed a lady to express her feelings in an otherwise restrictive or inappropriate environment.

Selections from the "language of the fan" that might have been used during the Restoration:

Fan Gesture	*Meaning*
Carried in right hand, in front of face.	Follow me.
Carried in left hand, in front of face.	I'd like to meet you.
Closed fan on left ear.	Not listening. Go away.
Carried in right hand.	You are too eager.
Twirled in left hand.	We are being watched.
Closed fan drawn through hand.	I hate and despise you.
Open and shut quickly.	You are too cruel.
Yawning behind the fan.	You bore me.
Drawn slowly across right cheek.	I love you.
Closed fan, held horizontally to the heart.	You have my heart.
Resting on right cheek.	Yes.
Resting on left cheek.	No.
Fanning slowly.	I'm married.
Fanning quickly.	I'm engaged.
Fanning very quickly.	Catch me, I'm going to faint.
Closed, with tip of fan to lips.	Hush.
Closed, with handle to lips.	Kiss me.
Drawn across the eyes.	I'm sorry.

It appears that a lady could carry on an entire "fan conversation" with a gentleman, if he is conversant in the "language." It would certainly be to his advantage to know at least a few "words" or "phrases," particularly if he desired the lady's acquaintance or wished to pursue a relationship.

The use of the fan is a perfect example of the contradictory function of gestures mentioned in Chapter 1. A lady might say "No," but her fan may say "Yes." A lady might say "I'm married" or "You are too eager," but her fan may say "I'd like to meet you" or "Kiss me, you fool."

Few modern actors are familiar with "fan language," yet it is an easily acquired skill that serves the actor well when performing Restoration comedy or one of Molière's plays. It is unlikely the audience will know immediately what a particular fan gesture means, but in context they will understand its use means something. In time, they may come to understand the actual meaning. The use of "fan language" can enhance the onstage interplay between characters, which is in itself a worthy use of an arcane skill.

The costuming, props, and other extrinsic physical elements of the production of Restoration plays offer actors considerable opportunities for inventive movement and for wonderfully elaborate, if wholly superficial, physical characterizations.

Representative plays. ■ Dramas: *The Conquest of Granada* and *All for Love* (Dryden), and *The History of King Lear* (Nahum Tate). Comedies: *The Country Wife* and *The Plain Dealer* (Wycherly), *The Way of the World* (Congreve), *The Man of Mode* (Etherege) and *The Beaux' Stratagem* (George Farquhar). Restoration dramas and tragedies are seldom performed, primarily because the comedies are more popular (and because most of them are formal, stuffy, and excessively emotional). One exception is Dryden's *All for Love,* a reworking of Shakespeare's *Antony and Cleopatra.* In contrast to many Restoration dramas, *All for Love* is a romantic, heroic tragedy, structurally sound, and not overly sentimental or melodramatic. In fact, in the Prologue of the play Dryden takes the Restoration theatregoer to task for being too easily impressed by the prevailing mode of dramatic presentation. *The Country Wife, The Way of the World,* and *The Beaux' Stratagem* are the most often produced of the comedies.

Mention must be made of Richard Brinsley Sheridan's *The School for Scandal.* The play is often attributed to the Restoration, although it was written nearly a hundred years later. The play is certainly reminiscent of a Restoration comedy of manners, with its apt character names—Sir Oliver Surface, Lady Teazle, and Sir Benjamin Backbite, for example—and its send-up of contemporary fashions and customs, but do not be misled. Actors need to be aware of the essential differences between Sheridan's play and plays of the earlier period, in order to represent characters appropriately within the actual (rather than the perceived or imposed) world of the play. *The School for Scandal* may be performed in a Restoration style, but it is not a Restoration play. For one thing, fashion and custom had changed considerably by the time of its writing. The play is also less bawdy, less cynical, and less morally compromising than a Restoration play. Virtue and sentimentality triumph, representing the social attitude of the increasingly middle-class audience of Sheridan's time. His audience rejected the Restoration notion of social artifice and easily compromised moral values in deference to sound moral judgment and ethical behavior. The values inherent in the plays of either period should not be considered intrinsically right or wrong, nor should the values of one period be imposed on the other. The plays are simply a reflection of the times.

Period Plays in Perspective

High school and college acting students are called on to perform in many period plays during their educational careers. In a typical university-level performance season, there may be four, five, or even six plays, most of which will be period plays, usually "classics," with a musical thrown in to sell season tickets and to make up for the expected financial losses of the less popular classical offerings. The prevailing theory visited on unsuspecting acting students is that acting in period plays will help prepare the aspiring actor for work in the professional theatre.

The aspiring actor discovers, however, sometimes to his dismay, that the majority of plays produced in the professional theatre are not period plays, but modern, realistic plays, for which he has obtained little practical experience. There is the odd production of Shakespeare, of course, but in many cases the popular theory simply doesn't hold true. Period plays are the exception rather than the rule for all but the most enlightened (and solvent) professional theatres. Professional theatre is a business (an *artistic* business, but a business nonetheless), and period plays (other than Shakespeare's more well-known plays) simply don't "sell." Modern, realistic, small-cast, simple-set plays and musicals do sell. For the professional theatre producer (or one who wishes to remain so), the choice is quite simple.

Still, acting in period plays can be instructive and rewarding in its own right, and acting experience of any kind can only help the aspiring actor to learn her art and craft. Acting in period plays provides the actor with new challenges, new ways of looking at the challenges, and new ways of meeting those challenges, but will not give an actor preferred entry into the professional theatre world. There is no "shortcut" to the top of any profession. Superior acting ability, range of experience, talent, and above all, perseverance are (and always have been) the keys to professional success.

Transition to Realism

The period from the end of the seventeenth century to the mid-nineteenth century has been referred to as the "Romantic Period,"

"The Age of Melodrama," "The Age of Sentimentalism," and the "Pre-Realism Period." It was all of these. A great portion of the Western world was undergoing significant turmoil and change, adjusting to major advances in science, industry, and culture, all of which was reflected in the plays of the period.

It is nearly impossible to categorize the style of movement during this transition period because techniques in acting ranged from the mannered Restoration style to early attempts at realistic acting. Advances in theatre architecture, lighting, production facilities, and staging techniques affected acting styles throughout Europe and America. Actors moved back from the audience for the simple reason that advanced lighting techniques allowed the actors to be seen clearly at a greater distance. The audience was also moved farther away from the actors. Spectators accustomed to sitting on the stage were removed to the auditorium. Moving the actors farther from the audience (or the audience from the actors, whichever way you look at it) meant that the actors had to speak up. This gave rise to a declamatory style of acting—the "stand-there-and-shout-down-the-walls" school—that was popular in Europe until the mid-1700s, and which persisted on the American stage well into the 1800s.

By the end of the eighteenth century, however, acting in Europe had developed into a less bombastic, less declamatory, less presentational, and considerably more natural style that emphasized a true-to-life representation of characters and situations. The overall style of production became increasingly representational as well, a precursor to the more realistic style that would follow within the next few years.

Nevertheless, the "old school" of acting was still very much in evidence, particularly in the "provinces" and the "colonies," where advances in the dramatic arts had not yet been adopted. Actors still declaimed their lines and exaggerated their movements. The audience might interrupt the performance to applaud an actor's speech, whereupon the actor might repeat it, or, if the audience response warranted it, repeat the entire scene. Realism was not practiced on the provincial stage, nor was it expected.

The following are general notes on the style of movement in plays of this transitional period. Romantic drama—plays by Johann von Goethe, Friedrich Schiller, Edmond Rostand, and Victor Hugo—requires an intense, emotion-based style of acting. Movement and gesture are reminiscent of Elizabethan tragedy: selective, controlled, and restrained, but with a heightened emotional base. Movement was motivated primarily by emotion rather than reason, and the production style was predominantly presentational.

Melodrama—particularly plays by René Charles de Pixérécourt and August Friedrich von Kotzebue—employed what might be considered a fairly realistic style of acting. The style was representational, and movement and gestures were reasonably true-to-life, except for an occasional aside or other conventional holdover from earlier times.

It should also be noted that new forms of theatrical entertainment developed during the eighteenth century. The *ballad opera* (for example, *The Beggar's Opera* by John Gay); the English style of *pantomime* (dancing and mimicry performed to a musical accompaniment, made popular by John Rich); the *burlesque* (Henry Fielding's *Tom Thumb*); and the *comic opera* (a comic, romantic play with musical interludes), all appeared during this period. Advances in technical theatre gave rise to *spectacle*—enormous moving panoramas, treadmills (for the chariot race in *Ben Hur*, for instance, with live horses and a moving panorama behind it), and, with the introduction of gas lighting, special lighting effects. All these changes affected the style of acting, which now competed with these technical developments.

Representative plays. ■ Romantic drama: *Mary Stuart, William Tell* (Schiller), *Cyrano de Bergerac* (Rostand), and *Hernani* (Hugo). Melodrama: *The Stranger* (Kotzebue), and *The Child of the Forest* (Pixérécourt). Of these plays, *Cyrano*, which best captures the "romantic ideal" of the period, is the most often produced, particularly at the regional theatre level.

REALISM AND NATURALISM

The nineteenth century brought acting from the age of romanticism and melodrama to the age of realism. Advances in theatre architecture and stage lighting, and an increased emphasis on historically accurate costuming and design influenced acting techniques significantly. The bravura display of acting that occurred so often at the beginning of the nineteenth century on an immense set in an immense auditorium was decidedly out of place in the more intimate theatres and more realistic sets in use at the end of the century. The introduction of gaslight meant that the audience area could be dimmed without sacrificing the lighting on the stage. Actors could be seen clearly wherever they went on stage, and from any seat in the theatre. Exaggerated movement and gestures were no longer necessary and appeared ludicrous in the context of new production techniques.

Theatre production companies also changed. The "star system" of the eighteenth century—every man/woman for him-/herself—was replaced by ensemble acting. The success of a production depended not on the star's drawing power alone but on a balanced production, all of the elements, including the acting, worked together in a common effort. No one element of the production took precedence over any other.

The terms "realism" and "naturalism" are often misused and misunderstood. *Realism* is not a period, as such, nor is it a movement. It is a style, an approach, a manner of presentation. A realistic play is one that is written in prose, in colloquial, everyday language (even if it is set in another period or an exotic location), in which the situations of the play occur and events transpire (for better or worse) in a natural, believable way, just as they might in real life.

In contrast, naturalism is a movement that first took hold in France in the 1870s. The major tenets of naturalism are that man's fate is based on heredity and environment, and that since man's behavior is determined by forces outside of his control, he cannot be held responsible for his actions. Society, not man, is to blame for man's behavior. A naturalistic play is also written in colloquial language, but the situations and events of the play emphasize the environmental influences exerted on the characters' lives. The characters lack "free will." Their lives are controlled by heredity, by the environment, or by the Darwinian concept of evolution. (Darwin's *On the Origin of Species,* first published in 1859, was the major impetus for the naturalistic movement.) In this rationalized and rather pessimistic view of the world, the characters cannot escape their fate. No matter what they do, they're doomed.

In a realistic play, the plot progresses in a dramatically interesting way. The playwright selects and organizes the events of the play, condensed or expanded in time and space, for the greatest dramatic effect. In contrast, a naturalistic play might be considered an extra-realistic play, an actual "slice of life," a scientifically accurate moment-by-moment record.

To Emile Zola (the leading exponent of naturalism) and other naturalistic writers, the essential elements of dramatic invention were unnecessary. The situations and events of the play were to be recorded as truth, not as art, and certainly not as dramatic art. The problem with this approach is that if the events the playwright chooses to replicate on stage are not very interesting in and of themselves, neither is the play. Zola tried to prove his naturalistic theories by dramatizing his novel *Thérèse Raquin.* What he proved was that even a sensational story (a wife and her lover murder the wife's husband and then commit suicide because they are haunted by the unremitting gaze of the wife's paralyzed mother-in-law) could become an exceedingly dull play. There are few notable naturalistic plays. *The*

Vultures, by Henri Becque, is considered one of the best, but it can boast of no sympathetic characters, no dramatic progression of scenes, no apparent climax, and a cynical, ironic, and pessimistic outcome. Not surprisingly, it was not well-received at its original production (there have been few productions since), nor did it contribute significantly to the naturalistic cause. The play simply did not state its naturalistic case strongly enough to challenge traditional values.

Clearly, then, "realism" and "naturalism" are not synonymous terms. An actor should know the difference.

Following is a brief overview of some of the major playwrights of the late nineteenth and early twentieth centuries. These are the playwrights with whom the modern actor is most likely to come in contact and with whose plays every actor should be familiar.

CHEKHOV

The plays of Anton Chekhov (1860–1904) transform the seemingly insignificant details and random fragments of daily life into compelling, realistic drama. At first reading, the interrelationship of events and personalities in Chekhov's plays is not readily apparent. Chekhov builds his plays slowly, bit by bit, until a larger pattern begins to emerge. The plot is often subtle, yet simple and straightforward, and events occur in a tightly woven cause-and-effect progression. There are no startling revelations or climactic moments in Chekhov's plays. In fact, nothing much seems to happen at all (except in retrospect), but there is always a central, all-encompassing theme that unifies the action of the play. Every speech and every event, no matter how insignificant, reveal character or contribute to the theme.

Chekhov's characters are clearly defined, believable, and human. They behave realistically, yet the relationship between characters seems distant, ambivalent at times, and often discordant. Even characters who like each other don't seem to get along very well. Their motivations are intellectually based rather than emotionally based and reflect mental attitudes and beliefs that the characters find difficult to express or translate into positive and effective action. Quite simply, none of Chekhov's characters actually knows herself (or anybody else, for that matter), and none of them can comprehend the great mystery of her existence. Each character aspires to a better life, to better herself and her situation, yet none of them knows quite how to do it. Even when they are provided an obvious choice, they seem confused and unable to act. They continually founder in their halfhearted attempts to pursue their ill-defined goals and eventually give up and resign themselves to their monotonous, frustrating existence. Chekhov's plays are not dramas of hopeless despair and desperate hopelessness, however: in every play there is a glimmer of hope.

Naturally, the actor needs to understand Chekhov's world to enact one of his characters. Each of Chekhov's major plays—*The Sea Gull* (1898), *Uncle Vanya* (1899), *The Three Sisters* (1900), and *The Cherry Orchard* (1904)—is set in rural Russia near the turn of the century, and accurately (if somewhat pessimistically) depicts the lives of the land-owning class, the Russian "landed gentry." Chekhov's notes and stage directions are brief and to the point. The *details* of characterization are vitally important. What the character does and how he does it, particularly the "little things" of daily life, are the foundation on which the characterization rests and from which the action of the play evolves. Repetitive daily tasks and seemingly insignificant movements and gestures, if performed realistically, can enhance the physical characterization and contribute to the overall effectiveness of the play.

To portray a character in a "foreign" play (one originally written in a language other that English), the actor should seek out and compare several available translations for insights into the play. Different translators emphasize different elements of the play, which can alter its meaning or change its focus. A good translation can actually enhance a play, whereas a poor translation can quite literally destroy it.

IBSEN

Henrik Ibsen (1828–1906) wrote in several different styles, romantic, symbolic, naturalistic, even fantastic, yet each of his plays portrays the ordinary events of daily life using colloquial dialogue and contemporary settings, reflecting his fundamentally realistic approach to playwriting. His plays progress in an unambiguous cause-and-effect manner, moment by moment and scene by scene, to a logical conclusion. Like the dialogue and setting, the costumes and stage business Ibsen describes in his notes contribute directly to the realistic approach of the play. Ibsen uses none of the common "tricks" of his contemporaries—inventive (and often highly implausible) turns of events, sudden revelations, and coincidences—that would strain the play's credibility. His plays represent true-to-life human experience.

Ibsen's characters dress, speak, and act normally. They are not heroic or larger-than-life, but live an essentially prosaic existence. They are ordinary people struggling to find their place in the world. Each character acts from a well-defined psychological base, although the influence of environment and heredity are apparent (most notably in *Ghosts*, written at a time when Ibsen was greatly influenced by Zola and the naturalist cause). The characters behave logically, and for the most part, reasonably. Each character has a distinct personality shaped by the past and present circumstances of her life, which, if clearly understood, can add immeasurably to the actor's characterization. Many of Ibsen's plays are termed "retrospective" in the sense that the present circumstances of the play are, to a considerable extent, the result of the characters' past behavior—the present is a consequence of the past. Retrospective plays (like *Ghosts* or *A Doll's House*) employ a small cast, a single setting, a tightly structured plot, and take place over a relatively short time span. Economy is the key: there is little to distract from the action and the theme.

Economy is also the key to enacting an Ibsen character. Where Chekhov fills his plays with a wealth of what appears to be insignificant incidents and extraneous characters, Ibsen uses both sparingly. The cause-and-effect relationship of events in his plays is clear, almost transparent at times. Much of the conflict flows from within the characters themselves as they struggle to "do the right thing," even in the face of societal pressure and other external forces. The actor needs to find ways to portray that struggle realistically—without resorting to tortured looks, a halting gait, or a withered arm.

The influence of nature is felt throughout Ibsen's plays. The characters are never far from the forest, the mountains, or the sea. Ibsen isolates his characters only briefly from the outside world. No matter how "civilized," protected, and secure they may appear, Ibsen reminds us that the wilderness (natural, social, and spiritual) is just outside the door.

An important, often overlooked aspect of the plays that can be very helpful to the actor is Ibsen's reliance on personal props to define his characters. Hedda's pistols are an obvious example, and Nora's macaroons a less obvious, but equally important one. Using props in this way may seem somewhat contrived to modern actors, but Ibsen provides them as something for the character to "hold on to," something that embodies the essence of the character. The actor's challenge is to discover that "essential something."

Ibsen's more well-known, more often produced plays include *A Doll's House* (1879), *Ghosts* (1881), *The Wild Duck* (1884), and *Hedda Gabler* (1890). Ibsen's stage directions are helpful to the actor, director, and designers. His descriptions of the set, the costumes, and suggested stage business are designed to reveal the world of the play, and provide a substantive base for characterization. (Ibsen wrote his staging notes from the perspective of the *audience* not the actor. Directors and designers who wish to re-create Ibsen's staging directions usually get them backward.) As with Chekhov, the actor should compare several translations of Ibsen's plays, since they can be substantially different from one another in tone, style, and focus.

SHAW

Like Chekhov and Ibsen, George Bernard Shaw (1856–1950) was concerned with the social problems of this time. Shaw believed in the influence of heredity and environment on the individual, as did the naturalists, but he also believed in free will and freedom of choice. He wrote in a pointedly subjective style: his opinion is the correct one, and it is his opinion that he wishs to persuade the audience to accept. In contrast to Ibsen, who believed that characters were a medium for the expression of human behavior and experience, Shaw believed that characters were the medium for the expression of ideas—preferably his.

Shaw wrote what appear to be comedies of manners—plays that satirize conventional modes of behavior. Shaw takes society to task, but his plays are much more than social commentary: they are plays of ideas. Shaw created his characters and his plots to express his own particular (some might say peculiar) point of view about the world, the injustices he observed, and the societal values he wished to address. Shaw's plots and characters are "theatrical" in the sense that the plots are artfully contrived yet plausible, and the characters appear natural but are not. Plot and characters exist solely as the medium for Shaw's "message."

Shaw's characters are highly articulate. They speak in a slightly elevated manner (even when speaking in dialect), and never seem unable to say exactly what they want to say at exactly the right time (it is Shaw, of course, who is doing the talking). They have relatively straightforward and uncomplicated personalities but sometimes behave in contradictory ways. Shaw believed that people are what they think, and his attitude is apparent in his characters. At times, they seem to be nothing more than walking opinions. The actor confronts a considerable challenge in portraying one of Shaw's characters: to meld those seemingly incompatible contradictions into a believable and compelling characterization.

A familiarity with the manners and customs of Shaw's time would benefit the actor in developing his character's movement. Note that Shaw wrote plays for more than fifty years, however, and things change. His plays are topical and address issues that were of concern to Shaw at the time. Although Shaw set plays in distant times and places, they remain firmly rooted in his own era. His intent is to make a point about his own social, economic, or political environment, *not* to write a period play.

The plays of Shaw and Ibsen include strong roles for women. Both were ardent supporters of women's rights, and their attitude is reflected in their plays. In contrast to Ibsen, however, Shaw's plays are unfailingly optimistic. Even though Shaw vigorously (often unmercifully) attacked the conventional thinking and behavior of his day, he believed in "setting a good example" in his plays. Few of his characters are beyond "redemption." They are misguided, perhaps, or misled by society, but each possesses some redeeming quality. Shaw believed in the inherent dignity and goodness of humankind. His objective was to help build a "good society."

Pygmalion (1912) and *Saint Joan* (1923) are two of Shaw's more famous plays. *Arms and the Man* (1894), *The Devil's Disciple* (1896), and *Heartbreak House* (1919), subtitled *A Fantasia in the Russian Manner on English Themes* (subtitling is a conceit of Shaw's worth noting), are produced occasionally. Shaw provides sometimes voluminous notes and stage directions that can help the actor to understand his point of view and give substance and life to his characters. An actor's research should include reading the notes, introduction, preface, or epilogue to the play, and a selection of Shaw's nondramatic writings.

BRECHT

Bertolt Brecht (1898–1956) was a playwright, dramatic theorist, and stage director who formulated a personal vision of theatre he termed "Epic Theatre," a form of theatre that he felt would be most closely related to epic, narrative poetry. Brecht rejected the Aristotelian concept of unity of time, place, and action, as well as the prevailing notion of illusion-based theatre, which is highly dependent on the audience's empathy for the characters. Brecht did not reject realism per se, or reject realistic elements of playwriting and play production, but he employed these elements to a different effect. By portraying a situation realistically and objectively, Brecht hoped to cause the audience to analyze the situation and to study the characters. Brecht's Epic Theatre juxtaposed realistic and symbolic scenes with staged debate, discussion, narrative, poetry, and interpolated songs, and his multiple plots were organized episodically, all in an attempt to distance the audience from the play and from the characters.

Brecht originated an approach to theatrical production commonly referred to as "alienation" or "alienation technique," but which might better be termed "detachment." Brecht wanted the audience to remain fully aware that they were sitting in a theatre watching a play.

His intent was not to "alienate" the audience—to displace them from the theatrical experience—as is commonly assumed, but to prevent the audience from identifying with any particular character, in order to better observe and analyze the action of the play dispassionately, from a distance. Characters in Brecht's plays do what they believe is "expedient," not necessarily what they feel is "right." Brecht wished to focus the audience's attention on the character's motivation for action—the social conditions that impose certain attitudes and behaviors on the characters that are often in conflict with the character's own feelings and better judgment.

There are times when Brecht asks the audience to identify with the characters, to think about them, to try to feel what they feel (in an abstract way), and to analyze that feeling. Empathy implies a dissociation from one's self and one's objective sense. Brecht preferred that audience members not dissociate themselves from their objective selves. He reminded them periodically that they were observers, not participants in the play, and analysts, not the subjects of their own analysis.

Brecht devised a style of acting for his Epic Theatre, based on what he termed *gests*—a combination of physical attitude, movement, and gesture related to the social attitude prevalent in any given situation. As we know, physical attitudes change with social attitudes. We move differently in different situations and with different people, even with the same people under different circumstances. Brecht sought to emphasize the sometimes devastating effect societal influence can have on the individual and on interpersonal relationships. The underlying theme of many of his plays is that evil is imposed by the social order, and that man's natural tendency toward good is thwarted by a corrupt society. Brecht is telling us the audience that in order to change the moral order of things, man must change society. Unfortunately, a person cannot expect help from anyone else in that quest. He must affect the change by himself. Brecht's plays stress the adversarial relationship between the individual and society, and often conclude with the triumph of society over man: of inhumanity over humanity.

Acting in a Brecht play requires, first of all, that the actor know, understand, and accept that she is acting. The actor does not "feel" the part, "assume the role," or "become the character." There is no such illusion. Instead, the actor "demonstrates" her character, her character's emotions, and her character's actions to the audience—in the same way that she might "act out" a narrated story—with no attempt to convince the audience that she has actually "become" any of the characters described. Brecht believed that the actor must sustain a certain level of detachment from the character, so that the audience could adopt the *same* level of detachment. The character should appear no less human, simply appear more detached from the world around her. This style of acting is difficult for many actors, particularly those who have been trained in any of the prevailing "methods." "Acting out," "demonstrating," and "detachment" are not part of the "method" actor's working vocabulary.

Luckily, Brecht gives actors some help. The plots of his plays are episodic, even disjointed at times, which helps distance the audience from the play. The audience has to think about what it's observing rather than simply experience it: a character might address the audience directly, in a soliloquy, or comment on his own actions or those of other characters, or serve as a narrator; occasionally, the actor might drop out of a scene to sing a song or recite a poem. This helps members of the audience distance themselves from the characters. Apart from these instances, however, the character must appear to act naturally and realistically within the given circumstances of the play and in relation to the other characters.

Given the nature of "Epic Theatre," the stigma attached to the "alienation technique" (usually by those who have no idea what it means), and the extraordinary demands placed on the actor, Brecht's plays are not often performed. Again, an educational theatre (particularly one with a conservatory-style training program) or a professional regional stage is the most likely venue. *Mother Courage* (1938) is performed occasionally, *The Good Woman of Setzuan* (1940) less often, and *Saint Joan of the Stockyards* (1930), *Galileo* (1938), and *Antigone* (1948) hardly ever. More likely to be performed are Brecht's collaborative efforts on musical productions like *The Threepenny Opera* (1928), performed quite often, and *The Rise and Fall of the City of Mahagonny* (1929), performed rarely, both of which Brecht wrote with composer Kurt Weill. It's interesting to note that many modern musicals adhere to Brecht's theories: they include multiple plots loosely arranged in an episodic structure, interpolated songs and dances, elements of narrative (particularly in the songs), and a sense of detachment from the not-always-realistic characters and situations. For the most part, audiences "watch" or "observe" a musical production, they do not "experience" it as they do most nonmusical productions.

O'NEILL

Eugene O'Neill (1888–1953), son of actor James O'Neill, who was famous for his portrayal of the Count of Monte Cristo in the play of the same name, wrote about forty plays during his thirty-five-year career.

O'Neill's plays are considered by many to be uncompromisingly realistic. They're not. He experimented with many different writing techniques to attain the greatest possible theatricality in his work, not necessarily the greatest reality. He wrote plays in the classic Greek mode, for instance (the psychological melodrama *Mourning Becomes Electra*, a trilogy, is based on the ancient Electra myth), mask plays (*Lazarus Laughed* and *The Great God Brown*), expressionistic plays (*The Hairy Ape*), symbolic plays (*The Fountain*), and realistic plays (*Anna Christie, Desire Under the Elms,* and *A Moon for the Misbegotten*), and what might be termed a realistic autobiographical play (*Long Day's Journey into Night*). It is nearly impossible to restrict O'Neill's plays to one particular style or approach to playwriting, except to say that all share a common theme—the character's search for the significance of his own life and of life in general. This is not a new theme, of course, but it is common to all of O'Neill's plays.

Aside from one comedy, *Ah, Wilderness!*, O'Neill's major plays are unremittingly serious. (*The Hairy Ape* is subtitled *A Comedy of Ancient and Modern Life in Eight Scenes*. It may be "in eight scenes," but it is definitely *not* a "comedy.") Even comic events and situations eventually turn serious, sometimes even tragic. O'Neill probes the depth of often contradictory human feelings, and relentlessly pursues the search for truth—in the world and within one's self. He explores human desires and the often futile effort to attain those desires, the nature of truth, and the recurring conflict between reality and perception.

O'Neill's major characters feel alienated from the world around them. They struggle with their environment, their fate, and themselves, trying to find their "place" in the world, trying to "belong." The quest for self-realization is the key to many of O'Neill's characters, not in the sense of personal achievement, success, or the attainment of material wealth, but in the sense of personal awareness. Above all, they want to know who they are.

O'Neill's plays are not performed often outside the educational theatre or professional regional theatre stages. Several reasons can explain why. First, O'Neill's estate won't allow the plays to be cut—not a word. They must be performed in their entirety, a daunting proposition for most organizations. *Strange Interlude* has nine acts in two parts (plan for a dinner break), and *Mourning Becomes Electra* has twelve acts (lunch *and* dinner breaks). Second, O'Neill's plays need to be performed by gifted actors, or by gifted actors-in-training. "O'Neill" and "amateur theatricals" are anathema. Finally, O'Neill's plays are very demanding for an actor. Acting in his plays can be emotionally draining and physically exhausting. The dialogue may be colloquial, poetic, artificial, elevated, and occasionally downright indecipherable to the modern actor (like some of Shaw's English dialects). O'Neill's characters are culturally specific, occupationally specific, ethnically specific, environmentally specific, or all the above. Research into the role is essential. A cursory reading of O'Neill's plays is insufficient to glean essential elements of a character. *Everything* is essential.

There are many more playwrights with whom an actor should be familiar, but this brief discussion of the giants of modern drama should give some sense of the depth and range of acting experiences available. In terms of contemporary drama, look to regional theatres for the direction of modern playwriting. New playwrights of consequence (those who write plays of substance with characters of universal appeal) emerge more often from the ranks of the regional theatres than from any other theatrical forum.

Contemporary Plays

The actor must take special care when acting in plays of recent vintage. Consider, for instance, plays related to the North American culture of the 1960s and 1970s. We may think we know how people behaved during those years—"peace and love," the war in Vietnam, "hippies," Kent State, "flower power," and all that jazz—but there is as much method to the style of movement in those years as in any other historical period. Not every young person in the 1960s was a "flower child," nor was every adult a "square." The 1980s is typified as a time of three-piece suits, button-down collars, and corporate greed, but not every businessperson dressed or behaved that way, or moved in a way that might be dictated by such a "costume" and social attitude. Be aware, too, that change in the modern era is rapid. What was "all the rage" yesterday may be considered hopelessly outdated today. (A computer with technology more than six months old is considered a "dinosaur." Judge accordingly.)

The challenge? To determine how people really moved and related to one another. The solution? The same as for any other period: research. The director will likely have prepared herself for rehearsals with the relevant information, but if she has failed to do her homework, then it falls to the actor, the person who will embody the character, to discover the information for herself. In fact, it's a good idea to do your own research anyway to supplement the director's research and provide yourself with as many alternatives for character development as possible.

This discussion of period movement is intended to encourage the actor to learn to perform "period" movement and gestures naturally and effortlessly, not to draw attention to himself or the activity, or distract the audience from the flow of the production. Any period movement performed awkwardly, self-consciously, or inappropriately will compromise a character's believability. An actor must practice the movement many, many times prior to actual performance so that it becomes as much a part of the character's physical behavior as any other aspect of the characterization.

Advice for Players-in-Training

The development of your acting skills will depend to a great extent on the following factors:

- *Awareness:* a realization that there are, indeed, skills to be learned, and that no matter how much training or experience you've had, you still don't know all there is to know about acting.
- *Motivation*: a vigorous pursuit of knowledge, and a passionate desire to learn and learn well; not just a passing interest or a "quick fix" mentality ("How to Audition," "How to Do Voice-overs," "How to Act in TV and Commercials"), but a compelling "need to know" pursued actively at every possible opportunity.
- *Attitude*: a positive, self-motivating, "I can do it" frame of mind, coupled with an inordinate amount of self-discipline. There is no guarantee that you will "make it" in acting, even with a fervent desire and strong motivation, but there *is* a guarantee that you *won't* make it if you quit trying.
- *Knowledge*: Knowledge of acting skills can be acquired on one's own, by reading, for instance, or by observing other actors. Most performing artists learn their skills from other performing artists, those with practical and continuing experience in the chosen field of endeavor. Choose your teachers wisely. You've heard the saying "Those who

can, do, and those who can't, teach." The best acting teachers are those who do both—who act *and* teach. Be wary of any acting teacher who rarely, if ever, sets foot on stage, or who is living on "past glory."

■ *Experience:* Human beings learn practical skills by only one proven method: "trial and error." Acting skills cannot be learned in isolation or without *practical* application. Actors need feedback, coaching, encouragement, and constructive criticism in order to grow in their art. Few beginning actors manage to "get it right" the first time they try. Skills in any field are acquired as much (or more) by making mistakes as by doing it right.

A performing artist learns by doing, by performing. The greater the range and variety of your acting experiences, the more you will learn. *Any* acting experience, no matter what size the role or the professional level of the performance groups, can provide valuable practical experience. Be wary, however, of wasting your valuable time in trivial pursuits. Search for opportunities to grow in your art, not just opportunities "to act." Not all acting experiences will be *positive* ones, of course, but you will learn something from every worthwhile experience, even if it's what *not* to do.

Understanding a skill is one thing. *Doing* it is quite another. In few other fields is there as much "on-the-job training" as in acting. A person with no prior training or experience is cast in a role he has little or no idea how to enact, in a play he probably never read and does not fully comprehend. He attends rehearsals and is given directions on how to move about the stage in a language that he does not understand. He does not know how to use his voice and body expressively (either separately or together), has no concept of theatrical production techniques, styles, or historical periods, and couldn't "find the light" if a thousand-watt fresnel dropped on his head. Yet we call this person an "actor"! Would we extend the same courtesy to a painter who has no sense of color, a sculptor with no sense of three-dimensional composition, a dancer without technique or sense of rhythm, or a musician who can't read music, has no vocal or instrumental training, and has never heard of Johann Sebastian Bach? No wonder people think anybody can act! Certainly anybody who makes the attempt can be called an actor, if by no one other than himself, whether he has any idea of what he's doing or not. Still, he's got to start somewhere.

You've probably noticed that little has been mentioned about *talent*. Talent is important in acting, certainly, but talent is not the defining element of a person's artistry, her personal and artistic integrity, or her achievements in her chosen field. A person with limited talent who works to enrich that talent in appropriate and self-respectful ways will succeed to a far greater extent, and reach a higher level of personal and artistic accomplishment, than a person with greater talent who squanders it on trivial or frivolous pursuits.

The greater the devaluation of an art by the general public, the greater the value of personal, individual artistry. The fewer who have it, the greater its worth. Ironically, the way to the top of any profession is to be one of the few, not one of the many. There are lots of people in the supporting cast, in the crowd, and in the chorus. There are relatively few leading characters. Aspire to be one of the few. Face it, being famous is easy. Being good is not. If being famous is most important to you, give this book away. There's nothing in it for you, and you don't need it. If being good is most important to you, read it again.

Appendix

List of Physical Behaviors

E very person's physical self is composed of a unique combination of movements. This is by no means a comprehensive list of all possible body movements, but it does include many that can be explored and used in physical characterization. In and of itself, no movement or gesture is expressive, but in the context of a play every movement can be made expressive.

HEAD

- *Full nod:* Head moves up and down (or down and up) in one complete, unbroken motion
- *Half nod:* Head moves up or down, with a pause before returning to previous or centered position
- *Bounce:* Multiple nods of any speed
- *Pan* (or *Head Sweep*): Head moves from side to side
- *Full pan:* Head moves from center to one side, then to the opposite side, then back to center
- *Half-pan:* Head moves from the center to one side, then back to center

The classic "take" or "double-take" is composed of "pans." A take may be fast, slow, or a combination of fast and slow, and may be composed of single or multiple pans—a "single" take, a "double-take" or, less often, a "triple-take" or a "quadruple-take." The take begins with a normal-speed half-pan to the right or left, followed immediately by a quicker or slower half-pan to the same side. This might be followed by yet another fast or slow take. The movement of the eyes might precede the movement of the head, or the eyes and head might move together.

- *Head shake:* Repeated little pans
- *Swoop:* Like a "pan," but the head moves up, over, and down (or down, over, and up) in its side-to-side path
- *Tilt:* The top of the head moves right or left
- *Dropped:* Head moves down and forward, and is held in that position
- *Raised:* Head moves up and back, and is held in that position

FACE AND EYES

The classic facial expressions have been discussed in Chapter 1. The following is a list of various facial movements to explore within the context of facial expressions in the overall development of a physical characterization.

- Blank face
- Raised eyebrow (one or both)
- Lowered brow (one or both)
- Brow contraction
- Wide eyes
- Blink (single or repeated)
- Squint (one or both eyes)
- Sidelong glance
- Stare (focused or unfocused)
- Rolled eyes
- Slitted eyes
- "Shifty" eyes (slitted eyes with side-to-side eye movement)
- Eyes upward
- Fluttered eyelids
- Wink
- "Smoker's eyes" (squinted eyes with raised cheeks)
- Flaring nostrils
- Pinched nostrils
- Nose wrinkle
- "Bunny nose" (repeated flared nostrils or nose wrinkle)
- Sneer (right or left)
- Rolling sneer (moves from side to side)

- Smile (multiple variations)
- Tense mouth (a slight tightening of the muscles around the mouth)
- Pulled mouth (one corner of the mouth pulled down)
- Drooping or frowning mouth (both corners of the moth move downward)
- Tongue in cheek
- Cheeks sucked in or puffed out
- Pout (a frown and a protruding lower lip)
- Clenched teeth
- "Toothy" smile or grin
- "Tight-lipped" grin
- Square smile (generally lacking emotion—the "beauty queen" smile)
- Open mouth
- Lip lick (fast or slow, mouth open or closed)
- Moistening lips
- Biting lip (upper or lower)
- Protruding lip (upper or lower)
- Whistle (silent or with sound)
- Pursed lips
- Puckered lips (pursed lips that protrude slightly)
- Pressed lips (lips pressed together, pulled back at the corners of the mouth)
- Relaxed open mouth
- Protruding chin
- Retreating chin
- Lateral chin thrust (protruding or retreating chin moves to right or left)
- Dropped jaw (open or closed mouth)
- Chin wag (chin moves rapidly up and down, mouth open or closed)
- Yawn (normal, stifled, absent-minded, or exaggerated)
- Tongue protruding through closed lips

FINGERS

- Relaxed state (slightly curved)
- Extended (tense or relaxed)
- Hyperextended
- Angled (finger straight from joint, but moved off-center)
- Bent (slight movement)
- Crooked (larger curving movement)

- Curled (finger partially closed on itself)
- Closed (finger curled into palm)
- Touching (one or more fingers touching another finger, another part of the hand or body, or another object)
- Grasping (one or more fingers)
- Tapping (one finger, or two or more fingers moving simultaneously)
- Drumming (sequential tapping of fingers)
- Wiggling (up and down or side to side)
- Circling (tip of the finger(s) inscribes a circular pattern in the air)

Hands

One Hand

- Hand at rest: Fingers usually slightly curved, hand droops slightly from the wrist
- Extended: From the wrist, relaxed or tense, fingers touching one another or not; palm up, down, or to the side
- Open
- Cupped
- Closed
- Fist: Tightly closed hand, thumb position varies
- Touching: Hand as a unit
- Grasping: Hand as a unit
- Hand sweep: To right or left, up or down
- Circled: From the wrist
- Wave: Repeated up-and-down or side-to-side motion of the hand from the wrist

Two Hands

- Fingertips touching: Fingers straight, angled, bent, curved, or cupped
- Praying hands: Palms together, fingers extended, touching along their length; thumbs straight or overlapping
- Fingers intertwined
- Twiddling thumbs: Fingers intertwined, thumbs move around each other
- Tapping thumbs: Fingers intertwined, thumbs touch one another repeatedly
- Hands overlapped: Fingers straight, bent, curved, or cupped; both palms down, or one up and one down

- Fist in cupped hand
- Cupped hands: One palm up, one down; "opera singer" hand position
- Hand grasps opposite wrist
- Wrist rubbing or wringing: Hand moves around wrist, or wrist rotates inside hand
- Kneaded hands: One hand squeezes or kneads fingers of other hand
- Hand rubbing: One hand rubs palm or back of other hand with a circular or back-and-forth motion, fingers only, or entire hand
- Wringing hands: Repeated kneading, squeezing, or rubbing of both hands
- Nail picking: Purposeful, nervous, or absent-minded
- Clapping hands (many variations)

ARMS

- Folded arms: Many variations—hands visible or not, arms intertwined or flat on top of one another, hand grasping forearm, elbow, biceps, or shoulder
- Arms behind back: Folded, hands together, grasping, or overlapped
- Arms at side
- Arms across the body
- Hand in pocket (one or both hands)
- Thumb in belt (one or both thumbs)
- Hand in belt (one or both hands)
- Hand inside clothes
- Hands on hips (many variations)
- Extended
- Bent
- Arm circle
- Arm Sweep (and Half-sweep)
- Chopping motion
- Arm swing
- Wave: Many variations—with or without hand wave, from the wrist, elbow, or shoulder, arm bent or extended, side-to-side, up-and-down, or circular motion

NECK

- Relaxed or tense
- Straight or bent: Forward, back, or to the sides
- Swallowing

- "Gulp": Exaggerated swallowing

SHOULDERS AND TRUNK

- Bump: Upper body moves as a unit stiffly forward, back, or to either side and back again
- Waver: Upper body undulates forward, back, or to either side.
- Upright: Relaxed or tense (stiff)
- Slump forward: From the waist or lower chest
- "Rared" back: Hyperextension or curvature of the back, head pulled back
- Leaning: Upper body straight and aligned, leaning forward, back, or to either side
- Contracted: A "sunken in" position—shoulders hunched, stomach and chest contracted, spine curved or bent forward
- Curved: Upper body curved to the right or left from the chest, waist, or pelvis
- Expanded chest
- Raised chest: Expanded with a slight back extension
- Sunken chest
- Rotated: Upper body turned as a unit to right or left

SHOULDERS

- Relaxed position
- Hunched: Shoulders pushed forward, tense
- Shrug: One or both shoulders
- Raised: One or both shoulders lifted and held for a period of time longer than a "shrug"
- Drooped: Shoulders dropped forward and down
- Rotated: Shoulders rotated (turned or twisted) to right or left
- Pushed forward or pulled back: Either or both shoulders move forward or back in a straight-line motion
- Rolled: Shoulders move forward or backward in a circular motion

STOMACH

- Relaxed or tense
- Protruding: Purposefully thrust forward, with or without a curvature of the spine
- "Sucked in": Stomach muscles held tight and tense, and pulled in toward the spine

PELVIS

- Thrust: Pelvis moved forward
- Bump: Pelvis moved sideward
- Tilted: Asymmetrical alignment of the pelvis to one side
- Bounce: Repetitive thrust, bump, or tilt of the pelvis
- "Grind": Circular motion of the pelvis

LEGS AND FEET

- Standing: Many variations, depending on overall alignment and positioning of body as whole—legs together or apart, knees straight or slightly bent, various foot and leg positions, weight on one leg or the other, pelvis straight or tilted
- Rocking: Body moves as a unit forward and back or side to side
- Foot shuffle: Foot movement from the ankle
- Dangling leg: Weight on one leg, other leg moves in a random pattern
- Leg swing: Movement from the knee or hip, forward and back, or side to side
- Legs crossed: At ankle, knee, or thigh
- Foot on foot: One foot placed on other foot
- Standing on inner or outer side of one or both feet
- Stoop: Body in an upright or slight forward curvature, legs slightly bent, knees together or apart
- Squat: Knees fully bent, heels off floor or ground or in contact with floor or ground. Body upright, curved, or hunched; many variations of arm and hand positions
- Step: One step in any direction
- Walking: Continuous "stepping," many variations on length of stride, speed of movement, "type" of movement (normal, exaggerated, bouncing, gliding, swaggering, marching, dancing), straight or bent knee, on flat of foot or on tiptoe, and so on. "City folk," used to walking on flat, even surfaces, generally walk with a straight-knee, stiff-legged gait. "Country folk," more likely to walk on uneven ground or otherwise rough surfaces, often walk with a fluid, bent-knee motion.
- Running
- Skipping
- Sitting: Many variations in alignment and positioning of legs and feet as well as upper body, arms, hands, and head
  Feet: Together or apart, side, heel, or ball of the foot touching
  Knees: Together or apart

Legs crossed at ankle, knee, thigh; ankle or foot on knee or
thigh; fully or partially crossed

Leg wind: Legs crossed at thigh, with foot wrapped around calf
or ankle

"Tailor" position: Legs crossed, sitting on heels

"Yoga" position: Intertwined legs, knees part, feet on opposite
knee or thigh

- Sitting on heels: Knees together or apart, toes or top of foot in
contact with floor
- Leg dangling or swinging: Crossed-over leg moves in a random,
back-and-forth, side-to-side, or circular pattern.
- Leg kick: Noticeable "kicking" motion of the crossed-over leg
away from the support leg
- Bouncing leg: Bouncing motion of crossed-over leg, support leg,
or both
- "Nervous" legs: Legs crossed at the ankle; knees move repeatedly together and apart (almost a bouncing motion)

FEET (STANDING OR SEATED)

- Nod: Non-repetitive foot movement
- Foot pat or tap: Repeated motion
- Rocking: Heel-toe or toe-heel motion with slight shift of weight
- Sweep: Foot moves in a side-to-side motion with the heel in
contact with the floor
- Dig: Foot moves in a side-to-side motion with the toe in contact
with floor
- Shake: Repetitive, small movement of the foot, up-and-down or
side-to-side motion
- Circle or curved motion: Toe or heel inscribes an arc or circle
- Turned: Foot turned as a unit to either side
- Side foot: One or both feet rested on inner or outer side
- Toe raise: Toe lifted from the floor, heel in contact with floor
- Heel raise: Heel raised from the floor, toe in contact with floor
- Roll: Foot is rolled from inner-to-outer or outer-to-inner side

Further Reading

Alberts, David. 1995. *Rehearsal Management for Directors*. Portsmouth, NH: Heinemann. Includes a short discussion of the director's concept, the director-designer working relationship, and the overall process of rehearsal and production.

Chisman, Isabel, and Hester E. Raven-Hart. N.d. *Manners and Movements in Costume Plays*. Boston, MA: Walter H. Baker.

Crawford, Jerry L. 1983. *Acting: In Person and in Style*. Dubuque, IA: Wm. C. Brown.

Duchartre, Pierre Louis. 1966. *The Italian Comedy*. New York: Dover Publications. The standard reference on the *commedia* that includes an exhaustive study and description of all the major characters.

Gordon, Mel. 1983. *Lazzi: Comic Routines of the Commedia dell'Arte*. New York: Performing Arts Journal. Contains 250 *lazzi*, two complete *commedia* scenarios, and a descriptive list of *commedia* characters.

Harsh, Philip Whaley, ed. *An Anthology of Roman Drama*. New York: Holt, Rinehart and Winston. Includes major plays by Terence, Plautus, and Seneca.

Knapp, Mark L. 1978. *Nonverbal Communication in Human Interaction*. 2d ed. New York: Holt, Rinehart and Winston.

Moore, Sonia. 1981. *The Stanislavski System*. New York: Penguin Books. A concise guide to Stanislavski's approach to teaching acting.

Morris, Desmond, Peter Collett, Peter Marsh, Marie O'Shaughnessy. 1979. *Gestures*. New York: Stein and Day.

Russell, Douglas A. 1980. *Period Style for the Theatre*. Boston: Allyn and Bacon.

Saint-Denis, Michel. 1960. *The Rediscovery of Style*. New York: Theatre Arts Books.

Salerno, Henry F., ed. 1989. *Scenarios of the Commedia dell'Arte*. New York: Limelight Editions. A compilation of fifty *commedia* scenarios, which also includes an interesting appendix that traces the sources of many of the plots and plot devices of many of the plays of Shakespeare and Molière, among others.

Stanislavski, Constantin. 1963. *An Actor's Handbook*. New York: Theatre Arts Books. A compilation of Stanislavski's writings on various aspects of acting.